SUCCESSFUL DRUG-FREE PSYCHOTHERAPY FOR SCHIZOPHRENIA

Successful Drug-Free Psychotherapy for Schizophrenia offers a close examination of how to treat schizophrenic patients using psychotherapy rather than drugs, applying derivatives of psychodynamic principles in treating patients. The author provides real examples throughout of how therapists can resolve patients' emotional conflicts with better outcomes than by resorting to drugs. She presents methods that allow patients to avoid the neurological damage and obesity that can often result from the use of anti-psychotic drugs. The practical techniques and advice in this book enable therapists to resolve the chaos of schizophrenia using psychotherapy alone. Theoretically, this book can also be useful for work with depressives.

Revella Levin, Ph.D., is a psychotherapist based in New York.

SUCCESSFUL DRUG-FREE PSYCHOTHERAPY FOR SCHIZOPHRENIA

Revella Levin

First published 2018
by Routledge
711 Third Avenue, New York, NY 10017

and by Routledge
2 Park Square, Milton Park, Abingdon, Oxon, OX14 4RN

Routledge is an imprint of the Taylor & Francis Group, an informa business

© 2018 Taylor & Francis

The right of Revella Levin to be identified as author of this work has been asserted by her in accordance with sections 77 and 78 of the Copyright, Designs and Patents Act 1988.

All rights reserved. No part of this book may be reprinted or reproduced or utilised in any form or by any electronic, mechanical, or other means, now known or hereafter invented, including photocopying and recording, or in any information storage or retrieval system, without permission in writing from the publishers.

Trademark notice: Product or corporate names may be trademarks or registered trademarks, and are used only for identification and explanation without intent to infringe.

Library of Congress Cataloging-in-Publication Data
Names: Levin, Revella, author.
Title: Successful drug-free psychotherapy for schizophrenia / Revella Levin.
Description: New York, NY : Routledge, 2018. | Includes bibliographical references and index.
Identifiers: LCCN 2017048627 | ISBN 9780815376255 (hbk : alk. paper) | ISBN 9780815376262 (pbk : alk. paper) | ISBN 9781351122313 (ebk)
Subjects: LCSH: Schizophrenia—Treatment. | Psychotherapy.
Classification: LCC RC514 .L397 2018 | DDC 616.89/8—dc23
LC record available at https://lccn.loc.gov/2017048627

ISBN: 978-0-8153-7625-5 (hbk)
ISBN: 978-0-8153-7626-2 (pbk)
ISBN: 978-1-351-12231-3 (ebk)

Typeset in Bembo
by Apex CoVantage, LLC

This book is dedicated not to a person but to a concept. That concept is separating the wheat from the chaff.

Sigmund Freud, John Rosen, and Wilhelm Reich have made important contributions to the field of mental health, but have not only been roundly criticized, but all too often dismissed because some of their ideas have been condemned and some of their important contributions have been neglected. At the present time, Freud's ideas are the most obvious example in the general culture. His most important contribution, the importance of the unconscious, is rarely spoken of today in a discussion of mental health.

This book is not a paean to any of these gentlemen. Indeed, one of the jokes I tell about myself is "I read Freud and keep telling him where he has made a mistake, but he ignores me and keeps making the same mistake. I get so tired of his not listening to me, that I just slam the book shut." I also have differences with Rosen and Reich.

But I insist we are not so inundated with good ideas of how to help the mentally ill that we can afford to waste them if they can be helpful to patients, especially when what we most frequently have to offer them are drugs (at least in the United States) that are at best cosmetic and, at worst, dangerous and so frequently rejected by patients. To me, that is pure spend-thriftiness (to borrow a joke from Stephen Colbert). There are far too many people suffering the agonies of schizophrenia that we can afford to throw away theories with genuine contributions to make, even if flawed.

So, this is a plea to extract the valuable ideas from the useless or dangerous ones from the same contributors. Let us, for example, be more patient with Freud. Yes, in many places he despaired of helping schizophrenics but in "Constructions in Analysis," he offered a brilliant architectural framework of how to help them without naming them. Further, I have never heard anyone express sympathy for the fact that the poor man had no one to analyze him. Certainly, this is a great handicap for the founder of psychoanalysis. The importance of having someone besides the patient analyze the transference and resistance is far too essential to be omitted.

Indeed, I (who was more fortunate) would ask the reader to offer me that grace throughout the present contribution, though I do not put myself in the class of the above-mentioned theoreticians. Before dismissing my work out of hand (or swallowing it whole), please separate what you think of as my wheat from my chaff.

With thanks to the late John Kerr, who brought my attention to that concept in his book "A Most Dangerous Profession" (Alfred Knopf, p. 183) and has so often inspired me.

CONTENTS

Acknowledgements ix

1 Introduction 1

2 Awakening the Schizophrenic Dreamer 10

3 The Difference Between Infantile Omnipotence and Grandiosity 27

4 Bathsheba: A 19-Year Recalcitrant Case of Schizophrenic Requiring 20 Months to Get to the Neurotic Level 44

5 "Black Hole" Phenomenon: Deficit or Defense? A Case Report 56

6 Addendum to "Black Hole" Phenomenon: Deficit or Defense? A Case Report 68

7 Faith, Paranoia, and Trust in the Psychoanalytic Relationship 72

8 John Rosen: Genius or Quack? Historical Reflections of a Former Student 90

9 Five Errors in Freud's Structural Theory and Their Consequences 108

10	Communicating with the Schizophrenic Superego	119
11	Communicating with the Schizophrenic Superego Revisited: A New Technique	143
12	Identification with the Schizophrenic Superego	167
13	"Out, Damned Spot! Out, I Say"; or, Karl Abraham Revisited	174
14	Opposing Opinions as to Treatment of Wishes and Hopes Pathology: A Response to Salman Akhtar	189
15	The Excuses for "Supportive" Rather Than "Active" Psychotherapy	202
16	Toward a More Optimistic View of What Analysts Can Achieve	210
17	The Burned-Out Therapist	224
18	How to Decrease Your Chances of Getting Hurt or Killed When Working with a Schizophrenic Patient	229
19	Technique: Dos and Don'ts	241
20	Side Effects of Anti-Psychotic Drugs	249
21	Epilogue	251
Index		*253*

ACKNOWLEDGEMENTS

This book was completely edited by Saideh Browne, for which I am most grateful.

1

INTRODUCTION

When I was 14, I was one of those fortunate people who knew what I wanted to do when I grew up. The story is rather amusing. A couple who were both social workers happened to be visiting at our home. They asked me what I wanted to do when I grew up. I said shyly, as adolescents sometimes do (surprisingly, I can still hear the sound of my voice in my mind when I said it), "I don't know." They persisted with "Well, what do you like to do?" I replied, "I like to figure out people and I like to help them." They replied, "That is social work." I said, "That's a job?" I was very surprised and said, "Do you mean they pay you for that?" They laughed. From an emotional point of view, it took me many years to get over my surprise that I could be paid for doing something I would enjoy so much.

As the years went by, my interests gradually became more specific. But it was in my Master's Rorschach class at City College of New York that I discovered exactly what I wanted to do. Again, I was fortunate because our professor was Ruth Monroe, the foremost expert in the city on Rorschach at that time. Near the end of the semester, she handed us the record of a hebephrenic, saying "I know you won't be able to do the dynamics of this patient, but do the best you can."

I read it, and, almost immediately, I felt I understood it. I was completely taken by surprise. But an argument started in my mind, "Ruth Monroe said it couldn't be done. How come I did it?" Her assistant graded the paper with a "C," writing "fancy." But I knew I had something. I consulted a senior analyst and she told me about John Rosen, saying "He is a Freudian but he likes his patients." I read his book and came to the conclusion that it wasn't the Freudian approach that cured his patients but the fact that he really liked them. (I had been studying the neo-Freudians at that time, i.e., Horney, Fromm, and Sullivan. And we students used to make jokes about Freud.)

But I was fascinated and decided I wanted to work for Rosen as one of the assistants he used. I got an interview and, in a few months, I was called and driven to a rented house in Bucks County, Pennsylvania, with a patient. The patient was so sick that she couldn't even form a coherent delusion. Again, fortune smiled on me. The psychiatrist fellow who was supposed to be in charge of her training with Rosen became ill, and I was put in charge of the patient. Rosen would come to visit three times a week to supervise my work. He was no feminist. I was expected to do four hours of housework and permitted to try to do therapy with my patient for another four hours. I was on duty 24/7.

I quickly learned that I had been wrong in assuming that his Freudian approach was irrelevant. My patient sounded, as I often said, as if she had read Freud in order to know the "correct" way to be schizophrenic. She was, as schizophrenics are, concrete. I had to learn the "language" in order to understand her and interpret so I would be meaningful to her. I came to call the language "schizophrenese." And I learned it the same way I learned German or French. I would translate what she said in my mind into regular English, then translate my English response into schizophrenese.

Often, I would make incorrect interpretations and I would be ignored. It was frustrating but I would wrack my brain until I find a correct one, to which she would instantly respond. That, to me, is one of the exciting things about working with schizophrenics. With neurotics, one generally has to wait, and/or the response is more likely to be partial or ambiguous.

I should say at this point that Rosen was a very intuitive person but not a good theoretician. Fortunately, I am the reverse. So, we made a good team. What was truly remarkable about him is the respect he showed for patients. I remember the surprise I felt when I first heard him speak to my patient. He approached her with as much respect as if she had come to his Park Avenue office with an intestinal problem. Until I saw this, I had not realized with how much contempt people usually talk to schizophrenics. To him, patients were truly human.

To my surprise, he treated my amateurish attempts with respect. The approach he had written about when he had treated schizophrenics was that their problems began in the oral phase. But my patient, a post-partum psychotic who had majored in English in college, seemed to constantly offer anal material. Rosen did not dispute me, and allowed me to proceed as I had been doing. (Of course, as a beginner, I was not at all sure I was working correctly.)

During the six months I worked with Alice, I took full notes. Unfortunately, those notes were "stolen." (I am sometimes shocked to think how naïve I was, as a young woman, that I would loan to someone what I now realize were terribly valuable notes.) But I have found a few notes that I took near the end that were separate from the lengthy, almost verbatim notes I had made through the treatment. I will offer a few of those notes that seem most instructive to me and some that I remember.

Alice was 5'8" and weighed 180 pounds (I was 5'4" and weighed 120). We kept her in a straitjacket for several months at first because when she first came into the house where we would live, she deliberately knocked a lamp over. Secondly, the precipitating factor had been that she had tried to kill her husband.

One summer day when she was much better, four months into the treatment, we felt that it was safe to let her out of the straitjacket. No one was in the house and the phone was out of order. She grabbed me and held me hard against her, with her hands over my wrists. I was startled. I spontaneously yelled "Alice!" We were near the back door. I thought I could certainly run faster than she could. I felt that if I pulled my hands down hard, I could get away and run to the village. But I feared that, standing next to the kitchen as she was, she might hurt herself with a knife. Further, four months of very intensive and valuable work would go down the drain.

Then, I remembered being told that if one was in trouble, one should kick the patient with one's knee in the belly. But I couldn't do that because Alice had me so hard up against her that I couldn't get my knee up. Then, I also remembered learning one could make a transference interpretation, so I yelled as loud as I could without hostility "I am not your mother!" (One has to yell in order to overcome the noisy superego in the patient's head.) She dropped her hands. We waited one hour till some men who lived in our house came home. (During that time, I suggested to her that she put her straitjacket on, which she used to feel comfortable in, but she refused.)

Needless to say, I did not risk any more interpretations till the men came home. But the incident had a salutary effect on me. First, I was angry with the more experienced men for having left me alone. But, prior to that, I believe I have always been more afraid of being hit than most people. Following that incident, I was never again afraid of being with a schizophrenic.

Of course, Alice was often verbally hostile. Indeed, once Rosen expressed concern about me for fear my feelings would be hurt because of it. But I knew it was only transferential hostility, so I had a firm conviction the hostility was not aimed at me. It belonged only to the transferential object. I replied honestly, "It's like water off a duck's back." Indeed, that attitude must be firmly in the therapist's emotional armamentarium, or the work will be erroneous, not to mention too painful.

People often ask me if my work is not depressing. My answer is, "On the contrary, it's very exciting. When the patient gets an insight, it is very dramatic." I don't deny that it is hard work, but it is very rewarding.

Alice's primary delusion was that she had not given birth to her child. She had many different theories as to how that had happened. Among them was that the "state" had given it to her. I could never figure out the meaning of that particular one until she came out of her delusion. When I asked her why she thought that, she told me it was the *state* of pregnancy. How correct Rosen was when he described schizophrenia as a walking dream. That concept has stood me in good stead through the years.

One of the symptoms of resistance is what I call dopiness. This state is when the patient appears half-asleep. In this state, Alice complained that something was the matter with her eyes. It appears useless to try to interpret when the patient is in that state. I, at least, have never been able to get through.

I interpreted it anally because she complained of emptiness. She said, "I see what Valerie (my nickname is Val) means when she talks of fear of losing shit." The feeling was, as I came to understand it, that when she got pregnant she felt full. But when she gave birth under anesthetic, the obstetrician had "stolen" her big belly from her. Worse yet, the baby probably was a demanding one, as most babies are. As a result, Alice became even more "empty." I believe that such "emptying out" may be the cause of post-partum depression in general.

As you see, the problem was an economic one. One delusion was a complaint that she had been forced into prostitution. I interpreted this as having given up her soul for food. After that, I heard no more about prostitution.

Rosen told us that psychotics don't dream except about food. After about six months, Alice had a dream. I don't remember what it was about, except that there was lipstick in it (she was approaching the Oedipal phase). In Alice's case, he certainly was right. I can't remember just how I came to know it, but the delusion was over. Her mood was quite changed. She accepted the reality of the delivery of her child.

One of the people in the house pretended he had her delusion. The portrayal was quite good. I wish I had a picture of her face when he did that. She was clearly trying to be polite, but she definitely looked at him as if he were quite mad. When we asked her how her child was born, she gave us a very accurate description. I was certain all was well when she told me she felt like Rip Van Winkle. (A few times since then, I have had the experience of patients using those exact words. I had not mentioned that character to her or my other patients. I can tell you, it is an eerie feeling to hear other patients use the same analogy.)

Alice did often speak of her fear of my leaving. I assured her a crowbar couldn't tear me away. She feared I would stop loving her if she became sane. She also feared her mother would hate her. I assured her that Rosen and I would protect her from her mother. Indeed, Rosen put her on the couch, as if she were neurotic, a few days after she had recovered from her delusion. (I have since learned not to do that. It produces too much anxiety. The patient being seated is quite adequate, although I heard that Hyman Spotnitz put his patients on the couch.)

I had been quite sincere in my promise not to leave her, but circumstances beyond my control forced me to. I subsequently heard that she had been correct in her fear of becoming sane. When I said goodbye, I was empathic with her pain and reassuring. I believe she knew I was heartbroken. But then, much later, I heard she broke down again.

Naturally, I felt terrible, but I knew nothing about transference then. Worse, I didn't think she was right that, if I left, she would have been sick again.

Of course, these days no one would hire someone to work 24/7. So, I knew I had a most fortunate experience. Nothing is so convincing as to see such change happen before one's very own eyes. Perhaps that was why people who came to see Rosen's work were so skeptical. They either insisted that the patient wasn't schizophrenic in the first place, or they weren't really recovered, or that the patient was one of the assistants. But some seasoned professionals were convinced of the validity of Rosen's work. For various reasons, Rosen later became unfashionable. All his work was done without psychotropic drugs, ECT, or hospitalization.

A Brief History of Madness

Centuries ago, the cause of madness was considered to be an invasion of demons. In 1817, McLean Hospital was established in Massachusetts. Bedlam, in London, was established even earlier. But in the late eighteenth century, the "moral movement" began. It was based on the idea that

> Mad people were trapped in fantasy world, all too frequently the outgrowth of an unbridled imagination. They need to be treated essentially like children, who required a stiff dose of mental discipline, rectification and retraining in thinking and feeling. The madhouse should then become a reform school.
>
> *(Porter, 1987) (2)*

Then, came electro-shock therapy and insulin therapy. In the mistaken idea that patients with epilepsy didn't have schizophrenia, it was thought that "giving them epilepsy would cure them of schizophrenia" (3). The brain damage caused by shock treatment was pretty well ignored. Paul Hoch, Commissioner of Mental Health Hygiene in New York, said, "Is a certain amount of brain damage not necessary in this type of treatment? Frontal lobotomy indicates that improvement takes place by definite damage of certain parts of the brain" (Hoch, 1948) (4).

But in 2001, Assemblyman Martin Luster, Chairman of the Committee of Mental Health, held hearings on the effects of ECT. I attended the hearings in both New York City and Albany. About 150 patients testified that they had permanent memory loss as a result of their ECT treatment. In some cases, the loss was so severe that they could not recognize their spouses or perform on their jobs. Six psychiatrists insisted that memory loss was due to their psychiatric illness and could not be permanent. This idea is quite inconsistent with the present understanding of depression.

I have also heard stories about psychiatrists changing diagnoses from schizophrenia to depression, in order to justify giving ECT to patients, because ECT is currently supposed to be given only to depressed patients.

The history of the treatment of mental illness is a strange one, in that it seems to learn nothing from either its failures or its successes. In ancient Greece, mental illness in women was attributed to their wandering wombs (The Nation, May 15, 2017) (12).

Treatment in the eighteenth century was limited to various forms of cruelty, i.e., restraints, chains, blood-letting, what we could call water boarding, etc. The patients included King George III, who, it was later decided, suffered from porphyria, a rare genetic disease which can lead to high levels of toxic substances that cause temporary delirium.

But such was not the case with most mentally ill patients. Treatment in France and England was of the physical kind, causing unimaginable pain to patients and curing no one. But Philippe Pinel, around the time of the French Revolution, had a different idea. "He noticed that if the patients were not treated cruelly, they behaved in an orderly fashion. The ranting and ravings, the tearing of clothes, were primarily protests over inhumane treatment" (Porter, 1987) (5).

During the same period, Quakers in York, England, instituted moral treatment. This led to remaking care of the insane in America (6). They opened small homes with all the domestic amenities, gardening, reading, writing, chess playing, etc. Poetry was seen as particularly therapeutic (shades of Freud's free association). The Quakers borrowed their 'medical' philosophy from the ancient wisdom of Aeschylus: "Soft speech is to distempered wrath, medicinal" (7). The discharge rate was 50%.

But the success of this treatment was ignored because it became more expensive than government would tolerate. Hospitals had to become larger. And perhaps more important, it threatened physicians' livelihood, since it could be managed by non-medical men. They complained that "such treatment was a product of Quaker religious beliefs that love and empathy could have restorative powers" (Ibid.) (8). Besides, such treatment did not require neurologists, since the cure did not require medicine. The fact that moral treatment was successful was irrelevant. The result was that treatment of the insane went backwards to physical means. And once again, attempts to treat patients were on the basis of how the patient appeared to the treater, how different he was from the ordinary people. That was the *objective* view. No one seemed interested in the *subjective* view, i.e., how the patient felt.

My papers are written as I began to understand or more clearly understand concepts, for example, the difference between omnipotence and grandiosity. As a result of that understanding, I learned not to interfere with omnipotence, however irrational it may appear, as an example of the utility of that concept.

I can hardly claim credit for being the first person to try to do psychotherapy with schizophrenics. Rather too often, except for Bertram Karon, Austin Riggs, and Chestnut Lodge, the idea has been discarded because drugs were easier and cheaper. The fact that so often patients hated the drugs and the drugs didn't cure anything was ignored.

When, for example, the idea of drugs was presented to the New York State legislature, as a way of emptying out the state hospitals and presumably saving a lot of money, drugs were seized on as a great solution. Clearly, the disadvantages were not presented or were ignored. At that time, the legislature presumably conceived of the idea of having clinics to help patients get their drugs and other help. But that concept was gradually neglected. The emergence of tardive dyskinesia was falsely attributed to the disease itself. It was many years before the psychiatric profession admitted that the grotesque and common symptom was finally attributed to the drugs themselves.

In the United States, another reason that psychiatrists were so eager to seize on the pharmaceutical solution was that they were threatened by the fact that other people in the mental health profession were starting to do psychotherapy. That was an economic threat to the psychiatrists. The concept of "chemical imbalance" was to support the idea of keeping schizophrenic patients within the realm of psychiatry.

Sociology of the Treatment of Mental Illness

Much as I would like to discuss the history of the treatment of mental illness, I think this has been done much better by others. Suffice it to say, it has been enormously varied. Theories have varied from an invasion of patients by demons to the present time, when scientists are looking for a chemical imbalance. (About the latter, I must quote a friend of mine who is a neuropathologist. He wrote to me that "schizophrenia is a graveyard for neuropathology careers.")

The search for the mysterious chemical has been going on for about 30 or 40 years now. I understand that no substantial progress has been made. Is it possible that this is because it isn't there? On the other hand, prior to about 1954, many people interested themselves and were successful to a greater or lesser degree in treating schizophrenia. Among them have been Jung (see John Kerr's book "A Most Dangerous Method"), Mosher, Breggin, Federn, Arieti, Byschowski, Fromm-Reichmann, Eigen, Murray Jackson, Giovacchini, Karon, and, yes, even Winnicott. I have doubtless omitted many others, to whom I apologize. (See footnotes.)

Most important, I believe, are the neglected Scandinavians. The drug companies say that psychotherapy with schizophrenics can't be done. But all four Scandinavian countries do it, each a little differently but with much better outcomes than ours. I have lectured in Sweden and done something I can't do in the U.S., i.e., played tapes. (I felt safe in doing it there because I was quite sure none of my patients were likely to go there or know anyone there.) I saw for myself how much more comfortable their patients are than ours. Patients there don't dread going to the hospital, as ours do. They know they will be listened to. Their therapists are trained for five years. They use almost no drugs and never use ECT. But my patients know that they can call me in emergencies.

I cannot leave this subject without mentioning the magnificent research of Robert Whitaker's "Anatomy of an Epidemic." Allow me to quote the blurb of that book:

> In an effort to prove that these new anti-psychotic drugs called 'atypicals' were more effective than the old. Whitaker proves that patients were long kept in the dark about the dangerous side effects, and were even encouraged to participate in experiments that exaggerated their delusions. (9)

Lest the reader think that Whitaker was mistaken, let me quote from the American Psychiatric Task Force Report #18 on tardive dyskinesia: "Prevalence rates of minimal abnormalities exceeded 60 percent, while the prevalence of moderate abnormalities was close to 30 percent" (p. 45) (10). The fact that "Tardive Dyskinesia exists is well documented and generally accepted" (Ibid., p. 25) (1).

(I'd like to know by whom it was accepted. I happen to know of a drug that can control it to some extent. But when the drug company offered it to psychiatrists, they refused, saying patients were not disturbed by tardive dyskinesia, the company representative told me. Since I have seen tardive dyskinesia, I don't find that credible.) Whitaker's book lists many other side effects of anti-psychotic drugs that horrify me. When the symptoms first showed up, drug companies attributed it to schizophrenia. Anyone who has some understanding of schizophrenia would have known that was impossible. Companies have been sued many times that I know of, but patients have always settled.

Nor must we forget neuroleptic malignant syndrome, which kills. I know of two people who had an acquaintance with that syndrome. One patient of mine was rescued from it (before I met her). The second person, not a patient, died of it recently.

A patient, who was very difficult for me, was being urged by friends to go on drugs. For her, I evolved what I called the "push down, pull out" theory of treatment. The "push down" theory of treatment tried to push down all the symptoms, which doesn't cure anyone but will hide the problems to some extent. But it keeps pushing its way up and the patient will continue to suffer to a large extent from her symptoms, feel dead or like a zombie, as patients like to call it, as well as have the neurologic effects. The "pull out" theory gets rid of the delusion, but she, of course, will have to face her anxiety. As I frequently say, "The drugs are for those in the patients' surroundings, not the patients. They make the patient more bearable for others."

I have met several people and heard about others who say they want to commit suicide, rather than continuing to take drugs. They could bear the schizophrenia but could not bear the medication. This is especially true when they have been told by psychiatrists that they will be on medication for the rest of their lives and have believed it.

Indeed, one such mother of a son, who called me after reading a letter of mine in the New York Times, said, "I wish I had seen such a letter before." In the letter, I had stated the above general position. She told me that her son had complained bitterly of the terrible way the drugs had made him feel. But, she said, she had not taken him seriously. He committed suicide.

There are, of course, many objections to psychotherapy. But unfortunately, when people do their research on whether it works, the research fails to state what *kind* of therapy the therapist is doing. They seem to think that all kinds of treatment that are not drugs are equivalent. This is categorically not true. I continue to learn more from my patients. As I have often said, "If I live another 50 years, I would still be learning more" (The Nation, May 15, 2017).

References

1. Freud, Sigmund. *The Standard Edition of the Complete Psychological Works of Sigmund Freud*, Vol. IV, Hogarth Press, London, p. xxii, 99n. and Vol. V, p. 4017, 298n.
2. Porter, Roy. (1987). Madness and psychiatry: A historical dialogue. In *A Social History of Madness: Stories of the Insane*, Phoenix Giants, Widenfeld and Nickelson, New York, p. 19.
3. Porter, Roy. *A Brief History of Madness*, Merk Tower, Oxford University Press, 2003.
4. Hoch, Paul. (1948). Discussion and concluding remarks. *Journal of Personality*, 49.
5. Porter, Roy. (1987). *A Social History of Madness*, Widenfeld and Nickelson, New York, p. 144.
6. Ibid., p. 182.
7. Ibid., p. 185.
8. Ibid. (pp. 2–10)
9. Whitaker, Robert. (2010). *Anatomy of an Epidemic*, Crown Publisher (a division of Random House, Inc., New York).
10. American Psychiatric Task Force Report #18. (1980). *Chapter III Epidemiology of Tardive Dyskinesia*, p. 45. American Psychiatric Association, Washington, DC.
11. Ibid., p. 25.
12. *The Nation*, May 15, 2017.

2
AWAKENING THE SCHIZOPHRENIC DREAMER

> A dream, then is a psychosis, with all the absurdities, delusions and illusions of a psychosis ... and we learn from it that even so deep-going an alteration of mental life as this can be undone and give place to the normal function. Is it too bold, then, to hope it must also be possible to submit the dreaded spontaneous illnesses of mental life to our influence and bring about their cure?
> *(Freud, 1940, S.E. XXII, pp. 267–268)*

The history of the treatment of schizophrenia is an example of a failure of civilization, much like the treatment of leprosy has been until recent times. A few centuries ago, schizophrenics were thought to be possessed by the devil and sometimes burnt at the stake. Later they were chained in Bedlam. In our century, they were given shock treatment. Some authorities have admitted that the purpose of the shock treatment was to *cause* brain damage (Hoch, 1948, p. 149). Insulin and metrazol shock treatment were also used, which have the same effect (Arnold, 1959, p. 215). Further rationale for using shock treatment is provided very succinctly by Viscott (1972, p. 356), who said, "Finding that the patient has insurance seemed like the most common indication for giving electroshock." The infamous lobotomy was also practiced, resulting in patients who appeared to be no more than walking biological organisms.

In the 1930s and '40s, inspired by Freud's work, psychoanalysts like Fromm-Reichmann, Sullivan, Bychowski, Federn, and Rosen began to understand that schizophrenics' strange behavior was a result of their suffering, not an attempt

(Originally published in *Issues in Ego Psychology, Vol. 10, No. i, 1987*. Reprinted with permission of Washington Square Institute for Psychotherapy and Mental Health)

to offend society. To my knowledge, except in the case of Rosen, the successes were never statistically documented, but many anecdotal reports gave evidence of some success in varying degrees. These variations were undoubtedly due to theoretical differences, the degree of illness of the patient, and the talent of the therapist.

However, before such treatment could become accepted for those other than the very wealthy, psychopharmacology came on the scene. For the psychiatrist who wanted removal from the irrationality, anger, and frequently unpleasant personal habits of the patient, psychopharmacology was a great boon. More and more drugs were developed, each one proclaiming a new "miracle." Further, like an autumn ritual the lay press would report new "proof" that schizophrenia was caused by some aberration in the brain chemistry.

Unfortunately, the "miracles" increasingly proved to have serious side effects. The Task Force Report #18 of the American Psychiatric Association reports that 60 to 65% of patients will get tardive dyskinesia (American Psychiatric Association, 1978, p. 43), a condition resulting in strange involuntary movements over which the patient has no control. It also causes bizarre grimacing. Damage to the eyes, as well as dangerously low levels of white blood cells (agranulocytosis, p. 5) are the result of continued use of some of these drugs. Indeed, there are no psychopharmacological drugs that do not have some of these side effects, including Lithium and Elavil. In fact, the problem is even worse than I have described because these drugs are often used not just for schizophrenics, but depressives, obsessive-compulsives, and the anxiety-neuroses as well, as the Task Force reports. Further, 50% of those who get tardive dyskinesia do not recover from this symptom, even when the drug is discontinued (p. 27). So that a patient may well be left not only with his mental illness intact, but having to suffer with additional neurological and other physical problems. In this instance, we may well wonder if the 'cure' is not worse than the disease.

Considering these circumstances, it would seem timely that we return to the psychotherapy of schizophrenia, whose potentialities were barely explored at the time of the psychopharmacological revolution. Contrary to what some people have said, Freud did envision the possibility of psychotherapy for schizophrenia. He said, "I do not regard it as by any means impossible that by suitable changes in the method we may succeed . . . and so be able to initiate a psychotherapy of the psychoses." (Freud, 1904, p. 264). As to concerns that psychotherapy can aggravate the situation, he says

> nor need you ever fear that the patient will be harmed by the shock accompanying the introduction of the unconscious into the consciousness, for you can convince yourself theoretically that the somatic and emotional effect of an impulse that has become conscious can never be so powerful as that of an unconscious one.
>
> *(Ibid., p. 266)*

Indeed, Freud has given us a complete, albeit condensed, recipe for treating schizophrenics in "Constructions in Analysis":

> Perhaps it may be a general characteristic of hallucinations to which sufficient attention has not hitherto been paid that in them something that has been experienced in infancy, and then forgotten, returns—something that the child has seen or heard at a time when he could still hardly speak and that now forces its way into consciousness, probably distorted and displaced owing to the operation of forces that are opposed to this return. And, in view of this close relation between hallucinations and particular forms of psychosis, our line of thought may be carried still further. It may be that the delusions, into which these hallucinations are so constantly incorporated, may themselves be less independent of the upward drive of the unconscious and the return of the repressed than we usually assume. In the mechanism of a delusion we stress as a rule only two factors: the turning away from the real world and its motive forces, on the one hand, and the influence exercised by wish-fulfillment on the content of the delusion, on the other. But may it not be that the dynamic process is rather that the turning away from reality is exploited by the upward drive of the repressed in order to force its content into consciousness, while the resistances stirred up this process and the trend to wish fulfillment share the responsibility for the distortion and displacement of what is recollected? This is after all the familiar **mechanism of dreams** (emphasis mine), which intuition has equated with madness from time immemorial.
>
> This view of delusions is not, I think, entirely new, but it nevertheless emphasizes a point of view which is not usually brought into the foreground. The essence of it is that there is not only **method** in madness, as the poet has already perceived, but also a fragment of **historical truth**; and it is plausible to suppose that the compulsive belief attaching to delusions derives its strength precisely from infantile sources of this kind . . . It would probably be worthwhile to make an attempt to study cases of the disorder in question on the basis of the hypotheses that have been here put forward and also to carry out their treatment on those same lines. **The vain effort would be abandoned of convincing the patient of the error of his delusion and of its contradiction of reality**: (emphasis mine) and on the contrary, the recognition of its kernel of truth would afford common ground upon which the therapeutic work could develop. That work would consist in liberating the fragment of historical truth from its distortions and its attachments to the actual present day and in leading it back to the point in the past to which it belongs. The transposing of material from a forgotten past on to the present or onto an expectation of the future is indeed a habitual occurrence in neurotics not less than in psychotics. Often enough, when a neurotic is led by an anxiety-state to expect the occurrence of

some terrible event, he is in fact merely under the influence of a repressed memory (which is seeking to enter consciousness but cannot become conscious) that something which was at that time terrifying did really happen. I believe that we should gain a great deal of valuable knowledge from work of this kind upon psychotics.

(Freud, 1937, pp. 267–268)

Unfortunately, many of the current writers on the subject have ignored Freud's advice to lift the unconscious material to consciousness, so that the patient improves his chances to gain control over those mental forces that are so threatening to him. Those who accept Freud's advice know how much easier, not to speak of gratifying, it is to deal with irrational anxiety—if the source is conscious—than it is to attempt to suppress these "demons."

The writers in what I call the "push down" school of therapy, like Werner Mendel, Robert Knight, and the Lidzes, advocate a "covering, rather than uncovering, supportive rather than interpretive, and structured, rather than open-ended type of treatment" (Allen, personal communication, 1982). These people appear to operate on two premises which are questionable—(1) that the schizophrenic process itself is something that cannot be understood, much less resolved, and (2) that the schizophrenic *behavior* is the most important issue because it disturbs those who are in the patient's environment. This view ignores the unconscious, the pain, and the panic that constantly pursue the patient.

As you will see, I am suggesting a return to an approach that addresses the *cause* of the problem, which can make important inroads in the schizophrenic process, and sometimes bring the patient to the point where he is no more ill than the average neurotic. Therapists need to recognize the *patient* as the one who has come to us for help, and our focus need not be the disturbed sensibilities of society, but rather, the human being sitting in our office. Our function can be therapeutic, not just cosmetic.

The question is, if we are to use Freud's work to solve this problem, how shall we proceed? Years of work in this area have led me to believe that simply taking Freud seriously may be the key. To do this, we must first define what a schizophrenic is. I have found the best definition to be a phenomenological one. To wit: a schizophrenic is one whose primary concerns are either literally or symbolically questions of life and death. They are subject to "panic" or "terror" as opposed to mere anxiety.

An example of this is the following patient who was always saying that if she did any one of many gratifying things, she feared she would be killed. At one point her placating tendency became apparent to me, and I said, "I think what you're saying is 'if my mother wants me dead, I'll have to die.'" She responded, "I hate to admit this, but you may not be totally off, because there's a big part of me that wants to appease the person who's jealous. Yes, I'd even die, if that's what someone wanted." She had formerly been in terror of the Devil. Now, she can express a wish to send someone *to* the Devil without panic. Her dreams no longer contain life-threatening content, as they always had previously. From this, it is clear how vulnerable such a patient is. It is a measure of her improved health that she now sees that the gun is in her own hand, so to speak, rather than only expecting the danger to come from outside.

From a structural point of view, we translate this terror as a dread of the dissolution of the ego, that part of the personality from which we get a sense of identity and which implements the wishes of the id. Which part of the personality is putting the ego in danger? The id in its most elemental state strives merely to live and to love, yet the study of schizophrenia always gives evidence of masochism, asceticism, and guilt. The id cannot be responsible.

If not the id, it must then be the superego. Clinical experience verifies this. Schizophrenics feel guilty not about such minor things as missed appointments, or failure to be considerate of someone else, as does the neurotic. They feel guilty for breathing, eating, and living. In short, their superegos are vengeful and cruel to a degree that makes the neurotic superego look like a wrist slapper.

Schafer's paper "The Loving and Beloved Superego in Freud's Structural Theory" is an important paper to discuss at this point for two reasons. One reason is that Schafer is such an influential writer. The second is that Schafer in this paper has catalyzed what I believe to be a negative effect on psychoanalysis, and especially on the psychotherapy of schizophrenia as I am discussing it. For example, he ignores what Freud says in a very clear statement: "What is holding sway in the super-ego is, as it were, a pure culture of the death instinct, and in fact it often enough succeeds in driving the ego into death, if the latter does not fend off its tyrant in time by the change round into mania." (Freud, 1923, p. 53). This statement is a perfect replica of what, in fact, happens in schizophrenia—except the schizophrenic has no recourse to mania, so he simply feels dead, dreads death, or commits suicide.

Further, Freud says, "The super-ego seems to have made a one-sided choice and to have picked out only the parents' strictness and severity, their prohibiting and punitive function, whereas their loving care seems not to have been taken of and maintained" (Freud, 1933, p. 62).

Schafer complains that Freud did not pick up the strands of his thought showing that the superego had a loving side too. I contend that, on the contrary, Freud did not sufficiently distinguish the superego from the ego. Further, I suggest the possibility that he did not take seriously enough his own statement that the superego was a "pure culture of the death instinct" (Freud, 1923, p. 53). If he had, he would have seen its more Machiavellian aspects. Schafer says that "it (the ego) is loved by the superego as one has wished to be loved by these parents" (1960, p. 172). Schafer, I believe, has been taken in by an excellent example of the guile of the superego. In effect, it *implies* it would love the ego, if only . . . But the number of conditions is endless. The gratification of that wish always remains in the distance. The message is a constant reiteration of "if you will only . . . then

I will love you." The accomplishment of the task is always beyond reach, never quite perfect enough, or done frequently enough. At best, completion of the task results merely in the *silencing* of the superego. It is only the *ego* that is capable of a "well done."

Freud is quite specific on this point. He says, "it is precisely those people who have carried saintliness furthest who reproach themselves with the worst sinfulness" (1930, p. 126). "Every renunciation of instinct now becomes a dynamic source of conscience and fresh renunciation increases the hitter's severity and intolerance" (Ibid., p. 128).

I have a borderline patient who is an excellent illustration of this point. She is very hostile to me, not as a function of the transference directly, but as an object who threatens her symbiosis with her mother. She is also very hostile to others in her environment. On the other hand, she has frequently expressed the wish to be Mother Theresa. I pointed out to her that no matter how many times we have discovered how destructive her mother was to her, she has never been able to complain about her mother or get angry with her. "I have to protect her," she finally admitted. "If I didn't, I'd be a bad person. That's why I can't judge her." (Her mother constantly complained she had no judgment.) I said, "If you admitted you *had* judgment, you feel you'd be a bad person." She said, "My conscience says I should be tolerant of others." I then recalled her wish to be Mother Theresa and said, "You are tolerant to the point of sainthood." In the following session, she told me that in an incident that occurred in her work, she felt confidence in her own judgment for the first time. This occurred even in the face of strong opposition by members of the group she was in. In this session it became apparent that her constant criticism of me was for the purpose of assuaging her guilt.

To return to Schafer, he confuses matters further by assigning so many similar tasks to both the ego and the superego that they become almost synonymous, resulting in their uselessness as constructs. One example is the pride that Schafer speaks of as emanating from the superego (Schafer, 1960, p. 179). But that pride, most frequently expressed as "I am better, purer, more moral than anyone else," is, in fact, grandiosity (Levin, p. 68).

The piece de resistance in Schafer's paper is his statement that "severity of superego function testifies to the inadequacy of superego formation" (Schafer, 1960, p. 184). Less may be more in art, but is most unlikely in psychoanalysis. In fact, the developing schizophrenic process is seen when the ego constantly surrenders to an insatiable superego, which grows ever stronger on the increasing flow of energy that it drains from the ego. It is important to stress this point for fear that the therapist, and, therefore, the patient may be misled by the deviousness of the superego.

Chasseguet-Smirgel also, contrary to the opinions of Segal and Bion whom she quotes, supports the value of the superego. She insists that Freud's search for truth when he discovered the Oedipus Complex was aided by the superego, because Freud discovered both at the same time. Yet she later admits that the resistance to truth "evidently comes from a super-ego that refuses to feel guilt" (Chasseguet-Smirgel, p. 32).

Certainly, it is true that resistance to discovering a death wish towards a parent comes from the superego. But the superego doesn't *feel* guilt. It threatens the *ego* with guilt.

The id, too, is, of course, suffering, in that fewer and fewer of its wishes are gratified. The process is most clear if one visualizes a superego constantly pressing down harder and harder with great weight until the ego experiences itself as being squeezed to the brink of death, while itself being forced to squeeze harder and harder against the id, until the whole unconscious erupts into delusions and hallucinations. These manifestations might not be so pathological if they took place in a dream. But what could ordinarily be expressed only while asleep is expressed in a waking state. Further, that which was previously conscious is now itself repressed. Thus, primary and secondary processes have been reversed.

Clearly, then, from a structural point of view, our task would be to siphon off energy from the superego, and return it to the ego. However, clinical experience shows that the therapist need make no effort to return released energy back to the ego. Released energy from the superego *automatically* goes back to the ego, and finds its appropriate "slot" with greater accuracy than the therapist is likely to attain. This view is supported by Bela Grunberger, who says,

> In the course of the analysis of his (the patient's) conflicts, as instinctual maturation progresses, he will spontaneously come to integrate his narcissism and acquire a sense of reality thereby reaching a better understanding of his capabilities. Those capabilities are, moreover, usually real, for one does not have to *inhibit what does not exist*.
>
> *(Grunberger, 1971, p. 181; italics mine)*

He is in agreement with Freud, who says "The psychosynthesis is ... achieved during analytic treatment without our intervention, automatically and inevitably" (Freud, 1919, p. 161).

Much more needs to be said about the nature of the superego to increase the efficiency of the therapist. See Chapters 10 and 11. I have two clinical examples of the relevance of structure. The first is from a patient who is *not* a therapist, but figured out for herself how structural theory works.

Roxanne is a musician in a commercial situation. She is a very bright young woman of 29 years old, with an older brother. Her family was in a state of constant hostility, with various members aligning themselves with others at different times. Roxanne has had seven previous therapists. Only one of these was left for practical reasons.

She was the kind of patient whom one would strongly suspect of being schizophrenic merely by looking at her. Her appearance was utterly devoid of any aesthetic value. I have no doubt that she improved psychologically to some extent in the course of approximately ten years of previous therapy. But when she came to me, the schizophrenia was still evident by intense hostility over minor matters, when she felt "possessed." Her improvement with me is exemplified by her decrease in "spacing out" and the fact that she is almost never embarrassed to talk to people as she used constantly to be. Her relationship with her mother has also strikingly improved. She is no longer obsessed by life and death matters. She has been my patient for two years coming once or twice weekly. The session I am going to provide took place ten months after I began with her.

R. Mother can't stand it that I'm not her. She tries to force me to be her. *I have guilt about existing.*
I. To whom is your existence damaging?
R. Mother saw it as a threat.
I. Will it really kill her?
R. No.
I. You may feel like it would.
R. I'm frightened because the last couple of years, she's using eye make-up and she doesn't know how to do it and it looks stupid. If I don't use make-up, I won't try to compete.
I. What if you did it better than she?
R. I'd be guilty and frightened (*she sits up*). She never compliments me on anything that puts me in a different league. She rewards me for being a slob like her. (*Lies down*) I had to get up because I get so mad.
I. You keep evading what you feel. What will happen to your mother if you wear make-up?
R. She will feel abandoned and left alone.
I. Do you want to get away from her?
R. Yes, I will feel like my own person finally, not a slave to her sickness.
I. Are you crying?
R. Yes.
I. Are you going to be controlled by your mother's sickness or be your own person?
R. I want to be my own person, but it's extremely painful. It leaves me alone.
I. Let yourself feel that.
R. (*Silence*)
I. You're making yourself alone by not talking.
R. I don't feel alone. I'm absorbing this. It's very heavy.
I. There's all kinds of alone. Tell me about it.
R. I feel separate from mother. The potential to be what I want is very real ... I feel enormous relief. I feel unburdened. There is an element of pain. I love her ... I feel like I've been run over by a truck except it doesn't hurt.

I. What is it that so shocked you?
R. How I could let go. This is what therapy is all about. But you (one) rarely see that. This is much more graphic and vivid than previous changes. This is a root.
I. Do you want me to see you as separate?
R. You better.
I. What would you like me to see?
R. Someone who deserves to exist. That's what you were trying to tell me from the beginning, when you said how repressed I was. I didn't know I didn't feel I deserved to exist.

   (*This is the unconscious superego. I should make clear I hadn't said anything about the content, since I didn't know she experienced it that way.*)

I. How do you think I feel?
R. You saw it all along. I stake my claim on the world and go get it. I'm lying here sort of stunned. I don't worry about how people see me. Just about what *I* want.

Next Session

R. I feel incredibly fragile. I have a core of myself in my hand and it's unprotected.
I. You're going to need to describe it to me, so I'll understand.
R. Those things in the ocean, like jelly, you see them on the beach. You see through it and it's formless.
I. You fear others see through you? Is that what bothers you most?
R. What bothers me most is that *I haven't been taking care of it.*
I. It's the baby of yourself and you haven't been mothering it.
R. Awesome.

Following Session

R. Before it was a fetus. Now it's a baby. I asked myself why I've never done that kind of thing before.

   (*The reference is having done something self-protective. I have from the beginning been aware that she is pathologically without defenses and thus gets terribly hurt.*)

R. The answer was because I never loved her (the baby) and I didn't think she was worth protecting. I had an insight in reference to my conscience. I learned to detach myself and listen to its nonsense. The baby is the id. The primitive savage aspect. The conscience is the superego.

   (*Note: I want to make it very clear that I never used the words "id" or "superego" with this patient. Indeed, I was quite surprised to discover she knew them.*)

Vivian

The second case is Vivian. She is a woman, over 70, of strict Irish Catholic background who had been a telephone operator until she retired. She lived in the same building, in a different apartment, as her widowed sister. She came to me hearing the voices of every tenant in the apartment building. At the beginning, there were over 20. The voices followed her everywhere. She would transfer from bus to bus in an attempt to escape them. Through work, we succeeded in getting them down to two. One was Mr. Nasty (her name) who was the superego. The other was Joan, who, much to my surprise, turned out to be the ego.

In one session, she spoke of her fears of what it would be like if her voices left her.

I said, "you may feel a kind of loneliness, not because Joan (the ego) is leaving, but because Mr. Nasty (the superego) is leaving. That's in a way, why you're holding on. Remember you used to say that, as awful as your father was, even if he didn't say anything, he was still in the house. You wanted to believe that if there was a body in the house, you weren't alone, but you really did feel alone."

This case was surprising due to the fact that I had never imagined that the ego could be heard as a split off voice. But the gentleness with which she addressed my patient and the veracity of her communications made it clear that "Joan" was a weak ego. Both these cases not only illustrate the validity of structural theory, but have a further value as well. I believe that by keeping clearly in mind the structure of the personality, the therapist is able to organize apparently chaotic communications of the patient, thus reducing the patient's and his own anxiety as well as increasing the therapist's efficiency. The stages of development are relevant to our discussion here. All are agreed that schizophrenia is at best a regression to earlier psycho-sexual stages. Indeed, it may be very possibly due to a fixation at those stages. At this point, an elaborated description of the emotional state of the patient can lead us to the point where we can accurately ascertain the developmental level that it occupies. The schizophrenic is either in constant dread of losing his life, in one form or another, or someone who already feels dead. Such a diagnosis may at times be easier to determine negatively, i.e., we can more easily determine what a schizophrenic is *not*. She is not very concerned as to whether her hair is set properly or the roast is overdone. That is, she is not worried about those things that do not threaten her existence either symbolically or physically. But she is terrified of being ignored, which she experiences as being killed, or people emptying her out, which she experiences as being in danger of starving to death, or becoming a non-entity (which is psychological death) through losing her mind because of being lied to.

These are clearly not Oedipal concerns. Indeed, the ease with which schizophrenics speak of what we consider sexual matters gives evidence of their desexualization of erotic terms. The panic and terror spoken of above point to the conclusion that the focus of emotional involvement is with oral and anal concerns. With these people, a penis is not a sexual organ; it is an organ for urinating and feeding, if we are speaking of its owner. For a woman, a penis is something that can feed her or destroy her, if the owner of it is hostile. A vagina to a man is something that can suck him dry or empty him out. For a woman, a vagina can be a vulnerable area open to attack or a substitute mouth.

Thus, all material must be viewed from an oral or anal viewpoint. It is incumbent on the therapist, therefore, to look at material in terms of whence the energy is emanating and what its condition is when it arrives at its destination.

An example of this is a child I worked with who was obsessed with his delusion that his urine could kill his mother. Further, he was so identified with his feces that he would search constantly for what had become of them. I have found that the superego concerns itself most often with anal material. But occasionally the material is oral, clothed in anal clothes, so to speak.

Now let us concern ourselves with technique. In recent years, I have heard many complaints from students that their instructors speak too much about theory and too little about what to do. So, I will try to address myself to that complaint in this chapter. If we attempt to treat a schizophrenic, we are instantly faced with the limitations of our patients. Asking such a patient to lie down and free associate, except in the most mild of cases, would bring either terror, withdrawal, mutism, or an exit. I understand that the Modern School of Psychoanalysis of Spotnitz encourages florid patients to lie down. I can't help but believe that, in so doing, the therapist is surrendering to his fear of the illness and has rationalized that it is to the benefit of the patient.

However, there is an exception to the rule of having the schizophrenic sit up. There are schizophrenics whose affect is still extremely repressed. These patients are most difficult in terms of reaching their unconscious and should be asked to lie down for that reason. This kind of patient, before becoming schizophrenic, was a classical obsessive-compulsive. So, the rule is, the more "uncivilized" the patient is, the more appropriate it would be for him to sit up.

As I said earlier, we awaken the schizophrenic dreamer by interpreting his "dream." This permits unconscious material to come to consciousness, making it easier for both therapist and patient to deal with.

In general, we concentrate more on the verb or predicate of the sentence than we do on the noun. Nouns are symbolic, therefore, interchangeable but interpreting them does little to affect structural change. For example, however tempting it may be to advise a patient that a faucet is a symbol of the breast, the patient will remain in the same emotional position after being told that. It is a knowledge of the means of how to defend himself against the "poisonous milk" that comes out of the faucet that will help the patient decrease the pressure from the superego and allow it to flow into the ego.

It is incumbent on the therapist to constantly be on the alert for the superego manifestations that so frequently *appear* benign and sometimes even rational. In fact, the superego consistently looks for excuses as to why the id should never be gratified, or gratified as little as possible.

The neutrality that the therapist displays toward the neurotic is not a luxury he can afford with the schizophrenic. The ego of the schizophrenic is too weak, and the superego too strong for the patient to be able to fight this battle without the overt loyalty of the therapist to the ego. The patient must feel that the therapist is on the side of the patient's life and against those forces that want to "kill" him. The therapist must be able to convey the message in one form or another, that the patient's conscience should not be allowed to be his guide, as Jiminy Cricket advocates. The patient must be informed that those guidelines are frequently misleading and may be advocating the conscience's interest in its own continued existence, rather than the welfare of the patient's ego.

Another task of the therapist is to identify which are the ego's and which are the superego's messages. This ability requires a good deal of experience to refine. For example, the superego's admonishment to the patient to "do his work" may very well be for the purpose of denying him appropriate libidinal pleasure. The ego in the real interest of the patient may give the same message.

It takes sufficient knowledge of both that particular patient and knowledge of theory to ascertain which is sending the message.

Needless to say, it is not desirable to use technical words with the patient. My practice has been that the superego is identified as the "conscience" and the ego as the "brain," the former designated as the "enemy" and the latter as the "friend." The id is identified as the "wishes."

There are a great many aspects to this battle which I cannot go into in this short space but which I am planning to write about in depth in the future. Suffice it to say that it is my contention that the schizophrenogenic mother concept, which is so out of favor these days, does in fact exist. She is a mother, or mothering figure, who has two essential characteristics: the combination of which is so destructive to the child. She is hostile *and* she lies about her hostility. Her tone of voice is frequently sugary behind which hides unknown depths of danger to the child. The destructive aspect of this lies not so much in the hostility, because were it straightforward, it could be recognized by even a fairly young child. It would be painful, and even produce guilt, to some degree. But the ego would not be so confused as it would by a mother who says "I love you and I am the only one who could love you. That's why I'm telling you not to laugh, because people don't like you when you laugh." Let us examine how much confusion results from this statement. Three different realistic statements contradict these two statements by the mother: (1) the mother does *not* love the child, (2) other people *could* love this child, and (3) it is the *mother* who doesn't enjoy hearing the child laugh, but most other people would.

These statements are very destructive in that by nature a child will rely on the parent to teach them what reality is. Here his natural infantile omnipotence (Levin, 1986, p. 68) betrays him, in that he expects that by mere wishing, he can rely on his parents to advise him as to what reality is. But a young child doesn't have enough knowledge to be aware of the narcissistic advantage of lying and other people's pleasure in hearing laughter. Since he will believe this lying mother, he will also think *he* is the strange one, since he does enjoy hearing laughter.

Now let us consider the problem of interpretation. In such a short space, I can give only the barest guidelines. We can begin with the suggestion of Freud himself, "there is not only *method* in madness . . . but also a fragment of *historical truth* . . . and it is plausible to suppose that the compulsive belief attaching to delusions derives its strength precisely from infantile sources" (Freud, 1937, p. 267; italics Freud's). This is where the therapist plays Perry Mason. He must find that kernel of truth that is inherent in every irrational statement.

With the child I previously mentioned who thought his urine could kill his mother, I made just that error, i.e., not looking for the kernel of truth. He told me his mother took his love away from him. I thought that was just too crazy to be understood. Later, working with another patient, I discovered the error of my ways. His mother had indeed "taken his love away" from him. Through his mother's rejection of any of his offerings or communications, he had lost his love. Only gifts that are received are not lost. In a condensed form, by not accepting his love, his mother took his love away from him.

It is incumbent on the therapist to find the correct interpretation. Freud says, "if it (the interpretation) is wrong, there is no change in the patient" (Ibid., p. 265). But one can flounder indefinitely if one is not in the right general ballpark. This is the problem with the interpersonal theorists who began early and heroically to work with these people. They do not work with the primary process, as David Glassman stated in a recent paper for the Psychoanalytic Psychotherapy Study Center. If one reads Sullivan's interviews with schizophrenics, one will see that he all too often interrogates the patient concerning definitions of nouns, rather than treating the material as a dream (Sullivan, 1962, p. 26).

It is John Rosen's genius that, rather than getting bogged down in translating the patient's language into understandable English, he interpreted the material like a dream. Rosen's reasoning was that if one could cure neurotics by interpreting their unconsciousness, why not do the same with schizophrenics? He says,

> what is the psychosis but an interminable nightmare in which the wishes are so well disguised that the psychotic does not awaken? Why not awaken the psychotic by unmasking the real content of his psychosis? Once the psychosis is stripped of its disguises, will not this dreamer too awaken?
>
> *(Rosen, 1953, p. 4)*

Objections have been raised that Rosen had an inadequate theory, that he relied too much on his intuition, etc. Ironically, perhaps it was his brilliant intuition that stood in the way of his work. Probably because of it, he waited too long before developing a theory. Further, some may object that even the theory he did produce may be dubbed inadequate. But these criticisms do not vitiate the value of the idea, nor eradicate the many people who have improved or been cured in his care. I have always operated on the premise that one could use those ideas that appeared to be useful, and ignore those that appeared not to be, regardless of who the originator was. No one, not even Freud, produced only useful ideas or ideas that stood the test of time.

In that spirit, I have used many of Rosen's ideas, discarded those that appeared not to be useful, and inserted bits of theory or technique in what appeared to me to be omissions. One of the more important of his deficiencies was his failure to recognize the idiosyncrasy of each patient in order to more tightly fit the interpretation to the material.

A woman who was the patient of a supervisee of mine was raised by governesses. The result was that some of the material transferred on to my student was that of a governess, not just a mother. Here there would be a difference in the emotional setting, in that because the governess was an employee, she was ultimately controlled by the mother, even though the child spent most of her time with the governess.

Frequently, the tight fit of an interpretation can be helped by examining the emotionally laden word and defining it and its function. One word that is frequently used and has important psychological implications is patients' complaining that they have been "poisoned." When we consider the relation of the body to poison, we see that poison is something the body cannot assimilate and continue to live. Unless the poisoned person can regurgitate it, or have it chemically rendered benign, he will die. Poison does not nourish. It damages.

What is the psychological equivalent of that phenomenon? Lies. The ego cannot integrate lies. They do not combine with what the person either has experienced or can deduce as the truth. If the lie is not regurgitated as in "You're lying," it partly hangs in suspension and partly wars with the truth already incorporated in the patient. But it cannot be assimilated and thus lies keep the patient in a constant state of tension (note that the patient will express the problem in the predicate form, as noted previously) (Von Domarus, 1954).

Another example of the importance of words and their idiosyncratic meaning come up in my experience with a patient I had when I worked for Rosen. She insisted that she had been forced into prostitution. Many weeks of useless interpretation led to my finally asking her for her definition of "prostitution." She told me that prostitution occurred when one sold one's body and soul for food. I responded that she felt she had to do just that in order to get food from her mother. The complaints ceased immediately and permanently.

This leads to another rule concerning interpretation. Even more watchful eyes must be kept on the transference than with neurotics. Freud was certainly in error when he said "sufferers from narcissistic neuroses have no capacity for transference or only insufficient residues of it. They reject the doctor, not with hostility but with indifference" (Freud, 1917, p. 447). Patients remain indifferent until one makes an interpretation that is correct on an emotionally laden subject. "Indifference" can quickly turn to either a strong positive or negative transference. The difficulty with schizophrenics is not that the transference is too weak, but rather that it is too strong, requiring constant alertness on the part of the therapist. One need not concern oneself about the positive transference for a long time but only be grateful that it is present to bind the patient to the therapist through difficult times to come. It is the negative transference that is so frequently the cause of fear to the therapist. But it is also the negative transference that has the most potential for possibilities of improvement if interpreted correctly and sufficiently.

For instance, a hypothetical patient complains to the therapist "you don't pay enough attention to me." (This could easily occur with a patient who talks very softly and is fearful of being a nuisance.) I would respond by saying "Why do you let me get away with it?" This statement accomplishes several things: (1) it avoids a useless battle, (2) it recognizes the reality of the patient's feelings, (3) it implies power on the part of the patient to remedy the situation, and (4) it supports the ego against the superego. Shortly after that, to put the matter in relief so that the patient sees clearly where the damage is coming from, I say "Your conscience is always telling you not to show off, isn't it?" Note that while I am fully aware that the mother paid insufficient attention to her child and probably, in some way or another, told him to make himself invisible, I ignore that for the moment. When the patient has sufficiently integrated the above message, he will tell me the manner in which his mother told him to hide.

The problem of the negative transference leads me to the question of what kind of person a therapist for schizophrenics should be. First, one must have a great tolerance for hostility. One's attitude must be that one is absolutely certain that all hostile manifestations are derived from the transference. One does not defend oneself or attack back, as one therapist I know does. When one hears an accusation, one's immediate response to oneself should not be the question of reality or non-reality but rather, as in the example of the hiding patient, "What does it mean?" Whether or not the hostile accusations are true is irrelevant. At this level, the only importance they have is the patient's experience.

"Aaron Green," the pseudonym given by Janet Malcolm for a psychoanalyst of the New York Psychoanalytic Society, has an interesting description of what he thinks a therapist for schizophrenia should be (Malcolm, 1980). He said,

> It bothers me sometimes. The reason is that I'm not very generous. I'm self-absorbed. I'm interested in my own ideas, my own worries, my own pains, my own pleasures. It's hard for me to give very much. The people who work well with schizophrenics are people whose center of gravity is a bit displaced, who can make another person the center of their lives, who are endowed with an unusual measure of intuitiveness and sensitivity and kindliness . . . it allows them to dispense with the rigors of analytic technique a little more easily. They can *afford* to do it. (Italics his) Whereas others like me, who are not so kind, not so sensitive, not so intuitive require more graphic demonstrations of data in order to be sure about what they're doing and where the patient is.

I would be inclined to agree with "Aaron Green" in general, but would disagree that one has to make the patient the center of one's life. However, I would say that it requires courage, the courage of being able to delve into the unconscious and, so to speak, be able to swim around in it. Of course, it is also necessary to keep one foot in reality at the same time. This kind of emotional acrobatics is required of the therapist. I consider that ability a true example of regression in the service of the ego.

One must also have conviction about the terror of the patient and really feel the panic of someone who fears he is being threatened with death by someone's stare, and leave aside for the moment the reality that no one was ever killed literally by a look.

One must have some facility for languages and be able to learn what I call "schizophrenese." It does require a different state of mind in the same way that speaking French would for native-born Americans. One gains a facility for "schizophrenese" in the same way one gains a facility for French. First, one translates in one's mind consciously into English, then translates one's response into French. Gradually, no translation from English to French is required.

Another requirement is that the therapist must *like* the patient. Here, I take strong issue with Searles, who seems to believe that the therapist must hate the patient (Searles, 1979). In my view, to work successfully with such patients, one's motivation must be high. This can hardly be the case if one dislikes one's patients, as Searles does, or misunderstands them so badly that one is jealous of them.

Learning how to do therapy with schizophrenics is like any other skill. If one has the talent and learns the skill, the ability to work successfully with schizophrenics is neither a miracle nor a mystery. It is something that I think can become nearly as commonplace as successfully dealing with neurotics. What is required is conviction that underneath that strange, weirdly behaving patient is a *real human being*.

But perhaps the most important requirement is an ability on the part of the therapist to be alone. A schizophrenic patient is in no way able to socialize. If the therapist cannot tolerate a patient who is unable to fill any need of the therapist's for relief of isolation, he will only find himself frustrated and angry when working with a schizophrenic. As Symington says, "the psychotic area also has within it that area of the mind which cannot be contained within a relationship" (Symington, 1986, p. 234).

If one likes one's patient, and fulfills the other requirements mentioned above, the rewards can be thrilling. Imagine for a moment the schizophrenic you are most familiar with. Then, imagine that person as someone who functions, communicates, expresses his feelings, and enjoys life. Would not such a change bring a warm glow of aesthetic satisfaction? Indeed, one of my chief complaints about Freud is that he never said what the therapist should do when she got so excited about the progress of a patient that she felt an almost irresistible urge to jump up and down in her chair. If the reader has a solution to this problem, I would be most grateful.

References

Allen, Robert E. (1982). Personal Communication, December 6.
American Psychiatric Association. (1978). *Task Force Report #18, Tardive Dyskinesia*, pp. 5, 27, 43.
Arnold, O.H. (1959). Results and efficacy of insulin shock therapy. In Max Rinkel and Harold E. Himwich (Eds.), *Insulin Treatment in Psychiatry*, Philosophical Library, New York, p. 215.
Chasseguet-Smirgel, Janine. *The psychoanalysts attitude towards ethics*. Unpublished paper.
Freud, Sigmund. (1904). On psychotherapy. In *The Standard Edition of the Complete Psychological Works of Sigmund Freud*, Vol. VII, Hogarth Press, London, pp. 264, 266.
———. (1917). Introductory lectures on psycho-analysis. In *The Standard Edition of the Complete Psychological Works of Sigmund Freud*, Vol. XVI, Hogarth Press, London, p. 447.
———. (1919). Lines of advance in psycho-analytic therapy. In *The Standard Edition of the Complete Psychological Works of Sigmund Freud*, Vol. XVII, Hogarth Press, London, p. 16.
———. (1923). The ego and the id. In *The Standard Edition of the Complete Psychological Works of Sigmund Freud*, Vol. XIX, Hogarth Press, London, p. 53.
———. (1930). Civilization and its discontents. In *The Standard Edition of the Complete Psychological Works of Sigmund Freud*, Vol. XXI, Hogarth Press, London, pp. 126, 128.
———. (1933). New introductory lectures on psychoanalysis. In *The Standard Edition of the Complete Psychological Works of Sigmund Freud*, Vol. XXII, Hogarth Press, London, p. 62.
———. (1937). Constructions in analysis. In *The Standard Edition of the Complete Psychological Works of Sigmund Freud*, Vol. XXIII, Hogarth Press, London, pp. 265, 267–268.
———. (1940). An outline of psycho-analysis. In *The Standard Edition of the Complete Psychological Works of Sigmund Freud*, Vol. XXIII, Hogarth Press, London, p. 172.
Grunberger, Bela. (1971). *Narcissism*, International University Press, New York, p. 181.
Hoch, Paul. (1948). Round table on ECT. *Journal of Personality*, 17: 48.
Ibid., p. 149.
Levin, Revella. (1986). Infantile omnipotence and grandiosity. *Psychoanalytic Review*, 73(1), Spring: 68.
Malcolm, Janet. (1980). The impossible profession. *New Yorker Magazine*, December 1.
Rosen, John. (1953). *Direct Analysis*, Grune and Stratton, New York, p. 4.
Schafer, Roy. (1960). The loving and beloved superego in Freud's structural theory. *Psychoanalytical Study of the Child*, 15: 172, 186, 179, 184.
Searles, Harold. (1979). *Countertransference*, International Universities Press, Inc., New York, pp. 590–591.
Sullivan, Harry Stack. (1962). *Schizophrenia as a Human Process*, W.W. Norton, New York, p. 26.
Symington, Neville. (1986). *The Analytic Experience*, St. Martin's Press, New York, p. 234.
Viscott, David. (1972). *The Making of a Psychiatrist*, Fawcett, Greenwich, CT, p. 356.
Von Domarus, E. (1954). The specific laws of logic in schizophrenia. In J.S. Kasanin (Ed.), *Language and Thought in Schizophrenia*, University of California Press, Berkeley and Los Angeles, CA, p. 356.

3

THE DIFFERENCE BETWEEN INFANTILE OMNIPOTENCE AND GRANDIOSITY

Throughout psychoanalytic literature, the words "grandiosity" and "omnipotence" have been used almost, but not quite, interchangeably. At the beginning of the century, the word "megalomania" was also used in the same connection. This interchangeableness may have led to some important confusions, not only of the words, but also as to which feelings or behavior are, or are not, pathological. And, of course, if there were questions as to pathology, then clearly there would be questions as to the approach of the therapist.

Freud (1909) himself contributed to this confusion. In the case of the Rat Man, he refers to the patient's "*omnipotence* which he ascribed to his thoughts and feelings, and to his wishes, whether good or evil" (p. 233, italics in the original). But only a bit later, referring to the same concept, Freud says "this belief is a frank acknowledgement of a relic of the old *megalomania* of infancy" (p. 234, italics added).

However, clinical experience leads to the impression that the emotional characteristics of grandiosity are very different than those of omnipotence. The most obvious example is the anxiety that accompanies the grandiosity of the patient compared to the peacefulness that is characteristic of the happy omnipotent baby. From a clinical point of view, the question arises as to whether it is desirable to give up one's omnipotence, if it really is not the same thing as megalomania or grandiosity.

That question, in turn, leads to whether or not one *can*, let alone *should*, give up one's basic wishes. Freud (1937) says,

> At no other point in one's analytic work does one suffer more from an oppressive feeling that all one's repeated efforts have been in vain, and from

(Originally published in *The Psychoanalytic Review*, Vol. 73, No. 1, Guilford Publications, Inc. Copyright 1986, N.P.A.P., New York. Reprinted with permission of Guilford Press)

a suspicion that one has been 'preaching to the winds,' than when one is trying to persuade a woman to *abandon* her wish for a penis on the ground of its being unrealizable.

(p. 252, italics added)

Given Freud's conviction about the immutability of the pleasure principle, his expectation that a patient would give up a wish on grounds of its being unrealizable seems most mysterious. Quite the contrary, it seems rather, that if a wish is *not* fulfilled, it becomes even stronger. For example, it is difficult to imagine that the recent recession *decreased* the desire of most people to be rich(er).

Given these contradictions and the thrust of Bettelheim's (1983) book questioning translations of Freud, research as to possible errors of translations seems indicated. This approach, however, was not rewarded in reference to either the last-mentioned quotation, nor in the following one: "We are justified in assuming that megalomania is essentially of an infantile nature and that, as development proceeds, it is *sacrificed* to social considerations" (Freud, 1911c, p. 65, italics added). However, research proved fruitful in the following two instances: In "Formulation Regarding the Two Principles in Mental Functioning," the statement is translated as: "Actually the substitution of the reality-principle for the pleasure-principle denotes no *dethronement* of the pleasure-principle, but only a *safeguarding* of it" (Freud, 1911a, p. 223, italics added). The statement as it stands implies that the wishes that compose the pleasure-principle *are* retained.

In addition, there appear to be two errors in translation. The original is "In Wirklichkeit bedeutet die Ersetzung des Lustprinzips durch das Realitatsprinzip keine Absetzung des Lustprinzips, sondern nur eine Sicherung deselben" (Freud, 1911b, p. 414). But "dethronement" is a distorted translation of "Absetzung." "Put down," "drop," or "discard" would be more accurate, thus vitiating the implication of rank. But most important is the unquestionable error of translating "durch" as "for." In fact, "durch" means "through" as in the sense of "to go through a doorway." On the next page, the original is "Die Erziehung kann ohne weitere Bedenken als Anregung zur Uberwindung des Lustprinzips, zur Ersetzung desselben durch das Realitätsprinzip beschrieben werden" (p. 415). This is translated as (1911a) "*Education* can be described without more ado as an incitement to the conquest *of* the pleasure principle; and to its *replacement* by the reality principle" (p. 224, last two italics added). Again, there is an error in translation. The German word "durch" is now translated as "of."

To add to this confusion, Freud's two statements, one following only a page later, whether in German or English, contradict *each other*. In addition, Freud (1913) makes the following statement:

A whole number of mental structures can ... be understood as attempts to deny whatever might disturb this feeling of omnipotence and so to prevent emotional life from being affected by reality until the latter could be better controlled and *used for purposes of satisfaction.*

(p. 186, italics added)

But there seems little profit in speculating what might have caused the contradiction in Freud's mind. Rather, I wish merely to bring to the reader's attention the fact that some question can legitimately be raised as to the idea of wishes being given up.

One could assert, quite understandably, that if wishes were never given up, of what value is psychoanalysis? If the essential wishes are uninfluenced, or undisturbed, is not the analyst helpless in his efforts to assist his patient?

The answer is that, when the gratification of a wish would no longer bring pleasure, the wish, so to speak, *dissolves.* For example, when a man who has had a fetish for women's shoes discovers its root, the cathexis changes from women's shoes to women's genitals. In that sense, the wish for women's shoes is dissolved. So, I would suggest that wishes are given up only when their fulfillment no longer brings gratification. But if a woman wants a penis and she attempts to suppress, repress, or deny her wish to have one, she will only succeed in suffering the pain of the suppression, repression, or denial of her wish, while her longing for a penis continues. How can one rid oneself of a wish, merely because it is inconvenient, or even painful to have it fulfilled? In fact, I have had patients who berate themselves for continuing to wish for what is unobtainable, but that only results in the painful feeling of "stupidity" or "foolishness." The wish continues.

Let us return to the question of infantile omnipotence and grandiosity. The interchangeableness of terms was repeated by many important theoreticians of whom the following are just a sample. Ferenczi (1952) says, "since it seemed to me probable that the fulfillment to which we are compelled by experience of the childhood *megalomania* by the recognition of the power of natural forces composes the essential content of the development of the ego" (p. 218, italics added). Klein (1935) says, "The *sense of omnipotence,* in my opinion, is what characterizes mania, and further, (as Helene Deutsch has stated) mania is based on the mechanism of *denial*" (p. 145). Kernberg (1967) states, "Underneath the feelings of insecurity, self-criticism and inferiority that patients . . . present, one can frequently find grandiose and omnipotent trends" (p. 671). Kohut and Wolf (1978) do the same thing: "However grave the blows may be to which the child's grandiosity is exposed by the realities of life, the proud smile of the parents will keep alive a bit of the original omnipotence" (p. 417). In *The Analysis of the Self,* Kohut (1971) goes even further: "these patients remained fixated on archaic grandiose self configurations" (p. 3). He later implies that the parent becomes the possessor of the omnipotence, a phenomenon which I will discuss later. Searles (1972) also uses "grandiosity" and "omnipotence" interchangeably as in "grandiose identification with technology" (p. 370) and "technology . . . seemingly omnipotent" (p. 371).

I find Searles' confusion between the two the most disturbing since he is known for his work in schizophrenia and the difference between these two concepts is especially important with those patients, as I will discuss later.

Both the ordinary language dictionary and the *Dictionary of Psychology* (Dreyer, 1952) make distinctions that, to the psychoanalyst, have important implications. The *American Heritage Dictionary* (Davis, 1970) defines omnipotent as "having unlimited power, authority or force, all powerful" (p. 496). Grandiosity is defined as "Affectedly grand" (p. 311), which implies to me that it has an unrealistic quality. Dreyer (1952) defines both "grandeur delusions" (p. 108) and "megalomania" as excessive overestimation of one's own importance, though the latter has the additional characteristics of an "overestimation of one's abilities" (p. 164). "Omnipotence of thought" is defined as a "conviction that a mere wish is effective in producing the event" (p. 189). He also attributes this characteristic not only to children, but to the beliefs of primitive people and obsessional neurotics as well.

Clinical Examples

Having worked with patients who run the gamut from hospitalizable psychotics to ordinary neurotics, I have no longer been able to ignore the overwhelming support for the idea that infantile omnipotence is healthy and grandiosity is pathological. I would like to give a condensed version of how Laura, a 50-year-old college English instructor, lost her omnipotence and became grandiose as a result. Laura's mother always told Laura that her judgment was bad. Since her mother obviously objected to Laura's having her own judgment and perception, Laura repressed her omnipotence in that area. She showed evidence of it by constantly professing to me that she was afraid of doing this or that, for fear she might be "wrong." It soon became clear to me, that she was more frightened of being *right*. But she ignored me and later admitted she didn't believe that interpretation.

Recently, when she finally accepted that interpretation, she described to me how that repression turned into grandiosity. "I'm so afraid they'll leave me." "*Everyone* will leave me." "I will lose *control*. If I admit I'm wrong (regardless of how right she may be), they'll stay. If I *make* (a typical grandiose word) them right, and I'm wrong, they'll stay."

But at another point omnipotence comes through.

I said to her, "You try to prove things to your mother in order to get her permission. Why do you need it?"

She responded, "Yes, that's true. That's good. (This from a patient who in this period of treatment is generally hostile or ignoring me.) I can do something without permission. That feels strong. I feel happy, relaxed. *I can do anything*. It's not the end of the world. That's what I had always felt, that it was the end of the world."

Note that "I can do anything" is not a realistic statement. But it does denote a feeling of confidence. Note also that it is not a *comparative* statement.

Merry, a 40-year-old, twice-divorced mother of two, experiences her grandiosity as being deflated in the following statement: "I feel exposed. For so many years, I pretended I was happy. The truth is I'm not happy. I feel embarrassed and stupid for pretending I was. (This is an expected response when a piece of grandiosity is exposed, since the patient has deceived herself.) Like I was something *special*. That's very deflating." Sam expresses the failure of his omnipotence by saying "I can't defend myself. I always wonder where the next smash is coming from." Maureen, a borderline schizophrenic patient, shows a little insight into her own grandiosity and resistance to sharing emotional material. "It may sound grandiose [a word I have never used with her] but I feel I'm so unique, that I feel you can't understand me." Note here is another characteristic of grandiosity. It is frequently, if not always, used as a kind of substitute identity. Later, with the characteristic insight of schizophrenics, Maureen says, "When you're growing up, you feel you can conquer the world."

Infantile Omnipotence and the Question of Repression

Let us now look at the original experience of omnipotence. In fact, infants can't even walk or talk, let alone have knowledge of how to fix their own bottles. By adult standards, no one is more helpless and less omnipotent than an infant. But let us, for a moment, try to put ourselves in the baby's place. Admittedly, this is a highly speculative attempt. No one can remember, at most, more than bits and pieces of the first year of life. But let us see how far we can go. The infant discovers that his wish generally brings a bottle. But, realistically, it is his crying that actually motivates his mother. We don't know if he actually makes a connection between his crying and the gratification of his wish. It is also possible that he makes a connection between his wish alone and the gratification. A third possibility is that no connection is made between his crying and the bottle before the second half of the first year. A number of combinations of these possibilities are conceivable. But for our purposes at the moment, the exact facts are not really relevant. Granted that the wish is not always gratified. But if his wishes were not gratified in a high enough proportion of instances, the infant would die of hunger or cold. In that case, he would never find out that he wasn't omnipotent.

One may protest that it is not *his* power that brings the bottle but the mother's. It is true that the immediate cause of a warm bottle is the mother's exertion. But the infant by his cry has the power to put the mother into action. His position is comparable to that of a monarch. The monarch hasn't the power himself to accomplish all his wishes. But he has been granted the power by his subjects to command them. Note with what a high degree of frequency babies are called "Prince" or "Princess," although the parents do not even jokingly allude to themselves as "King" or "Queen."

As the infant grows, he begins to learn to do things for himself. He learns that if he puts one block on top of another, he can gradually build a tower of blocks.

If he pushes, he can make them all fall down. That is the beginning of his education in direct cause and effect. But experientially, it is primarily felt merely as a different *means* of achieving satisfaction. He gained satisfaction earlier too, but it was his mother, rather than himself, who was the means. The *ends*, although they grow more complex, are not qualitatively different. But if he acts himself, the means are more direct.

If anything, as he grows more competent, the infant gains more of a feeling of power because he doesn't have to wait for his mother to build his blocks, as he may have to wait for her to bring his bottle. If he is cold, he can cover himself with a blanket without waiting for her to come. Learning the reality principle grants one an ever-increasing ability to gratify one's wishes immediately.

As the infant learns to speak he gains more efficiency in achieving satisfactions. If he can say "bottle," his mother won't have to wonder if the reason he is crying may be that he is wet. *His* acquisition of speech makes *her* more efficient in gratifying those needs he doesn't yet have the dexterity to grant himself.

The remaining question that is most pertinent to our discussion is: what happens at the time of infantile amnesia? We are quite certain of much of the answer to that question. The period before the amnesia is relegated to the unconscious. The ego boundaries begin to form. There is a definite distinction felt between mother and child. But to return to the issue with which I began this paper, the question of "giving up" of wishes, what happens to the infantile omnipotence? Klein (1923) says "When moved by the reality principle, he, the child, attempts to make painful renunciation of his own boundless omnipotent feeling" (p. 434). But I ask what the motive would be of this admittedly "painful renunciation."

Let us consider the possibility that Klein is right. Imagine, if you can, that a three-year-old child who has just newly separated out his own identity from that of his mother, can rely only on his own knowledge of reality. It becomes immediately apparent that the child would be paralyzed with anxiety. He knows enough about reality to know that it is far too complicated for him to handle. He is much too inexperienced in the ways of an extremely complicated world to feel any confidence in his ability to make it serve his needs and wants. If he has given up his omnipotence because he is past the state of infantile amnesia, what can a three-year-old fall back on? At that age, the world is still a very new, unfamiliar, strange place. It is rather like an Earthling going to Jupiter. One would wonder if the air could sustain one. Would there be nourishing food? How would one handle extremes of temperature? In a situation like that, what else could one feel but terror?

One may argue that a healthy three-year-old would probably have understanding and helpful parents. But the most understanding parents sometimes don't understand. And when such a moment occurs, the child has no one to rely on. I would submit that the fantasy of omnipotence prevents a feeling of *devastating* aloneness. If it were not for an unconscious infantile omnipotence at that age, I can think of no reason why the child would not be permanently traumatized.

We must at least postulate that there is something in him which cushions the blow of the parent's occasional failure to understand.

Now let us consider a second possibility: that infantile omnipotence is allowed to drop into the unconscious as the ego begins to form. But first let me digress to explain why I am using the phrase "allowed to drop," rather than repress. It is generally accepted that repression occurs when the material that is repressed is experienced as a threat to the individual.

In the case of omnipotence, this principle fits very aptly. Indeed, if the parent is jealous of the child's omnipotence, hostile to the child in general, intimidated by the child, and so on, the child would certainly be motivated to repress his omnipotence for fear of losing the parent if he retains it. Clinical experience has often shown variations of the attitude "My mother (or father) can't tolerate how strong I am." But I can see no reason why the normal child should be threatened by his infantile omnipotence.

Rather, the child merely discovers that the reality principle is a more efficient way of gratifying his wishes than mere wishing alone. Here Freud's (1911a) previously quoted statement applies so well. "Actually the substitution of the reality principle for the pleasure principle denotes no *dethronement* of the pleasure principle but only a *safeguarding* of it" (p. 223, italics added). Substitute "infantile omnipotence" for "pleasure principle," and the statement is just as valid. So that far from being a threat, the infantile omnipotence is normally a *catalyst* to the reality principle's pursuit of gratification. In dreams and in conscious states, we see the exaggerative character of the infantile omnipotence.

Freud (1900) quotes Jessen and Meier as describing the magnifying power of dreams. Meier dreamt he was being hanged when he felt his shirt rather tight around his neck. Another man, who was sleeping with a hot poultice on his head, dreamt he was being scalped by a band of Red Indians. A third man, who was wearing a damp night shirt, dreamt he was being dragged through a stream. Further, we are all familiar with how exaggerated split-off unconscious material appears when the source is finally discovered.

In a waking state, we are not considered mad if we express ourselves in exaggerations. How often does one say "I could have *died* laughing" or, in anger, "I could have *murdered* him" after the waiter spilled soup on one's lap. But I am certain that if the receiver of the soup had a gun thrust in his hand at that moment, he would have adamantly refused to use it. These exaggerations are expressions of the unconscious omnipotence manifesting themselves. Indeed, perhaps one of the criteria of improved health is the ability to use the expression "I could kill you" with complete confidence that there is no real possibility of actually doing it. Rather such "murdering" is tied to fantasy.

Freud (1911a) has the following interesting observation on this subject:

> With the introduction of the reality-principle one species of thought-activity was split off; it was kept free from reality-testing and remained

> subordinated to the pleasure principle alone. This activity *is fantasying*, which begins already in children's play, and later, continued as *day dreaming*, abandons dependence on real objects.
>
> (p. 222)

Because of the characteristic of exaggeration in the unconscious, the baby's realistic power in controlling his mother's behavior becomes expanded into a feeling of omnipotence.

But when infantile amnesia makes its appearance, the feeling of omnipotence comes to consciousness in the diluted form of confidence. Some support for this concept can be found in Freud (1914): "Everything a person possesses or achieves, every remnant of the primitive feeling of omnipotence which his experience has confirmed, helps to increase his self-regard" (p. 98). Again, in the same paper, "One part of self-regard is primary—the residue of infantile narcissism; another part arises out of the omnipotence which is corroborated by experience" (p. 100). Admittedly, self-regard is not exactly self-confidence, but the two do appear to be closely intertwined.

The child learns that the stove can burn him, but that learning is rationalized as a proof that he is right to be confident: "Now that I have discovered that stoves are hot, I am so clever that I know how to keep myself from being burned." One child, on hearing that his friend's mother had died, announced to his mother that if she died, he could go to the 'refrigerator and get the food himself. But the child is not anxious about things with which he has no experience. He will run out into the street until he has been taught not to. He will very likely have no reticence about finding out how a bottle of bleach tastes, unless he has been taught that this is dangerous.

His omnipotence gives him confidence that he is safe from danger until he is taught which things are really dangerous. It is this feeling of confidence that prevents what would be realistic anxiety until he becomes quite familiar with what he needs to know to preserve himself. Further, as he learns how to avoid dangers on a realistic level, that knowledge and the self-control he uses as a consequence give a realistic support to the fantasy.

Eugene Pumpian-Mindlin (1969) discusses the value of what he *calls* "omnipotentiality" for the growing or grown person:

> Omnipotentiality is transmuted recrudescence of infantile omnipotence which generally occurs during *later* adolescence and appears to be an essential and vital element in the maturation of certain aspects of ego development, particularly as these relate to the concept of the 'self.' It consists primarily of the feeling and conviction of the youth that he can do *anything in the world and solve any problem if only given the opportunity.*
>
> (p. 31, italics added)

Pumpian-Mindlin thinks omnipotence of thought is not limited to the child. He contends that "the fantasy of omnipotence remains a significant factor in all individuals and societies, regardless of the state of development, with only its relative dominance varying." "Infantile omnipotence is a major component of the most primitive core of ego structure around which primal psychic attention revolves" (p. 33). "The relatively free exercise of omnipotentiality is not only necessary but salutary. If not well developed, the child will be excessive conforming or his normal rebelliousness degenerates into insensate and self-defeating destructiveness" (p. 34).

Let us consider what life would be like for an adult, if, in fact, derivatives of infantile omnipotence were not conscious. Right at this moment we are all in great danger. I'm sure very few of you have inspected the ceiling of the room you are in to make sure it won't fall down on you. But ceilings have been known to fall. In spite of the far greater interest in the danger of nuclear weapons, realistically we are still too sanguine about the possibility that an accident could blow us all to bits. It is true that these catastrophes have a very low level of probability. But according to statistical theory, even if something has a million-to-one chance of occurring, one can never be sure just when that one chance will occur. Realistically, we should all be terrified at the number of dangers to which we are subject and over which we have no control.

On the other hand, we note that neurotic and psychotic people are quite anxious. It would appear, in fact, that the greater the pathology, the more likely that the patient will be anxious. Nor are all these anxieties unrealistic. It is quite possible that if you disagree with your boss, he may fire you. It is possible that if you get married, it may end in divorce. It is possible that if you get a divorce, you may be lonely. If you call a woman for a date, she may refuse. And by what means can we really prove to a schizophrenic that his food is not poisoned? Can we be absolutely certain that the F.B.I. is not after our patient? So, we are in the strange position of having to admit that the greater the pathology, to some extent, the more realistic is the patient, at least in terms of what dangers are inherent in our environment.

You may well object that the patient in the ward of a mental hospital who insists that he is Napoleon has a symptom that we could call *unrealistically* omnipotent. In fact, it is because he insists that he is Napoleon that he is locked up. My answer to this is that that symptom is not one of omnipotence but of *grandiosity*.

Grandiosity as a Defense

Grandiose people are contemptuous of those who cannot do what they can. A grandiose mathematician feels superior to those who have no talent in that direction. The immaculate grandiose housekeeper looks down her nose at the sloppy one. Grandiose people also assume that others can't do what they can, unless shown otherwise, and even then, find reasons to cavil.

The derivatives of omnipotence are experienced more as a *capacity* than an identity. The grandiose mathematician, for example, would feel "I am the only mathematician in this university who has worked in the space program." The non-grandiose man would feel "I am John Jones, and one of the projects I worked on was the space program."

Grandiosity also has a hostile quality. When delved into on a more unconscious level, it may be stated as "I am very dangerous to you. I am stronger than you." Napoleon was a man who was feared. In the neurotic form, patients are generally modest about it at first. They may even conceal it. But sufficient probing by the analyst will eventually unearth it. One of the forms that it frequently takes is "I can take more pain than anyone else." Again, these statements imply competitiveness, but also identity, as if the patient's name were "The Strongest Person in the World." A patient of mine recently had an insight, and in the course of her description of it, told me that she felt as if she were the *only one* in the world who had discovered the secret of how to live. Grandiosity includes sneering on an overt or covert level. *Most important, the therapist must recognize the apparent advantage of grandiosity to the patient, which must be discussed.*

Distinguishing Between Omnipotence and Grandiosity

To the extent that the omnipotent derivatives are intact, people think of their strengths as abilities that they take for granted, not as an identity. The question of whether others can or cannot do what *they* can do arouses either sympathy or happiness depending on the circumstances, but far less concern than would be aroused in the grandiose person. Omnipotent people are primarily concerned with increasing their own abilities. Further, that attempt to increase skills is not an anxiety-producing but rather a challenging experience. The above-mentioned imaginary grandiose mathematician could be traumatized by the discovery that someone else in his university also worked in the space program. He would even be upset if he had come face to face with a mathematician in *another* university who did the same work. It is almost as if that ability is his *raison d'être*.

Another way to distinguish between grandiosity and omnipotence is by the effect that these feelings have on others. When one is with a grandiose person, one will feel small and find that one is angry with him. He is frequently a "Mr. Know-It-All," who raises one's hackles. When one is with someone whose omnipotence is relatively intact, one will feel relaxed and inclined to like that person.

As we probe a specific grandiose attitude, we discover that power is very much involved. But the attitude of the patient toward this power is quite different from the attitude of a person who feels more or less confident. We find that the power of the grandiose person is restrained and controlled rather than used. It is generally kept as a *potential threat* rather than a kinetic power.

The most obvious example of the potential threat is demonstrated by the grandiosity shown in guilt. The person who feels guilty about criticizing others will keep himself from verbalizing his criticism. He feels that others could not bear the pain. Only *he* is wise enough to know this fault of the other person. Only *he* is strong enough to bear the pain of criticism. One part of his energy is attached to the impulse to criticize. The other part is devoted to restraining the impulse. In lay language, we could call this self-control.

But surely not all self-control is pathological. It takes self-control to accomplish anything. If one combs one's hair, one directs one's hand to a comb. One directs the comb to move in a specific way, and so on. The purposes behind combing one's hair and restraining oneself from criticism, however, have opposing directions. One combs one's hair in order to accomplish a *positive* purpose. One wants to achieve the goal of looking neat. The purpose of restraining criticism is a negative one. One wants to *avoid* giving pain to the other person. Even if one probes more deeply into the motivation of this restraint and discovers that the patient restrains his criticism for fear of losing the love-object, it is still an attempt to prevent a loss, rather than make a gain.

The implication of this behavior is that for the guilty patient, outwardly directed power is experienced as dangerous to the outside world, and therefore to the patient. And here is where we discover another connection between omnipotence and grandiosity. If power that is directed outward is dangerous, then omnipotence itself is dangerous. Our patient feels it will have a destructive rather than a constructive effect. If this is so, then grandiosity, far from being an equivalent of omnipotence, is an attempt to *cover up for its absence* or unavailability.

Therapeutic experience verifies this. Patients complain that their self-esteem is low when they are grandiose. Money-Kyrle (1965) refers to grandiosity as a "loss of confidence" (p. 142). Abraham (1923), in describing a patient says, "Severe and torturing feelings of" insufficiency with which she was later afflicted went back in their last roots very probably to this premature destruction of the infantile 'delusion of greatness'" (p. 404). Fenichel (1954) describes the corollary. "Every removal of feelings of guilt brings him close to his original feelings of omnipotence" (p. 158). In spite of the feelings of inferiority, we find that as the unconscious material comes forth, patients really feel they hold the fate of the world in their hands. They are responsible for the care and preservation of everyone around them. Frequently they cannot bear to disabuse the poor, helpless, naive analyst of his illusions. (Maureen, the schizophrenic patient mentioned earlier, who cannot buy a simple garment without horrendous guilt, has this attitude towards me.)

As the guilt dissolves, the patient experiences himself as less anxious and more confident but less bowed under the burden of taking care of everyone. The energy spent in repressing the omnipotence and the energy of the omnipotence itself is freed. The patient can use it with ego direction to satisfy his wishes. The compulsive restraint is gone. He feels less a combination of superior and inferior to others, and more on a par. He is happy about the power he has, instead of continuously repressing and suppressing it. But, in addition, he cannot quite understand why he feels *that* good. It doesn't seem rational even to himself. The reason for so much "irrational" happiness, I believe, is that the normal omnipotent feelings are freed and in a diluted form they have come to consciousness.

With psychotics, that relationship between grandiosity and omnipotence is even more important. Harris (1977) gives excellent examples of grandiose statements by psychotics (p. 347). He categorizes delusions in the following way: "Claim to *being* God', to 'God selected me' to 'My book will live forever' and 'Without me the world will collapse.' 'I can control people's minds.' 'I have the secret of life in my body.'" And then a most interesting delusion: "She believed that the rotation of the solar system depended on her staying awake and once she slept, rotation would cease" (p. 247). Taking into consideration that grandiosity results from repressed infantile omnipotence, I would have responded to that last-mentioned patient, "Your mother (or father) ignored you as if you weren't even in the same world." When this patient tried to have an impact on her environment, her parent must have ignored her. From this, the patient must have deduced that her power was so dangerous that her parent dared not even acknowledge what the child did or said. The child correctly saw that her parent was defending himself against his daughter by ignoring her. So, the patient repressed her omnipotence out of fear that she would destroy everything, if she used it. But lack of the availability of her omnipotence gave her a terrible feeling of helplessness. She responded to that by evolving the grandiose fantasy above. That fantasy, if we remove the condescension, says: "In spite of the fact that you treat me as if I were not in the same world as you, *I* am what makes the world go round." She is "undoing" her parent's reality, by reversing it.

The Cause of Repression in Omnipotence

In general, I believe that a child's feeling of omnipotence can be interfered with by a parent who too frequently fails or refuses to grant the child's wishes. Further, such a parent implies that the child's power (omnipotence) is to some degree destructive, as in "look what you did," "*you* did that," "you're *always* doing that," or "you did it again." How easily omnipotence can be discouraged is shown by the case of the previously mentioned Maureen. When she was little, she liked to draw. (I have seen her work and she is very skillful, especially considering that she has had no training beyond grammar school.) She had fantasies of being like Michelangelo when she was little, which I consider perfectly normal. Her mother told her that when she grew up, she would have to earn money. The implication was that this was unlikely, if one's activity were drawing. Maureen has drawn only once since then, and that was at my request. Since that time, she cannot make a career choice, although she is now 29 and has been working for the same company for about ten years.

These children soon learn that the parent resents the child's power and finds it painful. Pumpian-Mindlin (1969) says "Adults are threatened by it [omnipotence] and try vigorously to suppress it" (p. 34). The child himself begins to see his own power as destructive of the relationship between himself and his parent or even himself and the physical world. This situation, I believe, results in the repression of infantile omnipotence, thus leading to grandiosity.

On the other hand, if the parent appreciates the child's power, as in "you did a good job," "you rode your bicycle very well," or "you learned a new word," the child sees his power as constructive. One may then protest that one can't go through life successfully feeling that one's mere wish will bring gratification. This cannot be disputed. What appears to happen is that, as the child grows older, he learns that doing some things himself brings greater satisfaction than waiting for mother to do it, and makes him more efficient than she can possibly be, as stated earlier. As we get older, our tastes become more refined. We know exactly how much dressing we want on our salad, so the person most expert at fulfilling that wish is ourselves.

A few words about the situation where the child sees the parent as omnipotent and the child doesn't feel omnipotent at all. Pumpian-Mindlin (1969) says, "increasing awareness of the reality of his parents' power and of his helplessness causes the child to depend more and more upon his parents for self-esteem and consequently his omnipotence fantasy becomes repressed" (p. 33). It seems unlikely that infantile omnipotence would be repressed on mere observation of that reality. As previously noted, repression is painful and mere observing is insufficient motivation for it. It seems more likely that the child views the parent as omnipotent and represses his own omnipotence when he sees the parent as able to perform a task for himself but refuses to do so for the child. Further, he scolds the child for attempting to perform the task himself. Thus, the child comes to believe that in order to mollify the parent, he must accept the parent's omnipotence and deny his own.

Having made this distinction between grandiosity and omnipotence, we find ourselves in a difficult position from a practical viewpoint. Omnipotence sounds irrational but is not pathological. Grandiosity also sounds irrational but *is* pathological. Clinical differentiation seems very difficult. Indeed, it is partly because I found myself so often mistaking one for the other and being angry with myself later that I devoted myself to this problem. It need hardly be said that a psychoanalyst should be able to recognize whether what he hears is an expression of a problem or that problem's solution. If one mistakes omnipotence for grandiosity, one will question it instead of supporting it.

One of the most valuable clues that we can use to differentiate omnipotence from grandiosity is the affect that accompanies the statement. Indeed, I am surprised that Freud used the terms interchangeably (p. 233, 1909) since the Rat Man expressed such horror at his grandiose fantasies, something that would hardly be characteristic of the omnipotence of a baby. Another possible affect that could accompany the expression of grandiosity may be a note of bitterness because of the lack of freedom that accompanies it. One may also hear the resignation of martyrdom as having to restrain oneself for those "weak" other people, and the tension that goes with it.

In dealing with schizophrenics, I believe the question is even more pressing than in dealing with neurotics. All too often, analysts attempt to repress material that should be brought to consciousness with these patients. It is my conviction that, in these patients, more omnipotence is repressed than with neurotics, and the patient should therefore be encouraged to bring it to consciousness. Of course, here more than ever, the analyst should be aware of the difference between grandiosity and omnipotence.

Pia, a schizophrenic patient, has very grandiose ideas about people being jealous of her. These ideas show up as a great fear of demonstrating happiness. When she got a job, after much searching, she told me about it in a very small voice, near the end of the session.

In one particular session, I pointed out that she felt guilty about her happiness, and connected that with her ideas of making others jealous. Her response was, "You don't flaunt food in front of the poor. If I flaunt it, I will become conceited." (Here the *patient* is confused between grandiosity and omnipotence.) After much encouragement on my part, she finally tells me about her "dumb" fantasy in which she is a movie star. In the telling she uses the word "fun," a word she has never used with me. In fact, I was quite startled to hear her use it, since she always sounds like a Greek tragedy. I think it is most interesting that the patient herself (ordinarily most insightful) confused grandiosity and omnipotence. I have dim memories of other schizophrenic patients doing the same. This may shed some light on why Searles has such difficulty with his schizophrenic patients, since, as noted earlier, he has confused these two concepts.

I do not wish to imply that these descriptions will always make a differentiation possible. I find sometimes that I cannot differentiate until further elaboration comes. However, if one feels, for whatever reason, that a response is necessary, it seems to me that it is better to make an error on the side of omnipotence. When it is first expressed, it is generally new and the person does not as yet feel secure with it. To question it at the time may push it underground for a long time. On the other hand, if one mistakes grandiosity for omnipotence, the patient himself may very well tell you, you have made a mistake.

Once recognized, the difficulty then is how to get the patient to lift the grandiosity off, so the omnipotence can emerge. Berkowitz (1977) presents a very simple but helpful technique: "Helping the patient to bring into consciousness and experience the extreme grandiose fantasy of invulnerability . . . made it possible for the patient's observing ego to examine it and take appropriate action" (p. 16).

Mention must be made of Kohut's (1971) work in regard to grandiosity. The evolution of my theoretical approach to this problem was independent of knowledge of his work. My view differs from his in at least two important ways. One is, of course, a distinction between grandiosity and omnipotence. Second, in my view, mirroring is not required. A mere "lifting" of the grandiose fantasy and understanding of the reason for repression of omnipotence is all that is necessary.

Merry, one of the patients mentioned above, exemplifies how large a part the dynamics of the relationship of omnipotence to grandiosity could play. From the beginning of her treatment, Merry used to ask me repeatedly what the difference between a wish and a hope was, although she was very bright. Late in treatment, we discovered she felt she would have to give up all her wishes in order to stop feeling guilty, and she was unwilling to do that. At the same time, she felt she was "bad" for having any wishes at all.

This oral problem was in relation to her father, a narcissistic man with a psychotic wife and psychotic mistress. He physically beat the former whenever she expressed a wish, and perhaps beat the latter too. Merry's most deeply repressed wish was that her father not be "bad." Since that wish was guilt-ridden, she developed the unconscious fantasy that she had taken away her father's "badness," by "becoming" *his* wishes and using them as a mask behind which to hide her own secret identity. I interpreted that piece of grandiosity by saying he imagined she was killing him by "depriving" him of the reality of his "badness" and, in that way, was trying to "make" him good.

One day she told me she was going to have to stop treatment because she had gone into her savings so badly, she had almost nothing left. I interpreted that to mean that one way she got rid of wishes was by being extravagant. I said that by *buying* the things she wanted, she would no longer need to *wish* for them. She accepted the interpretation completely but then asked very sincerely "What will I do with all my wishes, if I don't throw them away?" I said, "You can imagine yourself in a new coat, going down the street in it, imagining someone saying 'How nice you look in your new coat!' etc." With great excitement, Merry said, "My God, that's a whole movie. I would never do that. The thing in my head says 'Shut-up.'" Note here the clear repression of omnipotence, in that the repressing force says "shut-up" to wishes.

The following session she reported with great delight what a wonderful time she was having saving money and how it didn't hurt at all, as she had expected. She reported that she was constantly wishing now. Further, for the first time since she can remember, she was consistently having happy dreams. She said, "Dreams are supposed to be wishes, aren't they? I've never let myself wish in my dreams." To myself, I wondered what Freud would have said to such deep repression.

Merry now comes into sessions consistently cheerful and enthusiastic, unlike her frequent depressions. She experiences herself as being taller than her mask and looking over it, seeing people as real. For the first time in her life, she tried to retaliate against someone who hurt her, instead of masochistically bearing anything as she has always done.

I want to specifically point out that in Merry I have presented at least three forms of grandiosity: (1) getting "rid" of her wishes; (2) "taking away" her father's "badness"; and (3) "changing" her identity to that of her father's wishes. Accepting her wishes, perceiving the world with her own eyes rather than that of her father's, and trying to revenge herself for an injury done to her are the beginning of the return to omnipotence.

Summary

A distinction is made between infantile omnipotence and grandiosity. The retention of the former is considered necessary for health and the latter is considered pathological. The former is described as feeling comfortable, though it can also be perceived both subjectively and objectively as irrational. The latter is viewed as ultimately distressing, though it can be subjectively experienced as necessary. Grandiosity is seen as a defense against repressed omnipotence. The repression of omnipotence appears to be caused by parents who are threatened by its power. Ways of making the distinction between omnipotence and grandiosity are discussed. Means of treatment and clinical examples are given.

References

Abraham, K. (1923). Contributions to the theory of the anal character. *Int. J. Psychoanal.*, 4: 400–418.

Berkowitz, D. (1977). The vulnerability of the grandiose self and the psychotherapy of acting- out patients. *Int. Rev. Psychoanal.*, 4: 13–20.

Bettelheim, B. (1983). *Freud and Man's Soul*, Knopf, New York.

Davis, P. (1970). *American Heritage Dictionary*, Dell Publishing Co., New York.

Dreyer, J. (1952). *A Dictionary of Psychology*, Penguin Books, Harmondsworth.

Fenichel, O. (1954). *The Collected Papers of Otto Fenichel* (Second Series), W. W. Norton, New York.

Ferenczi, S. (1952). *First Contributions to Psycho-Analysis*, Hogarth Press, London.

Freud, S. (1900). Interpretation of dreams. In *The Standard Edition of the Complete Psychological Works of Sigmund Freud*, Vol. 4, Hogarth Press, London, p. 24.

———. (1909). A case of obsessional neurosis. In *The Standard Edition of the Complete Psychological Works of Sigmund Freud*, Vol. 10, Hogarth Press, London, pp. 233, 234.

——— (1911a). Formulations on the two principles of mental functioning. In *The Standard Edition of the Complete Psychological Works of Sigmund Freud*, Vol. 12, Hogarth Press, London, pp. 222–224.

——— (1911b). Arbeiten zum Sexualleban und zur Neuorsenlehre. In *Gesammelte Schriften*, 5, Funfter Band, Zurich Internationaler Psychoanalytischer Verlag, Leipzig, Wien, pp. 414, 415.

——— (1911c). Psycho-analytic notes on an autobiographical account of a case of paranoia (Dementia Paranoides). In *The Standard Edition of the Complete Psychological Works of Sigmund Freud*, Vol. 12, Hogarth Press, London, p. 65.

——— (1913). The claims of psycho-analysis to scientific interest. In *The Standard Edition of the Complete Psychological Works of Sigmund Freud*, Vol. 13, Hogarth Press, London, p. 186.

——— (1914). On narcissism: An introduction. In *The Standard Edition of the Complete Psychological Works of Sigmund Freud*, Vol. 14, Hogarth Press, London, pp. 98, 100.

——— (1937). Analysis terminable and interminable. In *The Standard Edition of the Complete Psychological Works of Sigmund Freud*, Vol. 23, Hogarth Press, London, p. 252.

Harris, I. (1977). Psychotic grandiosity. *Psychiatry*, 40: 344–352.
Kernberg, O. (1967). Borderline personality organization. *J. Amer. Psychoanal. Assoc.*, 15: 641–685.
Klein, M. (1923). Development of a child. *Int. J. Psychoanal.*, 4: 419–474.
———. (1935). A contribution to the psychogenesis of manic-depressive states. *Int. J. Psychoanal.*, 16: 145–174.
Kohut, H. (1971). *The Analysis of the Self*, International Universities Press, New York.
Kohut, H., and Wolf, E. (1978). The disorders of the self and their treatment (an outline). *Int. J. Psychoanal.*, 59: 413–425.
Money-Kyrle, R.E. (1965). Megalomania. *Amer. Imago*, 22: 142–154.
Pumpian-Mindlin, E. (1969). Omnipotence, omnipotentiality, conformity and rebellion. *Bull. Assoc. Psychoanal. Med.*, 8: 31–34.
Searles, H. (1972). Unconscious processes in relation to the environmental crisis. *Psychoanal. Rev.*, 59: 361–374.

4

BATHSHEBA

A 19-Year Recalcitrant Case of Schizophrenic Requiring 20 Months to Get to the Neurotic Level

If one had a fantasy of the most desirable schizophrenic patient an analyst could wish for, Bathsheba would be that patient. When she came into my office, I saw a beautiful, tall 37-year-old woman with a magnificent figure, wearing a distorting bra and no make-up. I subsequently estimated her I.Q. to be 160. She is certainly the most intelligent person I ever knew. Amazingly for a schizophrenic, she can, at times, be utterly charming. But what makes her a fantasy patient is her ability to articulate. When she is willing to tell me truthfully what she feels, she can describe it so exactly, with such colorful metaphor, that I could believe I was present at the creation of a small work of art.

This same ability, of course, makes her a potentially wonderful patient to add to an analyst's abilities to treat schizophrenia, to correct one's incorrect ideas, and to add to one's understanding of theory.

Before going on to describe the treatment of Bathsheba, I will now present a very simplified view of the theory with which I have treated Bathsheba and other schizophrenic patients. I will use as a frame of reference Herbert Rosenfeld's paper "Notes on the Psycho-Analysis of the Superego Conflict in an Acute Schizophrenic Patient" (Klein et al., 1955).

Rosenfeld complains that Sullivan, Fromm-Reichmann, Federn, Knight, Wexler, Eissler, and Rosen all use reassurance. In more modern times, I would add Bertram Karon to that list. Rosenfeld says that they use reassurance to modify the superego, but he does not specify what objection he has to that approach, other than implying that it is not psychoanalysis. My objection to it is that it can be unrealistic and therefore contaminates the therapy, so I must infer that eventually it will add to the patient's anxiety. One can, after all, only depend on reality.

Rosenfeld quotes Pious (1949) as saying, "The fundamental structural pathology in schizophrenia most probably lies in the formation of the super-ego." That is a position with which I am in hearty agreement.

The first aspect of the superego problem that I would like to discuss is the problem of the feeling of imminent death from which schizophrenics suffer. At the very beginning of my training, I was much struck by a Rorschach response from a schizophrenic who said, "This is the expansion between life and death." Since there is, in fact, no space between life and death, one can see from this statement how precarious the patient feels his position to be. My experience has borne out how consistently valid that statement is.

Freud affirms that this problem is superego induced when he says, "What is now holding sway in the superego is, as it were, a pure culture of the death-instinct and in fact, it often enough succeeds in driving the ego into death" (XIX, p. 53). On the other side of the conflict, he points out that Eros is not just sexual, "but also the self-preservative instinct, which must be assigned to the ego" (XIX, p. 40). Indeed, in *The Ego and the Id*, he specifically says, "I believe that the fear of death is something that occurs between the ego and the super-ego" (XIX, p. 58).

Although, there has been much discussion in the literature about oral problems as a basis for schizophrenia, I have seen little about anality. Yet I find that most of what the superego concerns itself with are various aspects of dirt. Freud did quote Lou Andreas-Salome as saying, "What is 'anal' remains the symbol of everything that is to be repudiated and excluded from life" (VII, p. 187). It is just this repudiation and exclusion that I see as the function of the superego.

However, we find that those values that society deems most desirable, such as love, life, creativity, and beauty, are considered dirty by the schizophrenic superego. In the course of treatment, these views must be critically re-examined by the patient's ego and conscious decisions made as to whether or not characteristics or objects named by the superego as "dirty" would serve the patient's welfare if they are rejected. Indeed, as treatment goes on and the unconscious is more deeply probed, we discover that patients have a secret love of dirt for which they berate themselves. When this discovery becomes ego-syntonic, it adds to the patient's armamentarium in his battle against the "righteous" and guilt-administering superego.

I would now like to address myself to the question of schizophrenic speech. Rosenfeld points out that Eissler denies the importance of interpretations in schizophrenia. I agree with Rosenfeld's rejection of this position. He says very succinctly that the formulations of the analyst "are especially important in the treatment of schizophrenics who have lost a great deal of this capacity for conscious functioning, so that without help, they cannot consciously understand their unconscious experiences which are at times so vivid" (Ibid. p. 193).

My experience has been that the correct interpretation very frequently gets an immediate response. But an incorrect interpretation meets with disinterest.

Eissler's implication that caring for the patient is sufficient is at best the very long way around. I think Waelder is right on the mark when he says, "The old analytic rule of thumb is that the patient is always right, in a sense, and that it is up to the analyst to discover in what sense he is right" (Waelder, Robert, "The Structure of Paranoid Ideas," I.J.P.-A., 1951, Part 3, p. 171). And the analyst must be able to speak in primary process.

My last point in reference to Rosenfeld is in an area where I believe he does not go far enough. When a patient has such a weak ego, as does the schizophrenic, I think it is insufficient merely to interpret. I think the analyst must abandon his or her neutrality, actively battle the superego, and weaken it, so that the energy that properly belongs to the ego will return to it. Rosenfeld rightly points to "the appeasement of the persecutory super-ego by bluff," but neglects to mention that the superego encourages such bluffing, and itself bluffs the ego constantly. It is one of the functions of the analyst to call those bluffs. In the course of this presentation, I will give examples of how I specifically help the patient resolve his conflicts, rather than merely making interpretations.

The Referral

It was Bathsheba's boyfriend Ronnie who referred her to me. The only fact that Ronnie had to recommend me was that I was an acquaintance of his parents. He didn't know that I specialized in the psychotherapy of schizophrenia. In fact, I doubt he knew Bathsheba was schizophrenic. But he was at his wit's end when he asked me to take her on. She was extremely suicidal, screaming so loud that neighbors frequently called the police. Her psychiatrist would see her only once a week, for fear of her becoming too dependent. Ronnie assured me that frequency of sessions would be up to my judgment, since Bathsheba had an excellent salary.

I had never had a patient who committed suicide, and was reluctant to take one on who might spoil that record. I know full well how difficult the emotional sequelae of that experience are to bear. So, I suggested to Ronnie that I would do a marathon with Bathsheba to begin with, to see how it would go. In the back of my mind was the idea that I would see if I could attach her to me in some way, so that I could be reasonably certain she would not see me one day and commit suicide the next.

The Marathon

When she came for her appointment, she immediately told me that she was suicidal. She had planned to commit suicide several months ago, had taped the windows, and put on the gas. A month ago, she had taken overdose of Narvane. She said, "I got very angry and self-destructive and threw pills down my mouth. I screamed all this past week-end." (Ronnie subsequently told me that she always screamed on Saturday morning. He believed, quite probably correctly, that screaming was a response to her conflict about her Orthodox Jewish background and her not going to synagogue.)

Bathsheba continued: "Ronnie and I went to the local hospital emergency ward and that was horrible. I used to live with him, but then I got moral and I decided I couldn't commit suicide in his apartment, so I decided to get an apartment of my own to die in. When I get angry or frustrated, I want to commit suicide. I'm ashamed that everyone *is* more grown-up than me. I'm incompetent. I can't make small decisions."

Bathsheba had been married ten years ago. The marriage lasted eight years. From her description, her husband seemed to be a most bizarre kind of person, to say the least, but I cannot describe him any further, because it would be too identifying. Bathsheba said, "I thought if I left him, I'd be happier. But I'm not. He babied me. I hid behind the marriage." Since young adulthood, she had a series of men upon whom she depended, not only for emotional support but also for such things as laundry, super-market shopping, etc. Gradually, in her relationship with Ronnie, she began to do some of those things herself. But still sometimes she didn't eat a meal if one was not prepared for her.

Later I learned that Bathsheba had had 11 different therapists of various persuasions over the previous 19 years. She had been given anti-depressants, anti-psychotics, and Lithium, as well as psychotherapy. At the time she came to me, she was on 75 mg. of Palomar. The therapist who seemed to do her the most good, Lynn, was the one she saw for four years during her marriage. While seeing Lynn, Bathsheba was finally able to leave her loveless, almost asexual marriage. She took a six-month training course that prepared her for a high-level technical job during the time she was seeing Lynn. Then she advanced well enough in it to earn a very handsome salary. But Bathsheba left Lynn because she felt Lynn paid insufficient attention to their relationship. Bathsheba believed Lynn was an ego psychologist.

Bathsheba complained that she was permitted to see her present psychiatrist only once a week. I told her she could call me any time she was in trouble, as is my standard practice. I find patients almost never take advantage of my availability in that way even though I give them a phone number to call if I am away.

When I asked about her psychological history, she told me that her parents were extremely Orthodox Jews. She came from a large family of which she was the youngest. I subsequently discovered that only one of those children had not been severely damaged, although none appeared to be as damaged as Bathsheba. She said, "I was coddled and infantilized by both parents." She slept in a crib until she was five. Her mother combed her hair for her until she was 12 and cut her nails for her until she was 17.

This same apparently overprotective mother produced a very frightened child who constantly needed to hide behind her mother's skirt, literally. But her mother was absolutely indifferent to any problem the child brought up. At best, her response to Bathsheba's problems was to tell her to "go to sleep. It will be better in the morning." To a very minor extent, Bathsheba still does just that.

She said to me, "I have no place in the world. Even when I was young I felt that, but I was smarter than the others in my family. I am so alienated in Orthodoxy and out." Alienation was a constant theme for quite some time in her therapy with me. She said, "My upbringing was very moralistic. I was taught that anything having to do with the secular world was bad. The Orthodox problem is insoluble because of the guilt. My father is patriarchal and tyrannical."

Orthodoxy was not so much of a problem when she was married because her husband liked the ritual. But her father's response to Ronnie, her boyfriend, was, "You are ruining and alienating the family." I asked, "What is your picture of ruining and alienating?" She responded, "You're ostracized, not accepted. I'm alone. I can't approach people without shame. The only thing I know is Judaism. I don't understand what other people live for. What is life without a central passion?"

I asked, "you are using Judaism as a substitute for an identity." To my surprise, she responded with no resistance, "Yes, what do I matter? Only the family matters. How can I ever say, 'I don't like this school or that dress?' I have to keep sacrificing myself." I said, "If you do, then Judaism becomes your identity." With despair, she said, "Then I don't have an identity." I said, "In reality, your identity is really what you like and don't like. What stands in the way of that?" (I should insert here that that kind of question is a frequent technique of mine, i.e., to ask the patient what the subjective obstacle is to normal perception or feelings. This is what I meant when I said earlier that I help the patient resolve her conflicts not only by interpretation.)

To my surprise, she said (with great contempt), "The voices make fun of me. What do you mean, you like?" I said, "Will you do that voice and I will speak for you?"

What followed is what I call a brain-conscience dialogue when I speak of it to the patient. (See chapters on "Communicating with the Schizophrenic Superego") To you, my audience, I will call it the id-ego alliance against the superego. The patient plays the superego and I play the healthy ego and, so to speak, the cologne of the id perfume. I began using this technique over 20 years ago. I believe it has the following advantages:

(1) It greatly reduces the subjective chaos of the patient and not incidentally some of mine. It gives the patient somewhat of a map and a direction to go. In fact, it gives the whole therapy some direction, but always leaves enough of an opening so that new material can come through.
(2) It helps the patient see who is friend and who is foe, taking for granted the reason, which you will see later, that the superego is the foe.
(3) It allows me to see the nature of that particular superego.

(4) It breaks up the isolation in that the patient has the experience of someone speaking their language and siding with them in their conflict.
(5) It shows the patient that the superego is not invincible and one need not be in awe of it.

With this particular patient, the dialogue we had that day relieved the symbiosis with her father sufficiently to establish a connection between me and her. Later, I will give an example of such a dialogue. Suffice it to say that after this one, looking startled, she said,

> I never say these things out loud. I'm an object of ridicule. He really doesn't care about me as an individual. The rules are more important to him than being a human being. I do feel I'm seeing it in a new way, as if I were a separate person. I thought I was the center of his life.

She looked surprised enough for me to believe that some kind of delusion was broken. I felt some conviction that her surprise would be followed by enough curiosity in my work to divert her temporarily from her suicidal interest.

In this marathon, she added one more fact that was essential: "Everyone will tell you that my father is the villain, but I'm the only one who thinks my mother is." Bathsheba has not yet altogether come to terms with the validity of her own statement. After about two hours, we prepared to part, having agreed to three sessions a week. As I opened the door, she said, "I hate myself because I keep promising to be good. I'd love to be outrageous. I have no sense of humor because I have to be good." I said, "I'll help you be bad." The weighty cloud of depression that had hovered over my office since she had entered was lifted by her first smile. We both understood the symbolic nature of my statement.

The Treatment from the Marathon to the Trip

About a week after the treatment began, she complained, "When I leave here, it is just me and him (referring to her father)." Being aware of the difficulty that schizophrenics have in internalizing, I bought her a Lucy doll that said "Call me," which represented me, and a Snoopy doll that said "Hug me," which represented her as yet unexpressed yearning.

The following is a short example of a dialogue with the superego as God. (I-C here represents my statement to the conscience. C-I represents the reverse.)

I-C   Why are you so scared to let Bathsheba have what she wants?
C-I   You are not supposed to support or defend her.
I-C   If I do, what can you do?
C-I   I'll kick Bathsheba in the stomach. She should only listen to me because I am the only one who loves. Everything she does is wrong.

I-C   You are a liar. You don't love her. But a lot of people really do. You only enjoy her pain.
C-I   It's her fault she has pain.
I-C   Hey God, it is a sin to tell a lie."

Bathsheba then said, "It's a bad God." (During the first several months, the superego was interchangeably her father or God.)

Now as to the anal aspects of the superego: A few days after she began treatment with me, Bathsheba said, "If the police come, I think they are after me. You'll find out that I'm not a composed rational person. I regress to an infantile person with dirty diapers," implying that I should be shocked. I smiled. "I can't wipe myself clean," she continued. I said, "I know about babies coming into the world and having dirty diapers. Don't be in such a hurry to get clean."

Here Bathsheba clearly expressed her anal conflict. For this reason, and also because she and Ronnie had both told me that she screamed, although I had not as yet heard it, I decided that we needed a session in the park. I hoped that she might feel more free to scream there, so I could learn what she sounded like. I hoped also that I could work directly on her superego's rejection of dirt, if we went to a secluded wooded area. As it turned out, she did not scream then, though she began to do so soon afterwards in full volume on the phone. In the park, she was able to make mud pies without difficulty, but found it impossible to make me dirty. This problem was verbalized much later as her fear of being destructive to others, by telling the truth and honestly expressing her opinions.

It was difficult to ascertain the nature of her delusions due to her secretiveness. One delusion was, "I am the priest and prophetess of the religion of denying reality. I can't explain." There was also the religion-delusion of the sacredness of motherhood, which was later amended to the sacredness of her particular mother, and finally to the dissolution of the concept. But the ones that had the greatest cathexis were variations on the theme that God wanted her dead, so that He could have her in Heaven, that he beat her because he loved her and that eventually she would sit on His right side while Jesus sat on His left. Additionally, she had a mission that later turned into a compulsive need to give others pleasure. When I had enough information, I interpreted the mission by saying she needed to make her mother happy, so that she wouldn't have to face her mother's desire to kill her. But by that time, over a year later, we had pretty well dissolved the aspect of the superego that was her father, and were working on the more pernicious aspect of the superego as mother.

I would like to insert two points about her superego and superegos in general. One is that in my experience superegos are generally derived from one parent. But in Bathsheba's case I discovered the reason both parents were involved in the following interesting way: We were doing a dialogue when she, as her superego, said: "Your father will hear about this." So I realized the mother was the real superego but used the father as a stalking horse, making him look even more tyrannical than he was. This mother projected herself as a saint, but, as I got to know her, seemed almost incapable of sincerity. The second point about superegos is that they speak very loudly compared to the small-voiced ego, which necessitates that the analyst speaks in a loud voice (without hostility, of course), as if he or she were speaking to someone who is hard of hearing.

As therapy went on, Bathsheba experienced many improvements. One example was her statement: "I was trying hard to have the bad thoughts I usually have, but they weren't there." She wrote me a note saying, "Val, (me) has made me question the admirability and nobility of guilt, the source of punishment and the distrust of therapists and people who aim to help me." In session, she told me that she had begun to question the necessity of suicide. These improvements were almost all indirect results of our work. She claimed ignorance of the value of cause and effect, and reacted with astonishment when I used those concepts, even though her work was very much dependent on them. She preferred magical solutions.

Any contact with her mother would provoke screaming, while she denied the cause. But much to her surprise, she did finally manage to enjoy a lunch with her mother and sisters, whom she hadn't seen in years. However, the screaming reaction to contact with her mother did return at times. Two months after the beginning of treatment, she reported that she had said to someone in her office, "Calm down," a complete reversal of roles for her.

The piece de resistance came when, a few days after that, she announced that she was going on a trip without Ronnie. I had a sharp pang of anxiety, which I quickly squelched, saying to myself, "If she thinks she can do *it*, she most probably can." She had been asked twice before to go on a trip with a friend in earlier years, but had been unable to do so because of anxiety.

When she returned, she said, "I had a dream in which my association was that you might be angry that I had a good time." I said, "Perhaps you feel I'd be angry that you weren't dependent on me as your mother would have been." She replied, "It fits. I'm extremely gratified for being active." (She had frequently complained of feeling paralyzed.) "Why was I so crazy?"

When I heard that last statement, I speculated that if she could look at it in the past tense like that, perhaps the "craziness" was over, though I knew perfectly well the neurosis wasn't. But the delusions were still present, though far less prominent. She improved enough to write me a beautiful poem (see the end of the chapter).

From the Trip to the End of Schizophrenia

After the trip, there were many changes. Primarily, she became more socialized. Before, when she went to parties, she was silent and then used to come home and scream because she had been unable to talk. Now she was able to socialize and really enjoy herself. She called old school friends whose messages previously went unanswered. To her own surprise, she told one of them, "I'm tired of moral authorities." She began to wear make-up, high-heeled shoes, gave up her idea of a breast reduction and got herself a good brassiere, as her superego weakened.

She gradually let go of her two-year relationship with Ronnie. This was not a surprise to me, since Ronnie's main advantage was that he was willing to put up with her pathology. She then began a relationship with Harry, who although he was unable to communicate with her emotionally, gave her the first really good sexual experiences she had ever had and she "discovered" her body. That relationship necessitated an abortion, but she navigated it without too much difficulty.

The next relationship with Eli was a reversal for her. He was a bright but inadequate man who depended on her for emotional support. Here was a case where talking loudly availed me nothing, because she would not insist on his wearing a condom as protection against AIDS, and he resisted.

In terms of anality, Bathsheba said, "When I was a child, I was allowed to talk but not have a body, not get messy. There is no way around it, only death." Here we see how pertinent to survival prohibitions against dirt can be. When she became less fearful of dirt, she became fearful that she wouldn't be able to stop it from coming out. I replied in an excited, enthusiastic voice, "Yes, it won't stop for the rest of your life. Everything can keep flowing out of you, without getting stopped up." On hearing this, the listener may have fears that the patient will indulge in uncivilized conduct. Experience has taught me that such fears are unjustified. *Energy that was bound in the superego flows into the ego automatically.* The following dream is an example of that process:

She said, "I dreamt my landlord came to my apartment and there was shit in the sink and in the toilet." When I asked for her associations, she said, "You had said that one doesn't have to lose one's shit. The sink is where you clean." Groping, I said, "Do you think your dream shows you that you can be dirty and clean at the same time?" She said, "Oh yes, I didn't tell you that in the sink it was very neat. Like a work of art with a pink ribbon tied around it. A sculpture. It was odd that the landlord came. One tries to keep an apartment neat for him. A landlord represents the superego." (Needless to say, I don't use technical language with my patients, but Bathsheba was well read in Freud.) "Therapists belong in the basement because of the unconscious. I'm getting things out in the open. Yesterday, for the first time in my life, I realized there is a me." This last statement is an example of freedom from the fear of death that I mentioned in the theoretical part of my presentation. For lack of time, I can't go into some intensive work we did on rules, boxes, and contamination. But it concluded by her saying, "The whole system of rules is a sham," whereas before rules were considered sacred.

In February 1990, I had to go the hospital with what could have been a serious illness, but turned out not to be. I had to give her some idea of the gravity of it, because I felt it was necessary to refer her to someone else in the event I did not survive. She became depressed, anxious, and suicidal to an extent I didn't find out until later. When I returned to work, I could not work out the transference aspects of it, due to her continued resistance to admitting other people could affect her for good or ill. This caused the treatment to last many months longer than it otherwise would have.

Finally, 20 months after she began treatment, she visited her parents. Instead of keeping all her hostility suppressed, she breached her remaining resistance and expressed some of her real feelings, primarily toward her father. This autocratic man who attempted to control everyone said to Bathsheba, "Psychology is a threat to family structure." She responded, "I don't accept your moral or spiritual guidance. Only your advice about money." To me she said, "He reminded me as he always does, 'When you were 20, you said, "when you suffer, I suffer."' I said to him, "No more. I can't live like you." To me, she said, "Why did it take me 38 years?" and then jokingly, "You created a monster. Girl from Brooklyn goes to tell the chief rabbi to permit abortions."

The next day her father called, speaking in a most conciliatory tone, "dripping with honey," as Bathsheba described it. "He really heard everything I said. He even said, 'I'm not so old I can't change.'" (This from a man well over 80.) Her parents independently said, "We're glad you told us how you felt."

Just prior to and following this incident, there were many improvements. She said to me, "I realized my mother was weird not me. I am taking over God's role. He doesn't know what He is talking about. I feel like Rip Van Winkle. I used to feel, 'I can't survive without my mother liking me.' Now I feel, 'Who needs it?'" I reminded Bathsheba that she had felt she had a mission. "What mission?" she replied sarcastically "Not to tell the truth? To uphold the structure? He's a pretty fucked up God." Regarding her mother, she said, "She hides from me. She's silly. It's all bullshit. She is jealous of me." However, Bathsheba has not yet fully reconciled herself to the extent of that jealousy. She was able to say, "I won. God was wrong." Clearly, if God is wrong, the concept as an emotional, psychological construct is useless. Therefore, psychic energy is pretty well withdrawn and released to the ego.

Regarding her fear of death and suicidal wishes, I said to her, "Aren't you worried about getting killed anymore if you say something like that?" Her interesting response was, "It's too late. The cat is out of the bag. I thought it was normal not to be happy. God acted like it was a crime, so I took the abuse and made up a story like I was proud of it." (Note how the ego protects self-esteem from the shame of having had a delusion.) "I'm tired of being sick . . . I'm too normal to be noble." I concluded that the schizophrenia was over, especially since she calmly announced one day that she was an atheist now, as if it were an unimportant matter.

The Neurosis

Of course, I am fully aware that there is a large neurosis to be worked through. Some symptoms are still present but in neurotic form. For example, she will still go into depressions precipitated by happy events, as she had in the past, but they are not nearly so severe or so frequent and she can turn them around by herself. She still complains of not being able to do things (what used to be the paralysis), but now it is a feeling instead of a fact. She can cry now, but never screams anymore. Her biggest resistance is still toward accepting that others can affect her for her good or ill, but she does now to some extent, grudgingly. She can certainly be hostile toward me with no inhibition, which was unheard of before.

A few weeks ago, after some conflict, she called her mother to thank her for a gift. Her mother said, "I'm glad you're happy." Bathsheba responded, "It's difficult to compensate for what I've been through. I'd like you to know that I hold you responsible for my unhappiness as a child." Her mother said, "We gave you so much." Bathsheba said, "You were very cold and uncaring." Her mother asked for forgiveness but in the end hung up on Bathsheba, so it is clear that her saintly image was disturbed. Bathsheba told me that she felt she had taken charge and made her mother squirm. This is a patient who never before had done anything but tried to placate and entertain her mother.

A few words about the ongoing transference. Bathsheba is a wonderful entertainer and, as I have said, can be very charming. When she was not depressed, she certainly tried to entertain me. At the beginning, some of it was bizarre because she would laugh at tragic situations. But other than that, it was, and sometimes still is, difficult for me to separate out her real self from the transference entertaining, which is partly consciously supposed to prevent me from wanting to kill her.

She also frequently ignored me, which works in the service of her fantasy that no one can affect her. At first I made the mistake of assuming that this ignoring was merely part of the schizophrenic "tuning out." But I later learned that she felt she was "killing" people that way, in an attempt to escape what she was frightened to hear. It turned out that she felt she had a reciprocal agreement with her mother that each would give the other permission to live. But this is now something we pull out of the unconscious and which is ego-alien.

I don't want you to think I have neglected orality altogether. Quite the contrary, more and more is coming to the surface about her difficulty and guilt in taking, since her mother (and I in the transference) find it so painful to give. Her grandiosity should also be mentioned. She, more than once, told me she could take more pain than anyone in the world. She is no longer so interested in maintaining that achievement.

Shortly after the time when I believed she was no longer schizophrenic, she met the man who was to become her fiancé. He is a very successful archeologist, a widower. They have been living together for some months now and are planning a wedding and a baby. They occasionally have some problems in adjustment, but seem to find solutions without too much difficulty.

Bathsheba's fiancé believes she merely suffers from depression. Just yesterday, he said to her when she came home from her office, "I am so glad you come home from the office so calm and stable, when I feel so unnerved and harassed by my day."

For Val

daddy sterilized the bottles, the nipples
while momma laid the warp for the blanket

he warmed the milk
while she pulled the shuttle through the night-dark threads

he filled the bottles with rich warm liquid
while she wove the blanket so dense and dark

he fed me in silver-lined bottles
while she wrapped me in the blanket she wove,
and it was all so warm and soft and liquid

but the milk—it was laced with poison
and the blanket—it was wrapped around me so tight
i couldn't breathe, i couldn't speak, i couldn't see the sky

and i fell asleep, from the blanket, from the poisonous warm
liquid, i fell into a dream, into a night-dark haze

i cried out for help as i was falling,
but they all had gone to the synagogue, to pray
to god, in the haze
and the other children, they were dreaming and falling too

and when the fairy godmother finally appeared,
and held out to me the blanket and the bottle,
and said: drink and be warm

i lashed out at her, crying:
don't you know—
the milk is poisoned, and the blanket suffocates!

she said, i am a chemist.
and she took me to a laboratory where we analyzed the milk
separating out the poisons

and she said, i am a weaver too.
and she took me to a loom where we unwove the blanket
and loosened its grip.

and i breathed without gasping
and i drank without gagging
and it was real
and it was rich
and it was warm

All the metaphors in the above poem are Bathsheba's. They took me (Ravella Levin) completely by surprise.

5

"BLACK HOLE" PHENOMENON

Deficit or Defense? A Case Report

Grotstein (1990), following Tustin (1988), has recently described an important category of inner experience in psychotic states as "black hole" or "abyss" phenomena. He describes the experience as involving a "hapless or precipitous fall into endless space" combined with the "terror of nothingness and boundarilessness" (1990, p. 39). He cites Tustin's earlier conclusion that this experience is phenomenologically ubiquitous in psychotic states and that it represents the etiological factor of severe maternal deprivation or abandonment: "The 'black hole' emerges, in my experience, as a universal phenomenological image of the internal world of the psychotic and seems to represent the place where the mother used to be, but ripped herself away prematurely, leaving a 'gaping hole'" (Tustin, 1988, cited in Grotstein, 1990, p. 43). Pursuing Tustin's idea of maternal deficit further, Grotstein goes on to postulate that important neurobiological deficits, manifest in felt "meaninglessness," are involved. Accordingly, he argues that black hole phenomena should be dynamically understood in terms of deficits in primary narcissism:

> [A] deficient matrix of primary narcissism with a low threshold to experience and with a compromised ability to translate and transform it . . . predisposes the patient to-be to a vulnerability to stress, which eventuates in the traumatic state. If the traumatic state is experienced as intolerable, the patient 'disappears' emotionally from his or her body.
>
> *(p. 41)*

(Originally published in the *Journal of Clinical Psychoanalysis, Proceedings of the New York Psychoanalytic Institute and Society*, Vol. 5, No. 1 1996 International Universities Press, Inc.)

Beyond his sensitive description of the state itself, Grotstein also makes the clinically pertinent observation that it is often connected with a class of religious or quasi-religious delusions: "Following the descent into the 'black hole' . . . the psychotic patient feels the experience of delusional rebirth, generally with a religious format" (p. 43).

The purpose of this paper is to communicate the case of a woman who exhibited both the black hole phenomenon and an accompanying religious delusion that she had "God in her pocket," but who responded to an interpretive strategy that emphasized her dissociation and denial of unfulfilled wishes. Once these interpretations were worked through, moreover, the associated phenomena resolved themselves. Though the patient herself initially followed an implicit deficit model, after this stage of treatment was passed, she explicitly stated, "If I seemed empty in the past, it was a lie." As such, this report represents a contribution to the ongoing debate, recently summarized by Killingmo (1989), over the relative merits of deficit and conflict models of psychopathology vis-à-vis interpretive strategies.

The paper is also meant as a contribution to the understanding of what I have come to call the "overindulged" psychotic patient, as distinguished from the "deprived" or "neglected" psychotic patient. The two groups are to be distinguished in my experience by the typical transference attitudes they establish in treatment, which recapitulate important aspects of the parent-child relationships in earlier life. "Neglected" patients typically present as deprived and masochistic and enter into the treatment relationship with an air of hopelessness and despair that anything can be done for them. "Overindulged" patients, however, present as entitled and narcissistic, and they approach treatment with grandiose, almost miraculous expectations. With deprived or neglected patients, an attitude of a cautious but caring respect for their thoughts and feelings is often sufficient to mobilize a stable treatment alliance. But with "overindulged" patients, though they may initially present with an air of self-sufficiency, treatment quickly becomes complicated by their demandingness and devaluation. As will emerge in the case report below, "overindulged" patients will often have suffered subtle forms of neglect in childhood. Nonetheless, the principal lesson they have learned from their early years, and their principal form of relating to important objects, both internal and external, is predicated on the idea that they have a *right* to have all their needs met and they are shocked when this does not happen. Especially in psychotic states, this attitude can reach the extremes of a grandiose, entirely magical self-sufficiency. Ladan (1992) has described such an attitude in a patient who exemplified the psychology of the "exception": "She had no needs and was therefore never needy, because everything was already provided for before that point was reached" (p. 31).

In the context of this general distinction between the "overindulged" and "deprived" patients, it is significant that black hole phenomena, heretofore theoretically associated with deprivation and deficit, were manifest in a patient who clearly belonged to the "overindulged" category.

Case Report

Carolyn, aged 38, continues to be seen in individual therapy, three times a week. The following report concerns our first year of treatment. Carolyn was referred by a colleague, Dr. D, after ten years of treatment, when she began to develop prominent psychotic symptoms. For most of her adult life, Carolyn had worked in a semi-artistic area, but owing to persistent antagonisms with coworkers, she had recently lost her job and had been unable to find another in her field. In his treatment of her, Dr. D had been impressed by her seeming lack of basic socialization skills. He had tried to ameliorate this by continually investigating her perceptions of others and by suggesting alternative ways of dealing with them.

At the time of her referral, Carolyn had lost her apartment due to constant overspending. She had begun to feel that her food was being poisoned and as a result had lost 15 pounds which she could ill afford to lose. She also had developed the idea that somebody had urinated in her shampoo; this resulted in its imparting a "funny smell." Also, she felt that people were laughing at her. Her concerns about being poisoned and contaminated were related to growing concerns about impending cognitive deterioration. As she put it in her first session, "I feel the poison will seep into my brain and make me retarded." She also worried she might go blind.

Dr. D had warned me before I saw Carolyn that her father was an antisocial personality and he felt that Carolyn's behavior showed many of the same traits. The father was a compulsive gambler, had numerous questionable business dealings, and had even stolen money from his son. He had raised his daughter according to his own standards, namely, to manipulate, lie, and take advantage of others, to the point where she actually felt guilty if she did not behave that way. The issue of Carolyn's manipulativeness, furthermore, arrived quite literally before she did, as she called four times before her first appointment to check about trivial matters. I had previously discovered in other patients that an apparent fear of making a mistake—this is how the patients themselves characterized it—was a screen for a fear of being right. Accordingly, I engaged this behavior on Carolyn's part in the first session in the context of her initial complaints of an inner deficit. The following exchange took place almost at the beginning of our first meeting:

C: I have emptiness and loneliness.
I: Is *that* why you called me four times before you came?
C: I was afraid of making a mistake.
I: You were more worried about being right.

In the same session, I put down very firm rules about her calling me for reasons that were not emergencies, saying that if she called for other reasons, I would not accept any calls at all. After several weeks, she learned that I really meant what I said.

Carolyn was the fourth child in a family of two girls and three boys. She dated the onset of her illness from the age of 20 when her older brother, Larry, had died of an apparent drug overdose, which was denied by the family, a few days after he graduated from professional school. Carolyn had since acted as though it were her unresolved grief over his death that lay at the core of her illness. As I knew from Dr. D, she was ready to invoke Larry's death as an all-purpose explanation of why she didn't or couldn't do something along the lines of saying that nothing really mattered "since Larry died." It emerged after many months, however, that what was central about the brother's death was the pathological shift it occasioned in Carolyn's beliefs about God. Up until that time, she had believed in God more or less in line with the religion of her upbringing, and had regularly prayed to Him to look after her family. She also had some social relationships up until that time. But following Larry's death, she became angry at God for allowing his demise and, no longer praying for other family members, she developed the solipsistic, implicitly spiteful idea that God's *only* job was to look after *her*. From this point forward, ominously, she ceased to involve herself in social relationships outside the home, instead concentrating her energies entirely on her work. By the time she entered treatment with me, her belief that God's sole business was her welfare had reached delusional intensity. Her almost complete detachment from the day-to-day world was expressed in a recurrent feeling that she was hanging onto reality by the slimmest of filaments.

Carolyn responded quickly to the initial phase of treatment. After losing her last position, she had worked for a time in a very low paying retail job, but she soon mobilized herself to find a professional job, which paid better, though it was still outside her own area of special competence. She also "rediscovered" generous relatives who were willing to loan her money, a demonstration in itself of increased social competence and a necessity if she were to afford ongoing therapy. She even found a boyfriend, the first she had ever had.

Changes were manifest in her behavior in the sessions as well. She became markedly less anxious, and her hammering style of speech (a singsong, almost staccato style, delivered with great pressure, that left one feeling assaulted) gave way to more modulated tones. This latter change I construed as reflecting reduced superego pressure, which was also manifest in a lessening of her fears that she might go blind or become retarded. These fears I had confronted much as I had addressed her fear of getting the appointment time "wrong." Specifically, I had told her that the threat of going "blind" meant that there were things she was not supposed to "see" and then asked her what she thought that these things might be. She took this intervention very seriously and responded by determinedly looking at subjects that her internal prohibitions warned her against investigating. Only later did I arrive at the formulation that believing in God was much the same as believing her (lying) father. Carolyn felt that if she did not believe her father, and relied on her own conception of the truth, she would lose him. As she put it subsequently, "If I am right, I am alone." Only much later still did I grasp that behind the figure of the father lay the even more important figure of her overindulgent mother, who had compliantly supported the father's sociopathy.

Part of the consequence of her renewed reliance on her own sense of what was right was that Carolyn began to feel more independent and self-reliant; concomitantly, her relationships with her coworkers improved. Some four months into treatment, moreover, she also resumed a relationship with her mother, from whom she had been estranged for many years. It was not easy, however, to get a sense of who this mother was or what her relationship to Carolyn was all about. The mother had supported Carolyn's father in all his sociopathic endeavors, and at the same time she had regularly surrendered to Carolyn's childhood temper tantrums, though not to those of the other children. Carolyn's older sister had even tried to intervene in this special relationship, warning the mother that in the end Carolyn would suffer for that indulgence.

Interestingly, at about the same time Carolyn resumed contact with her mother, I began to appreciate that what appeared to be Carolyn's sociopathic aspects were, in fact, forms of *pseudo*-psychopathy. I was struck in particular by the fact that in one session, she paused to say "thank you" to me, and that in the next she volunteered that this was the first time she had ever said "thank you" to someone and meant it. She associated my attitude toward her with Annie Sullivan of *The Miracle Worker*, who had been stern with Helen Keller. She added that no one had ever been stern with her before: "I couldn't get my way with you. When I had temper tantrums with my mother, I could manipulate her. I had guilt because I could do that." Her sense of drawing closer to me was embarrassing to her. It was also connected by her to her brother's death: "I bottled up my love after Larry died. Now I have uncorked the bottle."

This initial stage of positive transference based on firm limit setting became the ground for a new round of difficulty in our relatedness some months into the treatment. Carolyn had gotten an apartment with three other young women so as to save money, but she soon began to antagonize them. This led, at approximately the six-month mark, to her suddenly beginning to call me repeatedly in her old way to talk about her problems with them. I responded to these calls the way I said that I would. In her next session, Carolyn seized the bull by the horns:

C: Shall we talk about the phone calls? You had said that an emergency means being upset.
I: The only thing you feel about the phone calls is mad at me because I hung up on you. The problem is that you feel you don't have to suffer like other people do.
C: (outraged) What am I supposed to do, sit there with knots in my stomach?!
I: Yes, neurosis is not a picnic. You wait until you have an appointment with me.
C: (looking shocked) I was scared, alone. I called seven people. There was blackness. I was falling through a *black hole*. I felt emptiness . . . The girls heard

me call out at night [in her sleep]. I was falling in a black hole and scared of dying ... (Crying) I want Mama. I'm scared. It's a black hole and I'm afraid of dying alone.

At this point, though Carolyn had three times used the exact phrase *black hole*, and though I had not long before heard Grotstein's lecture on "Notes from the Abyss," I did not connect the two. Instead, I suspected a connection with her dead brother. Specifically, I wondered if she were speaking of a symbolic grave that she might be sharing with him. This surmise informed my inquiry, which led only to a further description of the state:

I: What does it look like?
C: Black paint strokes, with some white or light. Other times it's like the inside of a coffee can or outside with the stars.

In the next session, Carolyn announced: "God is in my pocket because I am special." But it was some weeks before this theme reemerged with her telling me the story of Larry's funeral. After the funeral was over, the rabbi who had performed the service came to visit the family. He said to them: "Pray for me. I'm going to Israel tomorrow." Carolyn then recalled feeling powerless and saying to herself on the spot: "That's ridiculous. God didn't protect us from Larry's death, so he won't protect you." Later in the same session, she elaborated on her special relationship with God:

C: He needs me. He needs me. He needs his followers. Without them he wouldn't exist. If I take care of myself, I'll be punished for not believing God will protect me.
I: (seeing her expression) You are horrified by this discussion.
C: God doesn't want me to talk to you about Him, so I can't resolve this.
I: You don't want to expose Him.
C: Yes, because I will get well and there will be no God.
I: Did you hear what you said?
C: I want to jump out of my skin. I feel lousy that I don't have God in my pocket, unprotected.
I: You do have something to protect you, your brain.
C: (thoughtfully, then sounding surprised) Yes, I did a lot but nothing as important as getting out of that bad mental place [i.e., her intense anxiety] I was in.
I: (astonished) You had thought God did that?
C: Yes.

The next session she told me that I was waking her up and she was discovering that it was not so terrible to be alone—and without God. I said, "You felt when there is a God, there are no people and no death." She began to reflect on what she herself had done with her life—and on her 18 lost years. She recalled a poem concerning a man whose insurance company wouldn't pay when he died, because he had never really lived. The session following, she announced that her "coffee can" was no longer empty: "What is interesting is that the sands of time seemed to have filled it. So now I am full." The problem was not completely solved, she added, but she no longer felt so empty when people left her and her anxiety was still further reduced: "The light is the God within me. Before I was too doped up [not a reference to drugs, but to her mental state]. I was not conscious that I was dead. I was going to say something very dramatic like 'Thank you for giving me my life back,' but I am still angry at you for having taken away God."

It was at this point in treatment that issues pertaining to her recently found boyfriend supervened for a period of time. At the time of her intake, Carolyn had mentioned homosexual fantasies, also vague hypochondriacal concerns, as prominent problems, but I had paid little attention to these issues, instead addressing myself to her more frankly psychotic fears of being poisoned and going blind. Now, Carolyn began discussing her new boyfriend, Boyd. She enjoyed his company, she confessed, but she also constantly thought up various pretexts for wanting to drop him. I encouraged the relationship, feeling that whatever defects the young man might have, she should at least get her feet wet in a heterosexual relationship. At one point, I happened to inquire about her feelings further:

I: Do you enjoy your relationship with Boyd?
C: Yes, it is embarrassing. It's wonderful ... (Touching her cheeks, speaking seriously) I'm flushed. Should I see a doctor? (I laughed uncontrollably, and did not answer.)
C: (smiling) I feel so much like a woman, flowering. I'm like other women. I used to feel sex was dirty. It goes back to when Dad asked what I was doing, when I was kissing a boy behind the barn [at age 6]. I wanted to be Daddy's little girl and pure.

The following sessions indicated that homosexual fantasies were no longer a concern for Carolyn—seemingly they disappeared on their own without discussion—and I have not heard anything further about them since.

Some two months after the above discussion of Boyd, the subject of the black hole returned and this time I made the connection in my mind with Grotstein's depiction of the state as a kind of inner abyss. Carolyn introduced the topic by complaining about her need for love, a need which was being exacerbated by her having found objects for it:

C: I always needed love and it was painful and I never got it. It was a black hole and I had no love to fill it. (Complaining of the pain of feeling this) I need you and Boyd.
I: (responding to the implication that we were the cause of her need) If I died tomorrow, you would still have a need.

C: (frightened) Are you going to die?
I: Not that I know of.
C: I *like* having a need. Needs fill up the black hole, because they show that I am a human being.
I: (uncomprehending and incredulous): They do? How does it work?
C: I don't know.
I: (still looking for clarification): What were you before you were a human being?
C: A [expletive] robot.

Here I must digress to explain something about Carolyn and something about myself. On an intellectual level, Carolyn has an unusually clear mind. She does not embroider, nor is she ambiguous—provided she is not anxious. Her native inclination is to hit the nail on the head each and every time. This of course is apart from the times when she deliberately lies, which makes it easier for me to know when she is lying. But most of the time she does not lie, and when she makes a point, or comes to an idea, she sticks with it both during the session and thereafter. On my side, I must confess to wanting always to be slightly ahead of the game, so to speak, in working with severely disturbed patients. I like to feel ready to respond to whatever is said to me, and if I do not always know what something means, I like to feel that I am reasonably certain about what direction to go in order to find out. With Carolyn in particular, I had always felt quite confident in my ability to respond to the material she presented me. With her, as with other patients with psychotic symptoms, I feel that it is not only permissible but also desirable to be quite active, even confrontational.

But this interchange with Carolyn about the black hole being filled by needs brought me to an abrupt halt and left me feeling perplexed and full of consternation. For I conceived of the state in terms of an abyss, as something literally bottomless, and therefore as something which could never be filled up. Even less could I imagine how needs might somehow fill up any space, let alone a bottomless one. My perplexity was not helped by the emotional pressure I felt to have a response ready for my patient if only because I had always had one before. After the session, I continued to ponder the puzzle. I found I could not imagine a structure that had no boundaries at all, but I could imagine one that was bottomless, provided it had walls on either side. To Carolyn's assertion about needs, I associated to Hamlet's statement about his mother: "She would hang on him, as if increase of appetite had grown by what it fed on." But needs continued to suggest absence to me. Then I imagined a metal object in the form of a kidney-shaped sputum tray on top of the black hole. I realized then the relevance of needs as potential containers of objects. The kidney-shaped tray would prevent objects thrown into the hole from falling endlessly. The need tray would contain the objects, and in the process, provide a bottom where the abyss of the black hole provided none.

In the next session, when Carolyn again brought up the problem of the black hole, I drew a picture of my concept of the sputum tray and the black hole being covered by it. But Carolyn did not really respond to the picture, and we drifted to other topics. A month later, however, she again brought up the subject, saying that she felt gruesomely empty and lonely when she didn't get what she wanted. I volunteered: "When you can't get what you want, you 'give' the wish to the person who won't grant it. That way you feel you don't have the pain of the ungranted wish, but in reality, you lose yourself. Who you are is what you want." I again drew the picture of the tray atop the black hole for her and this time she asked to keep it, saying, "I'm getting the wish back."

The following session, Carolyn reported waking up with the feeling of the black hole: "I said to myself, 'I wish I could be with Boyd,' and the wish is staying with me. I felt a kerplunk in the tray. Then I realized I didn't have to be alone." The next session she again reported a similar incident, though it had left her puzzled:

C: I don't understand how it works.
I: What were you doing to yourself before you got your wish back?
C: I was splitting myself [I had never used this term with her]. The half I sent off is ghostlike. That is scary. Awful. On another occasion, I interpreted: "If you want something, you feel you have to have it. If you don't get it, *you throw away the wish. That is how you get a black hole.* That is how you die of not being able to afford to go to Bloomingdale's (a very expensive store)." A few sessions after this intervention, Carolyn volunteered: "The work on the black hole is worth a million dollars. It's connected with the fantasy about God." She also reported that the black hole was being filled with Amaretto (a liqueur) and it warmed her. As a result, she felt she didn't need God. Carolyn now began spontaneously to integrate the various facets of the God-black hole system with her day-to-day experience of people.

C: I am worried about my new job. I hate authority figures . . . I hate you because you are an authority. Rules. Rules. I have to follow them to be part of the world. I feel scared as I say this: With God in my pocket, there were only Carolyn's rules. I want to do what I want to do when I want to do it. I really believed I could get away with it. You helped me and you enforced your rules, especially at the beginning and even when I was sick. You said, "There are people who are sicker than you and I am not at your beck and call." My temper tantrums worked for me as a kid. At my jobs, I wanted to do it my way, like my father.
I: I don't see the connection between God in your pocket and the rules.
C: *God and I* made up the rules.
I: How do you feel about the rules now?
C: I hate having to follow them. It feels like being one with the herd. I got lost in my family.
I: It didn't sound like it. It sounded like you got a lot of special attention that the others didn't get. But now I see why you got lost. Your identity depended on getting wishes gratified from *others*, rather than merely having wishes as

part of your identity. When you didn't get what you wanted, you pretended you didn't wish it. That *really* made it seem like God was looking after you.
C: That is all connected to the black hole. I threw away the wish. It hurts having an identity based on others, because if I didn't get it, I threw it away.
I: In that system, you couldn't *not* like anything.
C: Now I have to sit on my temper tantrums. I used to scream, "I don't like it!"
I: What happens if I say, "It's okay not to like something"?
C: It feels wonderful. It also felt wonderful when you said months ago, "It's okay to be lonely." Loneliness makes me cry sometimes, but it's not empty.
I: What did you think was wrong with not liking something?
C: I felt I wasn't strong enough to deal with it. It was a pretend game. Real life was too painful. *My parents needed me to pretend I needed them.*

At this point in the treatment, Carolyn was educating me further about the meaning of wishes for what I have termed the *overindulged* psychotic patient. The deprived psychotic patient thrives to some degree on the therapist's merely having a respectful attitude, though more than this is needed for full recovery, of course. The overindulged patient, by contrast, so often seems unappreciative and looks for opportunities to take advantage of the therapist. I had previously found, in working with another such overindulged patient, that simply saying in a calm, reassuring way, "It's okay not to like it," had surprising anxiety-reducing effects. What Carolyn was making clear to me is that such statements might relieve an overindulged child from the need to pretend in order to satisfy the parents. Some months later, in describing a visit with her mother, Carolyn went further and in the process clarified how such a need to please could lead not only to a denial of frustrated wishes, but also to a sense of invisibility, of becoming a "ghost" in Carolyn's word, that prepared the way for the encounter with the abyss. Carolyn volunteered about her mother: "She says all the right things, but I don't believe her. When my mother says, 'I'm so happy for you,' I feel like a cartoon character, like when they show a baby crying and the mouth is black. I feel she doesn't know me. I felt invisible." By this time, my understanding had caught up with my patient. What began as a passive invisibility caused by her mother's essentially hollow responsiveness was transformed by the child to an active invisibility. The passive invisibility, paradoxically, was removed by simply wiping it out-though this required wiping out the wishes, too. In their place was left the black hole.

Discussion

The proposition that black hole phenomena represent the psychobiological anlage of having a mother "ripped" away in early childhood does not seem confirmed in this case. Nor does the idea that such a black hole, with or without an accompanying religious delusion, represents a deficit in primary narcissism seem to have much explanatory weight in understanding either Carolyn's dynamics or her phenomenological experience. Rather than represent a straightforward deficit in Carolyn's basic psychological makeup, her black hole clearly reflected an important defensive operation, namely her deliberately dissociating and denying those wishes that were not readily fulfilled by objects. Indeed, this dissociation eventually reached the point that it became habitual and Carolyn became unaware of wishes that had not been gratified, nor did she distinguish between wishes and the person who was capable of gratifying them. Such a defensive posture, though primitive in its all-encompassing sweep, requires a greater, rather than lesser, degree of psychological structure.

Some further clarification is perhaps in order. It is certainly true that Carolyn "lacked" something that ordinary people possess. But this "lack" was of the same order as a person "lacking" a capacity for full sexual enjoyment. In the great majority of cases of the latter kind of lack, one is accustomed to find that an underlying conflict, and not a basic deficit in hedonic capacity, is to blame. And so with Carolyn's "lack"—it reflected a conflict with regard to feeling her unfulfilled wishes together with a defense against experiencing that conflict, not a basic or primary deficit in the ability to have or feel wishes, unfulfilled or no. Were it the latter, one would not expect it to have resolved so readily with interpretation.

The same line of reasoning applies to the mother-child relationship in this case. Carolyn's relation to her mother, though it led to the inner experience of a black hole, was not of the kind that one would make one think of a mother having been "ripped" away. Deficits in maternal bonding or attachment come in many forms, to be sure, and no one could argue against the proposition that Carolyn's mother had shown a deficiency, albeit a subtler one than outright abandonment, in her relationship to her daughter. What is at issue is whether the deficit in the mother, her failure to respond genuinely to the child in a way that might make the child feel truly recognized, was the direct cause of the experience of the abyss or merely the occasion for it. And here I must take issue with the idea that Carolyn's black hole represented a loss of omnipotence in the face of trauma. Equally, I would dispute the idea that the black hole directly reflected the maternal inadequacy. To the contrary, it appears that in Carolyn's case, the maternal inadequacy, if not defended against, would have led directly only to a feeling of helplessness and overwhelming sadness. It was Carolyn's attempt to reinstitute a feeling of omnipotence (Levin, 1986) and restore a feeling of safety that caused her to construct her system of having "God in her pocket," and it was this in turn which led her to deny her wishes and thus herself. In short, here as with many other forms of psychopathology (see Gediman, 1983), it is not the maternal deficit that has the direct effect on determining symptoms, but it is the child's conflicted response to that behavior that leads to the experience of inner deficit.

With equal vigor, I would also dispute that neurobiological factors played a determining role in the creation of Carolyn's black hole. Grotstein (1990, p. 36) has supposed that the phenomenal expression of "neurobiology, especially when it presents itself as deficits, is that of meaninglessness." I would contend, rather, that if a patient experiences meaninglessness, it is because he or she does not dare to admit what the experience means to him or her. In all likelihood, there is no such thing as valid meaninglessness in the great majority of patients, including those reporting black hole phenomena, thus no need to posit a neurobiological factor.

Finally, though it is an old psychoanalytic moral, one should note the difference between the patient's external, and interpersonal, behavior and her inner reality. For Carolyn, the experience of the black hole led to the external expression of a great, panicky needfulness, directed both at her roommates and at myself. It would have been easy to imagine that she was searching for someone to fill up the black hole, to make good the supposed deficit in primary narcissism. But Carolyn's own inner experience was *not* one of felt needfulness. Rather, she experienced a loss of self secondary to the denial of her having unmet wishes and needs. In short, there was an important disjunction between her inner world and her outward behavior, a disjunction caused by the internal dissociation and denial operating in the context of a lifetime pattern of "overindulged" demands.

It remains to be seen, of course, whether the pattern of meaning regarding the black hole phenomenon revealed in Carolyn's case can be replicated in the treatment of other patients and, if so, in what percentage of cases.

References

Gediman, H. (1983). Annihilation anxiety: The experience of deficit in neurotic compromise formation. *Internat. J. Psycho-Anal*, 64: 24–36.

Grotstein, J. (1990). The "black hole" as the basic psychotic experience: Some newer psychoanalytic and neuroscience perspectives on psychosis. *J. Amer. Acad. Psychoanal.*, 18: 29–46.

Killingmo, B. (1989). Conflict and deficit: Implications for technique. *Internal. J. Psycho-Anal.*, 70: 65–80.

Ladan, A. (1992). On the secret phantasy of being an exception. *Internal. J. Psycho-Anal.*, 73: 29–38.

Levin, R. (1986). Infantile omnipotence and grandiosity. *Psychoanal. Rev.*, 73: 57–76.

Tustin, F. (1988). "The black hole"—a significant element in autism. *Free Assns.*, 11: 35–50.

6

ADDENDUM TO "BLACK HOLE" PHENOMENON

Deficit or Defense? A Case Report

Gradually, Carolyn's attachment to the idea that she had "God in my Pocket" began to diminish. Also, she became aware that she had made the "mistake" of having "given herself up" when she was a toddler to be loved.

C: I made an error when I gave myself up. Not admitting things is a way of making them not true. I can't have hope if I get bad news.
I: What are you hoping for? (startled)
C: That it was all a bad dream. I'm hoping I'm still special and I'm better than other people.
I: That is called wishing, not hoping. You can wish for anything. Hoping has to have some kind of rational basis. You lose your wishes by calling that hope. That is how you got into trouble with the "black hole."

To the best of my memory, I had not yet read Salman Akhtar's unpublished paper "Hope and Nostalgia" (see Chapter 16 "Opposing Opinions as to Treatment of Wishes and Hopes Pathology: A Response to Salman Akhtar"). He handles this differently. My first three sentences are pure dictionary definitions. Indeed, I can fault myself for responding that way because it is purely rational. I may have needed to say it, because I felt more pulled into psychosis at that point than I could handle with equanimity. Better technique would have been to say "Interesting that you who are so good with words are confusing hope and wish." But, my following two sentences are more appropriate. However, it is the beginning of my interest in this subject. That paper is cited above.

C: I am still dimly aware of the black hole. I exchanged my wishes for my mother's love and hope. Wishes are bad, bad, bad, (hitting a pillow with her fist). I'm

getting even with the world for my wishes not coming true. I thought hope would help connect me to other people. Wishes are connected to nothing. I thought it would control something. If it doesn't, I might as well have wishes connected to me. I feel sad that I threw wishes away. Why did I do it? Why didn't I think of wishes as precious? You can strive for things.
I: Like wanting to get well.
C: I felt my wishes were useless. I let my mother off the hook. I still have the wish that she loved me. If I have the wish, I add meat (sic) to myself. I *fill myself up* and make the wish of getting well come true.

The next session I got a letter from her saying in part,

> I forgot or neglected to tell you how wonderful, warm, filling and genuine it felt when I claimed my wishes and hopes and in the session before and the following days. Those following days I held on to all my wishes and hopes and acknowledged them and owned them. Then I felt truly, deeply, wonderfully sad for having given up those wishes all the years before . . . That acknowledgement and ownership of my sadness, pain and grief for the years lost and bad decisions made, freed me and liberated me in a way I'm not sure I can define or explain. I was **real**. (her emphasis) . . . A barrier is down. (It has since gone back up—I need to reconnect again to my pain) and sadness—the *two* of which I never thought I could own up to.

In the following session, she said,

C: Just because a wish doesn't come true, doesn't mean I can't have a wish . . . it feels good to say "I have a wish." Nothing happens (implying nothing negative happens). You just pile one wish on top of another and you **fill** yourself up with them (my emphasis). But I want to be sick and I want to be angry.
I: That is an interesting wish to have: to be angry.
C: Yes, a want is a wish, isn't it? (Therapist: Amazing ignorance for one as verbal as Carolyn is, but wonderful evidence for the power of the unconscious.) I feel like someone told me that if I wish for something I would get it. I don't really want to be angry. Something in me wants to be angry. *I* don't. It feels good to have a wish that doesn't come true.
I: For you it is an improvement.
C: Why did I throw it away? Yes, my mother gave me everything. (Therapist: This is the interpretation I would have made if she had not seen it herself.)

In the following session, she said "I didn't lose my wishes this week. It felt incredible. Wow! If I had known what good mental health was like I would have worked faster." During the whole of my professional life I have felt inadequate to describe what good mental health felt like. For the very reason Carolyn gives:

I would have liked to have been able to do it. The best description I ever heard came from an alcoholic who said, after a description I gave him that I unfortunately forgot, "It is like being drunk without having been drinking."

She continues: "The wishes *fill me up* (emphasis mine). Even if it didn't come true, it was great. The opposite of *being a shell with a black hole* (emphasis mine).

Following that, I received a letter from her that said, in part,

> I feel so full of myself-my true self, I feel that I truly have my brain, my heart, my courage. I have my hopes and wishes from the past and now of the present for the future. What I have now, no amount of money could buy. It's a most precious gift . . . I didn't know then how strong I really was . . . that I could face pain and sadness and loss. I didn't know then that if my parents didn't love me, I didn't have to give up myself and pretend for them. All I had to do was be me, love myself However, I feel compassion for myself. I forgive myself . . . I cannot be scared and shaking and cowardly and empty in *my* own skin. That is not me. I am intelligent, courageous, full of hope and wishes and desire . . . How sad to have been *not me* in myself. Better for now that I sit with this sadness. It carries me far to happy shores. (All emphases in this letter are hers.) In the next session, she says, "I feel incredibly solid, as opposed to being in an eggshell without the egg.

What is the significance of all this from a theoretical point of view? The idea that she had God in her pocket had a basis in reality, in that when she was a child, she would have temper tantrums and her mother would give her everything she wanted, unlike how her mother treated her other children (see Freud, S.E. XXIII, p. 268). So, in a sense, wishes became equivalent to hopes. All her wishes were granted, so it appears to be rational that they are equivalent to hopes. Even more, that they will be fulfilled.

But given this background she could not tolerate having wishes that did not come true. So she "threw them away" (denied them), thus "proving" she had "God in her pocket" and did not have any wishes that did not come true. This statement is an example of Freud's assertion that there is a fragment of historical truth in madness (Freud, XXIII, p. 267). I believe that there is more than a fragment. However, the denial of such wishes created the "black hole." Note how she clearly states that when she reinstates her wishes, she becomes "filled up."

Two things were a surprise to me. The first was that when I asked what she was hoping for, she answered, "That it was all bad dream." This is an impossibility in relation to time. One can wish that something had never happened, but a hope can never be connected to something past. It is impossible to hope retroactively (see Chapter 16 "Opposing Opinions as to Treatment of Wishes and Hopes Pathology: A Response to Salman Akhtar").

However, it has been my frequent experience that when a patient comes out of psychosis, they *say*, "I feel **as if** I had been having a bad dream." Indeed, more than one patient has said, "I feel like Rip Van Winkle."

The second surprise was the release of sadness. I had been struggling during the whole of her treatment (four years at that time) to get her to express sadness, but *up* to that point, I had failed. *Now* I understand that the expression of sadness requires that one be aware of having a wish that is not fulfilled. In Carolyn's system, that was not possible. I cannot help but wonder if such a system is not always the case in over-indulged patients.

References

Akhtar, Salman. *Opposing opinions as to treatment of wishes and hopes pathology: A response to Salman Akhtar.* Unpublished.

Freud, Sigmund. (1937). Constructions in analysis. In *The Standard Edition of the Complete Psychological Works of Sigmund Freud*, Vol. XXIII, Hogarth Press, London, p. 268.

7

FAITH, PARANOIA, AND TRUST IN THE PSYCHOANALYTIC RELATIONSHIP

I would like to express my deep gratitude to Dr. Neville Sumington for his helpful suggestions.

The history of Western civilization is, in one sense, a story of progress from faith to reality testing. Alongside the current tendency of a return to religious ritualism, man is gradually discovering more about nature and how to control it. Through reality testing, for example, we no longer accept the idea that one becomes ill because of evil spirits. We have advanced to the point where we can often pinpoint the exact bacteria that are the cause of many diseases. Further, we know enough about science to prevent and cure many others. Additionally, we have had an explosion in technology that exemplifies our ability to bend nature to our will, making what had previously been fantasies into reality. These are examples of man's direct control over our environment through scientific knowledge and our understanding of cause and effect, rather than illusory control through faith.

It is safe to assume that, in the foreseeable future, the part of our lives that is governed by faith will gradually be reduced as the amount of information gathered by science increases still more.

In psychotherapy, however, we have an interesting paradox. The stated goal for our patients is increased use of reality testing, that is, a greater reliance on a scientific approach to reality, and less reliance on magical thinking and faith. Because I work primarily with borderline and psychotic patients, my work requires me to be even more devoted to those factors than therapists who work with less seriously ill patients. But in general, we want our patients to experiment in order to discover whether the consequences of their behavior are what they suppose.

(Originally published in the *Journal of the American Academy of Psychoanalysis*, 26(4), 553–572, 1998. Reprinted with permission of Guilford Press)

On the other hand, we want a new patient to trust us, if for no other reason than that it is difficult to work with a patient who does not. Further, we often assume that a patient's skepticism is part of his illness.

Frequently, the literature supports us in these attitudes. The Grunebaums (1980) say, for example: "trust is the basis of mental health and the foundation of psychotherapy" (p. 817). Erikson (1963/1983) says: "It (trust) is a basic requirement for therapy in adults" (p. 248). Paolino (1982) is even more specific, saying: "In order for the patient to be capable of a therapeutic alliance, the patient must possess the capacity for trust, a phenomenon more profound than rapport and distinctly separate from transference" (p. 222).

In discussing Macbeth, Bachmann (1978) seems to me to be more realistic. She quotes Duncan as saying: "There's no art to find the mind's construction in the face. He (Macbeth) was a gentleman on whom I built an absolute trust." Bachmann comments:

> in such a world, this 'absolute trust' appears foolhardy and blind, since it seldom reflects an evaluation of the characters or situations themselves. In other words, such trusting does not seem to indicate a healthy mutuality, for it is the opposite extreme of total distrust-and likewise unhealthy.
>
> (p. 99)

It appears to me that what is called "absolute trust" would be better labeled "faith" because the dynamics of trust and faith are very different. This chapter attempts to differentiate trust and faith, and their relationship to each other and to paranoia. (When I refer to "paranoia," I will not be referring to the illness, but rather to the patient's *feeling* that someone wishes to harm him or her without evidence for it, or contrary to the evidence in that particular situation.)

Faith

On the distinction between faith and trust, Isaacs et al. (1963) say:

> With the development of stage-by-stage series of differentiations, the individual with broad lines of ego development becomes capable of new distinctions . . . the person who has not developed to the stage of trust does not perceive the distinction between faith and trust, or he will perceive the distinction as insignificant in itself or in its consequences. From the point of view of such primitive characters, the distinctions that the most mature persons make are seen as being without consequences, as perhaps a play on words, as a kind of naïveté, or as a preoccupation with trivia.
>
> (pp. 46–462)

If Isaacs et al. are correct about immaturity as the cause of being unable to distinguish between faith and trust, there is a plethora of immature people to be found. Part of the problem seems to me to be that the distinction between faith and trust is seldom made in common parlance. Even the dictionary (Webster, 1979) is misleading in that it uses "trust" as a synonym for "faith" (p. 650). The use of the word "faith" is usually limited to emotions applicable to religious matters. We fail to notice how often people feel it in many other areas, such as psychotherapy. Frequently, without being aware of it, we hope and/or expect our patients will have faith in us and our psychotherapy. What Grunebaum, Erikson, and Paolino are calling "trust" may in fact be "faith" if the patient has insufficient evidence to evaluate whether or not it is rational to trust.

Burton (1976–77) does not confuse the two, but insists that "it is existentially necessary" to have faith in a therapist (p. 609). Miller (1981) agrees, saying "Psychoanalysis can be seen as a new religion" and "therapy provides a forum for the emergence of faith" (p. 19). Freud, of course, disagrees. In a letter to Oskar Pfister (1963), the minister, he says, "I do not call for any act of faith on your part, but only a readiness to assess the appropriate material" (p. 23).

If we accept that faith and trust are different emotions, it must be emphasized that the therapist and the patient who has little or no knowledge of therapy are in different emotional positions. Therapists have seen how much psychotherapy has improved their own lives. They have seen the drama of its effect on their previous patients' lives and are so convinced of its efficacy that they expect it to be evident to others. Therapists have good reason to trust psychotherapy. But the patient who has little or no experience with it must use faith to accept it. Without evidence, he has no basis for trust.

Of course, if we do have wishes for patients' faith, they are sometimes fulfilled. A patient may come to us with faith in psychotherapy solely because of his or her own wishes. S/he may have been impressed by the story of a friend's experience in psychotherapy and, because of his/her strong wishes, assumes that therapy is always wonderfully successful. S/he may have met a therapist with a great deal of charisma and on that emotional basis acquired faith in psychotherapy.

His/her faith may also come about for negative reasons: for example, because of having a traumatic experience with another kind of therapy. Or the patient may be so desperate, s/he dare not think of the possibility of therapeutic failure. But in all these situations, no critical evaluation has taken place. The patient has not searched to find out whether there are other pertinent facts to consider.

Isaacs et al. (1963) eloquently point out the pitfalls into which a patient who has faith in therapy may fall:

> When a patient's affective attitude toward his analyst is faith-filled, there is a tendency to have complete belief in the analyst with an unquestioning expectation of (magical) results. The blind and unquestioning faith leads to a degree of credulousness which blocks perception. Such a person will undoubtedly try to accept any comment, interpretation, or suggestion of

the analyst. He will try strikingly different reformulations without question. Faith quells anxiety and forestalls close examination of a situation.

When the patient bases his expectation of analysis on a faith affect cluster, there is usually a blind and hidden grandiose expectation of a gratification. Such a patient believes that change will occur regardless of the kind or amount of his participation, and there is the expectation of magic or miraculous change brought about through an omnipotent analyst who is expected to perform miracles to enable the patient to be comfortable, content happy, satisfied, gratified, relieved and pleased, regardless of the circumstances in which he might find himself; and he expects that this will be achieved without his having to take any responsibility for the process.

(p. 467)

These writers deserve much praise for the point they make as well as for the breadth of their description. But to my surprise, they imply that this is not just another problem for psychotherapy, but call such a patient, "a poor prospect for psychotherapy and highly improbable risk for psychoanalysis . . . it is our impression that trust may rarely develop in the therapeutic situation, but forms an absolute prerequisite to integrative psychoanalytic activity" (p. 467).

To take such a dim view is to underestimate the potential efficacy of psychotherapy. Problems with faith and trust appear to me to be part and parcel of a large proportion of the illnesses we see. Why can't these problems be treated as well? Why can't we treat them as resistances, just as we handle other resistance? It seems to me that to do less is to underestimate both ourselves and our patients. Further, to do less is to deny treatment to those whose need is great.

Case Illustration: Glen

Glen is an excellent example of this point. If I were to have accepted Glen's evaluation of my statements, I would have believed I never erred. Glen is a 24-year-old, handsome, brilliant, talented transvestite. In the course of treatment, it became evident that his desire to dress in women's clothes was an attempt to appease his superego. Glen's father was inordinately jealous of him. Glen had the unconscious fantasy that if he "got rid" of his penis, his father would be less hostile.

I: When you pretend you have no penis, your eyes have to be closed? (He and I understand that this means, he has to "shut his eyes" to reality.)
G: Yes, I've been forcing myself to go into a situation completely unprepared to evaluate.
I: So you guide yourself by outside standards.
G: You are the outside standard. They come from you. (Needless to say, I have never proposed any standards at all. But since Glen has "closed his eyes," he is forced to have faith in what he believes to be my appraisals.)

I: You don't weigh what I say?
G: I torment myself with your statements. Either it's all true, or it's all not true.
I: I'm quite sure that some of my statements are wrong. Some are right and many are partially true.
G: Yes, there is something important about my relationship with you in this.
I: Why don't you check me out?
G: I have trouble doing it; when I look at myself, it's murky. I feel I gave you a twisted impression.
I: So if I'm wrong, it's because you gave me the wrong facts?
G: I don't trust what I tell you. On the other band, I don't trust what I *don 't* tell you either.
I: You can't figure out if I'm right, because your eyes are closed. And you keep them closed in order to go on pretending that you don't have a penis.
G: So, not trusting myself is pretending I don't have a penis. But I would sooner not trust myself than believe some of the things I know are true. (Here we can see that Glen finds normal perception and evaluation so painful, he would rather relinquish them, even if the consequence is to be forced to have faith in me.)

He confirms this in a later session, when speaking of how he tried to get himself to believe things there were not true, he said: "The way I did it, was I stopped trusting what was in my head, since I couldn't eradicate what was there." As the session went on, he became more aware that it was his superego that was demanding self-castration. He began to fight that with remarkably little ambivalence.

In the following session, he reported that the last session had been "great." "I've been riding high ever since. I was more out in the open. My mother, whom I saw afterward, remarked about it."

1: Which part of the session was so great?
G: Fighting my conscience.
1: What made it possible for you to fight it?
G: Trusting what I feel. When I dread coming here, I'm closing my eyes. I felt I opened my eyes and I knew something. (We can see from this, that the superego had forced Glen into a position, where he had to give up trust and was forced into faith.)

Since that time, Glen bas been far more questioning of my interpretations. I no longer get constant affirmation. In the following session, he said: "I look in the mirror now, and I see a man, not a boy."

A few sessions later, the problem showed up in the transference. He was able to tell me how angry he was that I had taken a week's vacation. He felt that I just went off because I felt like it and didn't care about him or whether it was an important time in his therapy.

G: I resent how little you show in exchange for what I show.
1: Are you sure you look at what I show?
G: I don't think I've ever looked. I took it for granted. I felt, "She doesn't care" and I haven't looked.
1: Yes, I suppose if one is sure of what one will see, one doesn't bother to look.
G: Of course you care. I know you do. I've seen the way you look at me.

Glen is now giving evidence of more separation-individuation. He is dating a few young women. His work is progressing considerably.

Steiner's (1985) quotation from Vallacott's "Sophocles and Oedipus" is relevant here. "When I come to the land of death-if I could see, I do not know with what eyes I should face my father or my unhappy mother, since against them both I am guilty of sins too black for strangling to atone" (p. 169).

Emotional Conditions that Encourage Faith

For Glen, not being able to see himself and also doubting my ability to see perfectly would have been a more realistic point of view, but would have cause intolerable anxiety (Levin, 1986). He is an excellent example of how not only evaluative abilities can go askew, but also how faith can come into being in the therapeutic setting. Because he couldn't use his own "eyes," he felt it necessary to have faith in me as a "seeing eye dog" (his words).

Another condition that may encourage faith is when the use of ego evaluative abilities is treated as immoral by a parent. Laura, a borderline patient, had a mother who lied consistently. Laura used to quote her mother's advice, in a tone of voice that is used in the movies to indicate that God has spoken. Not only have her mother's lies been introjected by Laura, but also introjected was the concept that it is immoral to tell the truth. Recently, after a few years of treatment, I learned of Laura's belief that the truth will not help her get well. She believed that only more and better lies would accomplish that. Her method of "therapy" is to try to convince herself that she feels differently than she actually did. Of course, because no repression is ever completely successful, she is also extremely paranoid.

In Freud's "The Future of an Illusion" (1930a) and "Moses and Monotheism" (1939), the dangers of faith are too well known to necessitate repetition here. I would only add that, in patients who are seriously ill psychologically, the feeling of being "dead" is almost pervasive. So that they, like those who are physically ill, may well reach for faith for the purpose of achieving immortality.

The Destructive Consequences of Faith

With the psychotic, we see the most glaring use of faith, which, in turn, can cause the patient even more damage. In psychotics, we can note the similarity of some aspects of faith to delusions. The psychotic may say "This man only *looks* like an ordinary man. In fact, he is really the Devil."

When the religious man says, "Death only looks like extinction, but it is really the beginning of a new kind of existence," he is saying as the psychotic says, "I know what this being looks like, but the 'reality' is hiding behind the appearance." *Undisprovability supports conviction.*

Faith may also present the possibility of changing one's identity, as Esther Menaker (1984) points out. She says: "Paul (the disciple of Jesus) was born into a new sense of self and became an ideal for others who, as he taught, could, through faith, be awakened to a new self" (p. 351). Symington (1986) points out another possibility.

> It is an interesting and seemingly paradoxical that . . . oneness, be it in religion or other ideological experience, delineates the self, *creates* (italics mine) the person as it were, while at the same time that merging with a collective ideal enables the individual to lose himself within a larger whole, thus guaranteeing him a measure of immortality.
>
> *(p. 47)*

But, in fact, such "creation" causes repression of the real self when one tries to make oneself "fit in." When this occurs extensively, the result is the loss of ego, and even the experienced loss of self as seen in the psychotic. These same dynamics are apparent in less ill patients who experience themselves as not "belonging" and feel rejected by the group. In order to ease their loneliness, they try to mold themselves into the image of someone whom they think will be accepted by a group through the means of adopting the same faith as the group espouses.

Positive emotions are also at risk because of faith. When faith is used as a denial of real helplessness, it presents the problems that any denial presents. Repression does not only repress the specific unwanted emotion or experience. Other consanguineous emotions will likewise be repressed.

All too often those emotions are tenderness, love, and sensitivity, the repression of which in turn would lead to a decrease in close relationships. Paradoxically, because of the lack of specificity of repression, the repressed helplessness, which originally was related to only a limited area, will spread unconsciously and govern a very large part of the person's life. We are all familiar with this phenomenon.

Ironically, some of the disadvantages of faith are evidenced by Meissner (1969), a Jesuit priest who is also a psychiatrist. He says: "Faith presupposes the resignation of all finite goods and the dissociation from all wish fulfillments. It is only in such an infinite resignation that man begins to catch a glimpse of his true validity" (p. 51).

The first sentence would appear to be particularly masochistic for a patient. Further, considering what we have been discussing, it would be difficult to accept the idea of a person's dissociation from all wish fulfillments because, in a general sense, wishes are precisely the inspiration of faith. Oddly, Meissner insists that "faith is not an emotion precisely because it requires resignation" (1969, p. 51). The logic of that statement errs in two ways: (a) anyone who has seen a supplicant with very strong faith cannot doubt his emotionality; and (b) resignation itself is an emotion, which one can see in the very depressed.

Meissner writes: "It (faith) is a gift to another, a gift of one's autonomy" (1969, p. 50). This is clearly a statement of the surrender of the entire ego. Who would think it is a desirable state of affairs to have only a superego and id? Fortunately, it is not entirely possible in any case. But it is very similar to the situation of a psychotic.

To summarize this section: Faith is generally an abrogation of the ego's evaluative and perceptual processes, which, on one level, puts the individual at the mercy of whatever one has placed one's faith in, while, on the other hand, placing responsibility on something that in all probability cannot meet that responsibility. Faith says: "My wish makes reality." But the price is loss of perception of reality and evaluative ability. It is also a threat to identity. It gives the feeling of unrealistic safety and can, therefore, be very dangerous to the patient. It also makes it more difficult for the therapist to reach the patient, in as much as it acts as an obstacle between the therapist and the patient's ego.

Paranoia

Much has already been written about paranoia. This discussion will restrict itself to pointing out the connections among paranoia, faith, and trust. We usually think of faith and paranoia as worlds apart. We think of people with faith as cheerful, on the surface bearing no ill will toward their fellow man. Certainly, the faithful are apparently less hostile than overtly paranoid people. We rarely think of them as dangerous to others. We do not usually associate the glower of the paranoid's face with the beatific smile of the faithful. In fact, paranoia is the obverse of faith, except for the superficial contents of the individual's perceptions. Neither the paranoid person nor the faithful one evaluates the object of his perceptions. Both arrive at their beliefs because of their emotional investments.

However, while the paranoid person is usually described as suspicious, this characterization is misleading. "Suspicion" implies doubt or skepticism. It leaves some room for another view. But, in fact, the paranoid person is as *certain* that others wish to harm him, as the faithful one is certain that he will be protected from harm. The paranoid person *depends* on his paranoid belief. Miller (1981) has an illuminating contribution to make on this point.

> Faith can . . . be succinctly defined as an irrational belief that things will improve or ultimately turn out well. Conversely, faith's obverse, despair, can be thought of as an irrational conviction that things will continue to worsen and deteriorate, and finally turn out badly.
>
> (p. 16)

It is not a large leap to substitute the word "paranoia" for "despair" in that context. In his usual succinct fashion, Freud (1930b) tells us what happens normally as the child grows and meets with disappointment. "The time comes when each one of us has to give up as illusions the expectations which, in his youth, he pinned upon his fellow men and when he may learn how much difficulty and pain has been added to his life by their ill-will" (p. 112).

But the patient with faith does not do that. He clings to his faith and becomes paranoid about people whom he sees as interfering with it. Thus, paranoia is a means of *maintaining* faith and its supposed "protection" and "safety." The outside world is seen as a plot against that faith. The current debate about abortion is a graphic example of that.

The person with faith can, of course, rationalize. For example, if one had faith that a particular course of medical treatment would cure a loved one and it failed, one could say, "It will work eventually" or "The medicine wasn't properly made up" and so on. In this way, one could continue to keep one's faith undisturbed.

But if the loved one dies and it appears that one must admit that one's faith is unjustified, one may feel forced to take more extreme measures to hold on to that faith. One may blame someone else for having been misled. This would be experienced as, "He led me to believe I could depend on him. He was trying to deceive me. He tricked me for his own ends. That proves he didn't care about me." Thus, paranoia becomes the response to faith, when reality totally contradicts it. Though perhaps not verbalized, the unconscious feeling is, "This faith is my possession of which others are trying to deprive me."

The result is both an increase and decrease in mental health simultaneously. On the one hand, it allows *some* reality to enter the wish system, that is, the death is not (usually) denied. But it is also a loss of reality in that it views the outside world as persecuting where usually what is involved is mere bad luck.

Case Illustration-Laura

Laura is a patient who constantly expressed the idea that I was exploiting her. She felt I was interested only in her money. She persistently ignored me defensively and attacked me when I offered her something she found truly valuable. Why did she want to see me in such a bad light? Laura had complete faith that her mother was devoted to her care. In fact, it was clear that nothing could be further from the truth. As mentioned previously, Laura's mother lied constantly and condemned Laura for telling the truth. She is borderline. The relationship between faith and paranoia can be seen in the following exchange:

I: You said last time that you want others to take responsibility, make decisions and then blame them if things go wrong.
L: I want *them* to make the mistakes.
I: That's a response to your wish to have them be the authority.
L: I wish to obey. I want someone to take care of me. But I'm also very frightened to turn decisions over to others.
I: You want someone to take care of you, so you obey them, like your mother.

L: She *has* to take care of me. It's her duty. (This "has to" is the foundation of Laura's faith.) It makes me feel betrayed if an authority doesn't take care of me. I have given up all of myself. It's a bargain. (Here Laura is saying she has surrendered her ability to evaluate reality in return for her right to keep her faith, but of course, she is often "betrayed.")
I: It's as if your obedience will force someone to take care of you.
L: I thought my agreement would do it. Then they always betrayed me.
I: Is there something to be learned from this?
L: You can't blindly obey. You can't force people to take care of you. Just because someone is an authority figure, doesn't mean you can put all your trust (read: faith) in them.

Case Illustration-Maureen

Maureen, during the first part of her therapy, constantly insisted that my interpretations were wrong, though surprisingly those same interpretations "acquired" validity in most cases by the following session. She was a compulsive borderline patient, with an underlying psychosis. She had a terror of connection with others, either physical or emotional. An acceptance of an interpretation was experienced by her as a connection. Her mother, although she offered Maureen very little connection with herself, made it clear to the entire family that anyone outside the moat of their home was the enemy. Maureen felt it would be a rejection of her entire family to form relationships with strangers, which included me.

Maureen had told herself when she was 12 years old that her parents loved her, but their love did her "no good." Through denial of her mother's indifference toward her, she convinced herself that her parents' sending her to a very restrictive parochial school did her no harm. The faith taught by the school was supported by Maureen's faith in her mother's "love."

However, I discovered that Maureen had an even deeper faith than I realized. Whenever I tried to interpret any of Maureen's irrational fears, she became angry with me. It gradually dawned on me, that she had perfect faith in her fears themselves. I had seen her fears as the problem. She had seen them as her defenders. That is, she felt it was safe and rational not to change jobs though her situation clearly warranted it. It was safe not to try to meet men, though she very much wanted a relationship with a man.

Most of all, she had faith in her fear of defending herself against people who attacked her. In the following session, after we had been discussing this problem for some time this interchange occurs:

M: I was thinking about why I'm so sure my fears protect me. In my family, any change is dangerous, so it wasn't a good idea to change. I bought it. I can't think about not being afraid. It ends anxiety when I give in to my fear. I *believe* in my fears. (I see that statement as a clear example of faith.) I had a dream in which I was physically fighting with my sister and mother. I know what it means: I am furious about people telling me what to do.

I: Maybe it also means that you are tired of having your fears tell you what to do. Maybe you want to decide for yourself what you should do.

Following this, there were two changes. She became less resistant to my interpretations and she came in *asking* for help in her difficulty about defending herself against attacks. It is clear that I had been an important source of her paranoia, in that I was "attacking" her faith in her fears.

From these two vignettes, I think it can be seen that paranoia is an attempt to retain faith, when it is being "attacked" by reality.

Trust

The question of trust in relationship to psychotherapy is one that has been discussed at length in the literature. No one surpasses Erikson (1963/1983) as its most famous exponent. "The infant's first social achievement . . . is his willingness to let the mother out of sight without undue anxiety or rage, because she has become an inner certainty as well as an outer predictability" (p. 147). "Trust forms the basis for a child's sense of identity" (p. 249). "It (trust) is a basic requirement for therapy in adults" (p. 248).

Trust at the Beginning of Psychotherapy

As previously discussed, trust is too often confused with faith. Boszornenyi et al. (1980) in their article "Trust Based Therapy" say that "trust is required as an initial investment in a relationship after which a person can take further steps toward trust building" (p. 768). "From the outset, the therapist receives trust through a client's contractions for help" (p. 773). Isaacs et al. (1963), in spite of their sensitivity to the differentiation between faith and trust, surprisingly make the same error. They say "trust . . . is an absolute prerequisite of integrated psychoanalytic activity" (p. 467). I have discussed my objections to this view previously in the section on faith.

I believe that the healthiest patients come to us with the view that they are *gambling*, because they have no evidence for any other attitude. Let us try for the moment to put ourselves in the patient's place prior to coming for treatment. Our friend or physician has referred us to a therapist. The referral source may even have given us some description of what a therapist is like. But how can we possibly know how this therapist will respond to us? How many times have we met people who have appeared to us totally differently than the way they have been described to us? We could also ask ourselves, "Perhaps this person is very competent, but can s/he help me with *my* problem?" This is certainly a realistic question, as most of us are better with some kinds of patients than others.

These and innumerable other questions can realistically occur to a patient prior to his or her first visit to a therapist. Is it any wonder that patients are very anxious in their first session? They are exposing themselves to a largely unknown quantity. What the previously mentioned writers are asking for is, in fact, faith, because there can be no trust without information.

Helping the Patient Discover Whether Trust Is Possible

Meissner (1976) writes:

> The question ... arises as to how the therapeutic alliance is established ... The basic issues, insofar as we are able to define them at this point, center around trust and autonomy ... The most important elements have to do with empathic responsiveness on the part of the therapist to the idiosyncratic needs, anxieties and inner tensions felt by the patient, such that the therapist responds to the patient in terms of the latter's own individuality, rather than in terms of the therapist's own needs or in terms of some preexisting therapeutic stereotype. Thus, important elements that might be focused on in this regard are the therapist's patient and attentive listening to the patient's productions. This involves a sort of active presence within the therapeutic situation and within the therapeutic relationship ... a consistent and available and 'present' object.
>
> *(p. 91)*

Lidz and Lidz (1982) are in general agreement: "Trust is established through the therapist's inherent thoughtfulness, and efforts to understand the patient's dilemma and grasp what the patient seeks to convey even as he or she seeks to hide thought or feelings" (p. 305). No doubt these writers were inspired by Freud's (1913) statement in this regard. "The beginning of a psychoanalysis ... must conform to its rules. There may perhaps be this distinction made, that in it one lets the patient do nearly all the talking and explain nothing more than what is absolutely necessary to get him to go on with what he is saying" (p. 124).

Later in the same article, in response to his own question—"When are we to begin making our communications to the patient?"—he answers: Not until an effective transference has been established in the patient, a proper *rapport* with him. It remains the first aim of the treatment to attach him to it and to the person of the doctor. To ensure this. nothing need be done but to give him time (p. 139).

Freud made these recommendations in order to avoid having the therapist tell the patient at the beginning of the treatment that he "is attached to his mother by incestuous ties," and so on. I question this technical rule. If we are merely listening, however attentively, the patient is given very little to test. He can have little knowledge as to what the response of the therapist is, unless the therapist tells him. Even if the patient is sitting up, the body language or facial expression of the therapist is far too amorphous as evidence on which to make judgments. The psychotic patient is much too anxious to tolerate this for long. If the patient is lying down, s/he has even less evidence to go on. Further, the analyst puts him or herself at an unnecessary disadvantage, because by saying so little for so long, s/he has no opportunity to correct erroneous assumptions. To assume that a patient can form a connection with an almost entirely silent therapist is to imagine that the patient can do precisely what some paranoid patients believe they can do: namely, read minds.

To give the schizophrenic patient an opportunity to discover whether or not s/he has some reason to trust the therapist to understand him, I suggest the therapist might do what I call "guessing," as early in the therapy as possible. By "guessing," I mean that the therapist should try to make a guessing interpretation about the patient's feeling, thoughts or behavior, for which one will no doubt have inadequate evidence. In other words, one may use the benefit of one's prior knowledge and experience. The value of this kind of guessing is supported by Symington (1986), who says, "I . . . think that an analysis cannot operate without both" (interpretations and guessing) (p. 34).

Of course, one would preface the interpretative statement(s) by acknowledging that one is guessing, thereby making the patient aware that the *therapist* is testing reality. This approach gives the patient something tangible to hang on to, if the therapist is correct. He is to that extent decreasing his gamble. Even if the patient rejects the interpretation, the patient benefits in two ways. S/he has seen that the therapist is really extending himself to help the patient. Further, the patient, in rejecting the therapist's statement, has an opportunity to clarify his feeling, both to him or herself and to the therapist on a particular subject. The patient has an opportunity to make some kind of judgment about how well he is conveying his or her situation, to evaluate the therapist early in the treatment, and to see whether s/he has some basis on which to base his or her trust.

Of course, I am not speaking of making an interpretation such as "You would like to sleep with your mother" in the first session. But there are wishes and other feelings that are far less unconscious than Oedipal wishes. One can speak to material that is slightly below consciousness, or material that has not yet been expressed, and still be useful to the patient.

One might object that this is "wild analysis." But what I am suggesting is that the therapist make such communications that will give a patient the feeling that he or she is being "seen." To allow the patient simply to talk without the therapist giving some *evidence* that (a) he or she is truly being understood and (b) that the therapist has something of value to offer the patient may give the patient the feeling that he or she is dropping his or her pebbles into a bottomless well. This prevents opportunities for reality testing for both the therapist and the patient, does nothing to decrease feelings of paranoia and/or faith, and heightens anxiety.

Case Illustration

When Maureen came to see me, she presented me with her delusion that the Devil was demanding that she sell her soul to him. In the course of the first session, I explained to her that the Devil was not really a part of her identity, as she had thought, but rather her conscience, which came from an external source. I felt such a statement would reduce her anxiety and begin to enable her to defend herself against the onslaught of paranoia that she was experiencing.

She responded by telling me that when she was 12, she began to question the teachings that she was learning at parochial school. "I was trying to find a way to agree with them." I said, "You were twisting your mind around to get yourself to agree." There in one sentence, I hoped to accomplish two things: (1) make her conscious of the pain involved in "trying to agree" (faith), rather than testing reality; and (2) point out that "trying to agree" was an inefficient way to discover what reality was, thus preventing the ability to see if trust was deserved. The net effect was to give Maureen a feeling of recognition and reduce her terror. "I had taken so much without questioning," she responded.

Case Illustration

A more dramatic example is the first session I had with Lynn. She had seen three therapists, prior to seeing me. With two of them, she did not return after the first session. The third, with whom she spent a few months, spent most of the time speaking about her own rose garden. I had been told only that she was a bright, homosexual alcoholic and she was clearly obese.

After stating a few initial facts, Lynn announced to me that she "doesn't talk." And truly, I didn't get much out of her, except "yes" and "no." Once, when I didn't hear her, she refused to repeat the sentence and often sentences were left unfinished. I said: "It must be difficult for you, a blow to your ego (in the lay sense), in view of the fact that you are so competent in your work, not to be able to handle your emotional problems." Fifteen minutes into the session, as she was preparing to leave permanently, she said: "It is a blow to my ego." (When I initially made the statement about her ego, I referred to her self-esteem, but the way Lynn said it, I realized *she* was talking about her superego.) I responded that in that case, I would talk to her "ego." I spoke to "it" as if I were talking to the *superego* and I were an ego. I spoke to "it," guessing as to how I thought it might be persecuting her and guessing as to what she might be feeling in response. As a result, Lynn stayed until the end of the session. Instead of coming the proposed once a week that I had suggested, she asked for four sessions a week. Further, she almost instantly changed from someone who "doesn't talk," to someone with whom I could barely get a word in edgewise. I had made a dent in her paranoia. To ask this woman to trust me, unless I gave some inkling of what I could do, would have been foolish.

The idea of the therapist taking a risk in an attempt to gain the patient's trust is noted by Catherine M. McKinnon (1953) in her review of John Rosen's *Direct Analysis*. She states: "Those direct interpretations (with psychotics) are believed to be effective in gaining the patient's acceptance of the therapist in the complicated relationship which is to follow" (p. 688). Surprisingly, Rosen had never stressed this advantage of early interventions with psychotics. But, in fact, patients do trust therapists who recognize their unverbalized feelings, as Rosen (personal observation) had shown countless times. When a patient says to a therapist, "How did you know that?" with surprise and even a little embarrassment, one can be certain that there is an increase in the quantity of trust.

Helping the Patient Trust Later in Therapy

The implicit idea governing this article is that faith and paranoia are both exclusive of trust and healthy skepticism. To put it another way: An increase in trust and healthy skepticism brings about a decrease in faith and paranoia. The first two are governed by reality testing and, of course, reasoning. The latter two are governed by wishes and irrational fear.

Surprising to me is that there are writers who imply they are helpless to have any influence in these areas. Curtis (1979) quotes Zetzel: "To accomplish this (regression), a therapeutic alliance dependent on stable mature ego functions of reality testing, object constancy, impulse control, tension, tolerance etc. is needed to contain and delimit the regression while analysis of the transference is taking place" (p. 167). I think that it is a great deal to expect of patients before they are finished with treatment. Zetzel admits: "Without such resources and achievements a suitable therapeutic alliance cannot be formed: examples of such cases would be borderline and psychotic patients" (p. 167). I rather doubt that whether many *neurotic* patients would fill that bill either. What such a view neglects is the therapist's role in assisting the patient to test reality. Paolino (1982) appears to share Zetzel's view. He says,

> Without basic trust, the patient will not make or maintain the most initial therapeutic relationship, since the patient will be unable to establish sufficient reality testing within the one to one relationship. Basic trust is necessary for the transference neurosis not to evolve into a transference psychosis.
> *(pp. 222–223)*

This writer also seems to expect his patients to be almost healthy when they come to him. In reference to the fear of a psychotic transference, must one not ask whether *all* transferences are not to some degree psychotic? A transference could not really be a transference if the patient were *completely* aware s/he was transferring. To the degree that there is a lack of awareness on the part of the patient, transference is a delusion. The difference between someone who is psychotic and someone who is in a transference is that, in the former, the psychosis is visible outside the transference. In the latter, only the area in relation to the therapist is psychotic.

I believe that Curtis (1979) takes a more constructive view of this problem. He describes how he helps the patient test reality in a very tangible way. He writes about a patient who is very anxious about using the couch. He allows the patient to decide himself when he can tolerate it. When the patient does lie down, Curtis speaks more often in order to make the patient more comfortable. When the patient hears a noise from the therapist, Curtis tells the patient that he has moved his legs or is taking notes.

Kanzer (1975) speaks of the difficulty of reality testing in the analytic situation. One of his patients had stressed in her first associations her professional inadequacy to judge the proceeding as compared to the supposed equipment of the therapist. Trust, under such circumstances, is not limited to the basic trust of the infant. The analytic situation in particular makes reality testing on the part of the patient difficult. Presumably, the analyst has realistic reasons which he is not prepared to communicate (p. 60).

To some degree, I would agree. The therapist's superior knowledge and experience do make it difficult to be challenged and is inclined to diminish the patient's confidence to do so. Further, the therapist has the advantage in that it is not his or her emotions that are under discussion.

The patient's ability to reason alone without specialized knowledge can go far toward helping the patient with reality testing. However, I think it is important for the therapist to encourage the patient to do so. Indeed, for the patient *not* to attempt to use his or her ability to reason and use the therapist's superior knowledge as an excuse to maintain the status quo in relation to his particular state of faith, can be a resistance. A patient may reason: "I don't know anything about psychotherapy. I have to rely on my therapist. He is trained, so he must know what he is doing." This is the typical kind of "reasoning" that faith-motivated people do in relation to authorities, thus abdicating responsibility for themselves. Nydes (1963) handles this problem with a wonderful rejoinder to a patient: "I am very much inclined to agree with you, but I am troubled by a very disturbing thought. Maybe both of us are wrong" (p. 52).

One final point must be made about trust. As the word is usually used in common parlance, it implies that one trusts another person not to deceive, mislead, or take advantage of him. However, I discovered by accident that a particular patient and I were talking about two different things, when we spoke about trust. It was this discrepancy that led me to inquire whenever a patient used the word "trust" to inquire "Trust to what?" I have found a very strange and surprising assortment of answers.

For example, Laura tried to use me as an authority on a great many subjects and then complained she did not trust me. I asked, "Trust to what?" She said, "To always be right." My response was, "Why should you? Since I am human, how can

I be trusted to always be right?" Ironically, Laura is a professional linguist. She later admitted putting me on a pedestal for transferential reasons.

Another patient, Roxanne, did not trust me to return from even a week's vacation. We discovered that the source of this distrust lay in the fact that she could not allow herself emotional intimacy with people even when they were *present*. The only closeness she accepted was touching. My vacation symbolized that problem. I have learned from these kinds of experiences never to assume that I know to what the patient is referring when he or she says he/she does or does not trust me.

Conclusions

I believe I have shown that we are expecting too much when we insist that a new patient begin treatment with trust in us. "Blind trust" seems to me to be an oxymoron. A patient may begin treatment with faith, but this needs to be treated as a resistance, as much as paranoia does. The terms appear to derive from the same root: certainly in the face of denial of reality, I believe that whichever one is on the surface, the other lurks behind.

It appears to me, however, that this view should lead us to optimism, rather than pessimism. Granted, we all feel more comfortable beginning treatment with a patient who *appears* to trust (read faith) us. But I believe I have shown that we can also treat a patient when the other side of the coin (paranoia) is exhibited. We need not restrict ourselves to the patient who appears to have faith in us, let alone the patient who makes clear to us, that he or she knows s/he is gambling.

Further, in pursuing our goal to have the patient trust us with validity, we can give evidence both at the beginning of treatment, and in the course of treatment, that we are worthy of that trust. Of course, a statement like "I don't lie" is asking the patient to have faith in us. We must give evidence by our attempts to understand that we *can* be trusted to have our patient's best interests at heart. Naturally, this can only be done gradually by dedicated work. At the same time, we can encourage our patients to use their own ego abilities to test reality. Even though we have superior knowledge and experience, they must learn that we *cannot* be trusted always to be right.

References

Bachman, S. (1978). Daggers in men's smiles-The trust issue in Macbeth. *Int. Rev. Psychoanal.*, 5: 97–104.
Boszomenyi, C., Nagy, I., and Krasner, B. (1980). Trust based therapy: A contextual approach. *Am. J. Psychiatry*, July, 137: 767–775.
Burton, A. (1976–77). The analysis of a therapeutic failure. *Psychoanal. Rev.*, 63: 587–614.
Curtis, H. (1979). The concept of the therapeutic alliance. *J. Am. Psychoanal. Assoc. (Suppl.)*, 27: 159–192.
Erikson, E. (1983). *Childhood and Society*, W. Norton, New York. (Original work published in 1963).

Freud, S. (1913). On beginning the treatment. In *The Standard Edition of the Complete Psychological Works of Sigmund Freud*, Vol. 12, Hogarth Press, London, pp. 121–144.

———. (1930a). The future of an illusion. In *The Standard Edition of the Complete Psychological Works of Sigmund Freud*, Vol. 21, Hogarth Press, London, pp. 3–56.

———. (1930b). Civilization and its discontents. In *The Standard Edition of the Complete Psychological Works of Sigmund Freud*, Vol. 21, Hogarth Press, London, pp. 51–145.

———. (1939). Moses and monotheism. In *The Standard Edition of the Complete Psychological Works of Sigmund Freud*, Vol. 23, Hogarth Press, London, pp. 3–137.

Grunebaum, J., and Grunebaum, H. (1980). Beyond the superego. *Am. J. Psychiatry*. 137: 817–819.

Isaacs, K. S., Alexander, J. M., and Haggard, E. A. (1963). Faith, trust and gullibility. *Int. J. Psychoanal.*, 44: 461–469.

Kanzer, M. (1975). The therapeutic and working alliances. *Int. J. Psychoanal. Psychother.*, 4: 47–76.

Levin, R. (1986). Infantile omnipotence and grandiosity. *Psychoanal. Rev.*, 73: 57–76.

Lidz, T., and Lidz, R. (1982). Curative factors in the psychotherapy of schizophrenic patients. In S. Slipp (Ed.), *Curative Factors in Dynamic Psychotherapy*, McGraw Hill, New York, pp. 298–320.

McKinnon, C. M. (1953). Book review of John Rosen's, Direct analysis. In *Annual Survey of Psychoanalysis IV*, International Universities Press, New York, pp. 686–692.

Meissner, W. W. (1969). Notes on the psychology of faith. *J. Religion Health*, 8: 47–75.

———. (1976). Psychotherapeutic schema based on the paranoid process. *Int. J. Psychoanal. Psychother.*, 5: 87–114.

Menaker, E. (1984). The ethical and the empathic in the thinking of Otto Rank. *Am. Imago*, 41: 343–351.

Miller, C. (1981). The role of faith in psychoanalysis. *Am. J. Psychoanal.*, 41: 15–20.

Nydes, J. (1963). The paranoid masochistic character. *Psychoanal. Rev.*, 50(2): 55–91.

Paolino, T. (1982). The therapeutic relationship in psychoanalysis. *Contemp. Psychoanal.*, 18: 218–234.

Pfister, O. (1963). *Psychoanalysis and Faith*, Basic Books, New York (letter by S. Freud, 1909).

Steiner, J. (1985). Turning a blind eye: The coverup for Oedipus. *Int. Rev. Psychoanal.*, 12: 161–172.

Symington, N. (1986). *The Analytic Experience*, St. Martin's Press, New York.

Webster. (1979). New Twentieth Century Dictionary (second edition). Simon and Schuster, Editorial Offices, New World Dictionary. Cleveland, Ohio, p. 658.

8

JOHN ROSEN: GENIUS OR QUACK?
Historical Reflections of a Former Student

This chapter will deal with my experiences with John Rosen and what I learned from working for him. I want to preface this talk by saying I have tried to be as objective as possible. Especially in terms of psychoanalytic theory, I have always tried to separate the wheat from the chaff. For example, the fact that Wilhelm Reich became psychotic in his later life does not invalidate his enormous earlier contribution. By the same token, Rosen's legal problems should not prevent us from utilizing the very valuable lessons he has taught us.

First, I will tell you a little about Rosen's professional growth and his theory. Second, I will discuss my experiences when I worked for him. Third, I will speak about his critics and what happened subsequent to my leaving his employ. Finally, I will offer my opinion of his value to the field.

I worked with him in the middle 1950s. He was 53 at the time, with a full head of gray, wavy hair, and incredibly penetrating blue eyes. (Show picture) His voice had the sound of gravel and he often spoke with the gentleness of a construction worker. He was about 5'6, of stocky build. His attitude was one that would discourage trifling with or lying to him. Everything about him was tough. His personality fit the name of his method. It was direct.

It was a time when there were important theoreticians trying to unscramble the mysteries of psychosis, a word Rosen preferred to schizophrenia, though he didn't think there really was such a thing as a manic-depressive until years later. He said,

> We regard the neurotic and the psychotic as different only in degree or stage of illness; one is simply sicker than the other . . . The admittedly neurotic is constantly warding off the unconscious in one way or another, by phobias, compulsive rituals, or hypochondriasis. Although it costs the neurotic tremendous amounts of energy to keep his unconscious where it belongs, he

may succeed in doing so for a lifetime. But if pressure from within or without proves too great, the unconscious surges out, inundates the conscious and the neurotic defenses give way to psychosis. (1)

I agree with this view based on my perception of what I saw when I worked for him.

In the 1950s, of course, ECT had been used for years, and the anti-psychotic drugs were just coming in. Rosen boasted that he would not so much as give an aspirin to a patient. That's the extent to which he was opposed to drugs and, as far as I know, there was only one patient who was an exception just prior to his death. This view is all the more striking, since the patients I saw when I worked for him were far more seriously ill than those at Chestnut Lodge who were described to us. The patient I worked with, Alice, was a perfect example. For the first six weeks, she couldn't even succeed in forming an organized delusion, speaking in chopped up phrases. Returning to Rosen's background, in 1962, he wrote,

> As recently as twenty years ago, there was little application of Freudian psychology to the treatment of the insane. At that time, when I entered this

field, Freud's work seemed to be either unknown or unacceptable to those who were dealing with psychotics. Apart from papers by Bleuler, Nunberg, Brill, Knight, Rickman, Federn, Fromm-Reichmann, and a few others, there was almost no interest expressed in the psychoanalytic approach to the psychotic.

Rosen's strength did not lie in intellectual pursuits, as did that of the above-mentioned workers. There was little indication that one day it would be taken seriously by an ever-widening circle of psychiatrists. There was nothing to encourage a beginner in this work; on the contrary, there was much to discourage him. He wrote:

> My own experience reflects the gradual change in attitude. In 1928, I began my career in internal medicine and pathology. A few years later, because many of the individuals who came to me for treatment of supposedly physical ailments turned out to have nothing the matter with them physically, I became interested in psychosomatic medicine and in psychoanalysis. I undertook a personal analysis with Nunberg (which lasted from 1939 to 1951). I enrolled in some courses at the New York Psychoanalytic Institute. Impressed and heartened by what I was beginning to learn, I ventured into psychiatry on a part-time basis, working in the Neuropsychiatric Clinic, Mt. Sinai Hospital. There, I was engaged in prescribing bromides and sedatives for every variety of neurosis or psychosis that came my way. Officially, the psychoanalytic approach to these problems was not encouraged. I decided I might be able to learn more, and accomplish more therapeutically, by going elsewhere and taking a psychiatric residency.
>
> Accordingly, I went to Brooklyn State Hospital in October 1943, as a resident in psychiatry. Despite the great popularity of shock treatment, particularly at this hospital, I began to observe psychoanalytically what the patients were saying and doing as I visited the various wards. From one individual, who I would probably describe now as being in the acute catatonic excitement phase of psychosis, I gathered some material which I presented in a class at the Psychoanalytic Institute, instead of dream-material such as that which my classmates brought in from the neurotic patients.
>
> Perhaps one or two other staff-members were trying out the psychoanalytic approach; if so, their interest was not known to me. Nobody seemed to object to the claim that 'our hospital does more shock than any other institution in the East.' After observing and administering hundreds of shock-treatments, I ceased to be impressed by such a boast. When families visited while I was on duty, I somehow failed to get consents signed for shock.
>
> *(Rosen, 2)*

Rosen's theory, such as it was, was rooted in the idea that one could treat psychotics using primarily oral interpretations. However, he started his career using genital interpretations. Later, he said, "The most that this will do is set the stage for improvement by demonstrating that you talk the patient's language, the language of the primary process." (However, I found it most interesting that Rosen often found it difficult to get off the genital level. And Nunberg found it even more difficult to focus on something other than castration.)

Rosen continues, "But now and then I made interpretations of anal cruelty and explosions, or its opposite, anal gifts of babies and wealth, with somewhat more success" (Rosen, 3). But he felt he was most successful with oral interpretations.

> I began to understand that the wish for the warm impregnating sun that was Schreber's delusion would ultimately spring from the need to put this sun in place of the cold sun that made him insane. Every paranoid patient whose insides were rotted by bad food pointed the accusing finger at his destroyer again and again.
>
> *(Rosen, 4)*

Rosen considered his "governing principle" to be that the "psychiatrist must be a loving, omnipotent protector and provider for the psychotic. He must act like an idealized parent who now has the responsibility of bringing up this neo-infantile individual all over again" (Rosen, 5).

But he did not mean "psychiatrist" literally. He said,

> I prefer the use of increasing psychotherapeutic manpower by utilizing a large number of young assistant therapists . . . In my experience, the difference between professionals and amateurs working as psychotherapists is not necessarily the difference between skill and lack of skill. I have found the ability for psychotherapy in people who had little or no training, and I have found some indication of inability among psychiatrists, psychoanalysts, clinical psychologists and other professionals, even among those who had enjoyed the best and most extensive training.
>
> *(Rosen, 6)*

I am inclined to agree with him about that view, though I might not carry it quite as far as he does. Having spoken to many colleagues about my work with Rosen, since leaving him, I came to the conclusion that the ability to regress in the service of the ego without anxiety is probably the major characteristic that would enable someone to work the way Rosen did. When I work with schizophrenics, I describe myself as straddling, keeping one foot in the unconscious primary process and the other foot in reality. The major difference between myself and the patient is that I can come out of the primary process at will. The patient is in a dream from which he cannot awaken. The therapist's ability to go back and forth is what makes it possible for him or her not to feel anxiety.

When I came back from working for Rosen full of excitement at what I had learned, it took me a long time to gradually accept the idea that many psychoanalysts are frightened of unconscious material or at least they are frightened of getting too close to it. I think, in fact, people who are unsuited to do this kind of work, generally filter themselves out, because they are simply too uncomfortable with it. But I do not agree with Rosen that people untrained in psychoanalysis can do direct analysis in an optimal fashion. His own work might have been better, if he had had more training. Theoretical knowledge is important.

Freud's greatest contribution was his ability to understand and use the idea of the unconscious for purposes of treatment. By the same token, I think Rosen's greatest contribution was to use Freud's idea that "the dream is a psychosis, differing only in its early morning non-reversibility" (Rosen, 7). Rosen's idea is that, if one interprets sufficiently and correctly enough, the patient will "awaken." I have absolute conviction that this is so, and find that belief indispensable to my work. Recently, I have discovered several people who suffer from "burn-out" in working with psychotics (see Chapter 16, The Burnt-Out Therapist). I believe that is due at least partly to the fact that they don't have that conviction. That is, it is my job to find the correct interpretation of the material with which I am being presented and, when I do, the patient will "awaken."

The aspect of Rosen's work that has received the most publicity, because it is so dramatic, is what he called "the trick against the trick." He describes a patient who believed that he was wanted by the F.B.I. for burning down the shrine of Ste. Anne de Beaupre. Rosen and his aides pretended that one or another of them had burned it down. Then "F.B.I. agents" took out a "list of suspects" and asked everyone's name. But they of course, were not on the list. Since no one's name was on the list, the "F.B.I. agents" walked out muttering, "A bunch of cheap publicity hounds." The patient, though shocked by this turn of events, was nevertheless interested in an exciting way as he had never been interested before. I talked with him further and still pretended I was angry when I sent him back to the ward. Four days later, for the first time, the patient uneasily accepted the fact that he was in a mental institution, that his ideas were crazy. Over the next five weeks, the delusional system evaporated completely, and in its place was a timid, frightened man, facing reality and being considered for discharge on convalescent status. Rosen admits that "patients are never cured by the trick against the trick, although the use of this device helps to push them toward great insight" (Rosen, 8).

I am quite critical of this technique. First, I see no reason why this material cannot be interpreted like any other material, if the therapist will only listen to the patient's productions, history, and his knowledge of theory. Using such a trick is an admission of defeat on the part of the therapist.

Second, I am opposed to it because it removes the patient's reason to trust the therapist. To whatever extent the patient trusts the therapist is, in my view, a desirable condition for the remainder of the therapy.

In a brochure put out by Roche Laboratories in 1974, (20 years after I worked for Rosen), he again denies reality to a patient who is in mortal dread, "I am the one that you think is going to kill you, and far from wanting to kill you, I love you and will protect you." I call this a denial of reality of the transference. Further, Freud says in "Constructions in Analysis,"

> there is not only **method** in madness, as the poet has already perceived, but also a fragment of **historical truth**; and it is plausible to suppose that the compulsive belief attaching to delusions derives its strength precisely from infantile sources of this kind.
>
> *(Rosen, 9)*

I have found that idea absolutely invaluable. I would say, in fact, that Freud understated the situation. There is **always** truth in it, except for those very rare occasions where a delusion is pure wish. I can say this with a good deal of conviction because where I have ignored it, I have been "punished."

Additionally, of course, there is the problem of Rosen's authoritarianism. I object to this, not just as his own personality flaw, but because I think it discourages the patient's ego from growing. Practical rules and rules of nature become confused with arbitrary rules, and again the patient has difficulty separating actual reality from someone's else's opinion. This goes to the heart of the superego problem, in the sense that it reinforces the superego, from the very person who presumably is trying to moderate it.

And, further, confusion is created by Rosen telling the patient that he was his father, that he loved him, and would not punish him and would not permit anyone else to punish him (Rosen, 11). This is a manifest denial of the patient's experience. It may help the patient temporarily but in the end the whole treatment is, I believe, compromised by it.

Nunberg, Rosen's analyst, belonged to the Viennese circle. He had a short analysis with Federn and they subsequently became friends. It was Federn who named Rosen's treatment "Direct Psychoanalysis." Federn understood psychosis well enough to see that it was not the result of excessive narcissism but rather an "ego disease" (Federn, 12). Nunberg studied in Burgholzi, Vienna, and Berlin. When he was younger, he had an interest in psychosis but gave it up as he got older, apparently because he thought his age made it too difficult. He also describes working with a case of acute catatonic excitement, which was the same kind of case Rosen first published. He was very prone to making interpretations about castration anxiety, but finally seemed to understand that oral and anal interpretations were more relevant in psychosis (Nunberg, 13). My view is that we don't die without sex, but we cannot live without food or the ability to excrete.

An example of Rosen's lack of theoretical talent is in the Roche essay:

> In the psychosis we note that the patient suffers frustration and even murderous rage directed against himself or the environment. But mainly it is a

> matter of the superego killing the ego, or the ego killing the superego as it is locked in relentless combat for the possession of the psychotic.
>
> *(Rosen, 14)*

There is no such pathology as the ego killing the superego, and the statement reveals Rosen's lack of theoretical underpinning. There is some evidence that he was aware of the lack. I inferred that from some brochures I received by a Charles Sullivan published by Rosen's foundation (15).

Now I will discuss my apprenticeship. I took very good notes of what my patient said and did, and what I said to the patient, whom I call Alice. One of the really painful things in my life is that I loaned those notes to one of my supervisors and he lost them. Fortunately, I did retain a few notes that I wrote up for Rosen himself, of the last few weeks I was there, Unfortunately, those notes contain little of what I said, but they do very interestingly describe Alice in some detail, as she came out of the psychosis. For the rest, I must rely on my memory.

Let me tell you first how I came to work for Rosen. My Rorschach class, where I was working for my Master's at City College, was given a protocol of a hebephrenic. As I wrote in the introduction, we were exposed solely to the neo-Freudian.

My exposure to Rosen's patients caused me to change my mind drastically. As I have frequently said before, it was as if the patients had all read Freud before they became ill, so that they would know the "correct" way to be schizophrenic. They certainly did not sound as if they had read Sullivan.

The plan was that a Cuban psychiatrist who was on a fellowship was to be in charge of Alice. But unfortunately for him and fortunately for me, he got an ulcer a few days after Alice and I came to the community. (I will remind you that ulcers were more serious in those days) and shortly afterward I was put in charge of the case.

When Alice came to us, for about six weeks, as I had said previously, she wasn't organized enough to have a delusion. She just talked in seemingly unrelated phrases. I can't remember how we handled that or who did. I do remember that I learned to talk what I call "schizophrenese" (more properly called the language of primary process). I called it schizophrenese because it was literally like learning a foreign language. At first one translates into English in one's mind and, then speaks the foreign language. As one becomes more fluent, one doesn't have to translate in one's mind anymore. I can't do it as fluently now as I did then, because the patients I have had since aren't as ill as Alice was and I am out of practice.

Alice's major delusion was a denial of the whole birth process. Rosen told us her psychosis began about four years after the birth of her child. It became overt when she tried to kill her husband. However much time had elapsed after the birth of the child, whom I will call Susie. Alice suffered from what was, in fact, a post-partum psychosis. Almost all the material she expressed had to do with conception, pregnancy, and delivery.

What became clear to me, within a few weeks of work, was that the material was not oral, as I had been led to expect by Rosen. It was anal. This is where I began to learn that while Rosen was marvelously intuitive, he was not a good theoretician. Later, I discovered that when his intuition deserted him, he became frustrated. He made stupid mistakes, which I believe is why his career and his reputation deteriorated. Lacking Rosen's intuition, I made up for it with my theoretical skill, the substance of which, for Alice, was: "You were so happy when you were pregnant, and your belly felt full. And when you had intercourse with your husband, he was feeding you 'milk' so your belly grew and grew. It didn't feel empty as it did when you were a child. Then you had to deliver, and you were unconscious when the baby was delivered. It was as if she were taken from you behind your back" (anesthetic).

"You felt the obstetrician stole the baby from you. You had suddenly lost that nice full belly which used to feel so empty, and worse yet, Susie always wanted to take more and more from you, like babies do. You were so drained it was unbearable. You had to deny the whole thing."

I cannot remember for sure, but I think it was while I worked for Rosen that I learned that oral and anal did not have to do with which organ might be involved, but rather in what *direction* the energy was going. That is, if the material is related to things going into the body, it is oral, and if it is related to things going out of the body, it should be considered anal. It is easy to make the error of offering Oedipal interpretations, as both Nunberg and Rosen did. Psychotic patients speak of sexual material much more easily than neurotics, but that is because for them sex is a symbol for pre-Oedipal material (sic). In terms of that view, in the usual sex act, the man is giving and the woman is receiving. I don't think it damages the patient if Oedipal interpretations are made. They are simply useless, and the therapist may be frustrated if she wastes her time with them.

Needless to say, this kind of work requires great patience, especially if one is new to it. You can well imagine how much thinking and repetition of the same interpretation I made since I worked four hours a day on one patient. My good fortune was that she was an English major, so that I got very precise answers to my questions. I cannot imagine having a better teacher than Alice.

Rosen used to come to visit us about three times a week. (He had a farm nearby.) I do dimly remember that he was surprised but interested in the fact that I was making anal rather than oral interpretations. And I do distinctly remember asking him once what I should do about a specific problem, and his saying "This idea is yours. You figure it out." I was most gratified that he had that much confidence in me. Looking back, I must consider the possibility that my whole approach was novel to him, and he might have been covering his ignorance. In material published later, he does mention that he also used anal interpretations, although he didn't use them initially.

I want to interpolate here that he was a very old-fashioned man in terms of gender. My job was to do therapy (if I wanted to) and housework. I spent about four hours a day doing each. The men in the community did "masculine" things. Of course, all this occurred before women's lib came along, and I didn't mind. But I think even for the time, it was a little archaic. Socially, it was difficult for me, because there was only one other single person in the community. I didn't drive. Looking back now, I wonder why I didn't get myself a bicycle in the spring. I should make it clear that we were on duty 24 hours a day, seven days a week. In six months, I got four days off. If it were not for the fact that the work was so fascinating, I might have been quite unhappy. However, I certainly never had a more valuable learning experience. What can replace a totally controlled experiment?! I know of no other situation in the field of mental health where such a thing could happen. The result of constantly being on duty was that I knew immediately which interpretations were right, and which were useless. I cannot think of any situation that brings more conviction than that.

I will give you two examples. Once, about three or four months into treatment, Alice's mother came to visit. We had our hands full the following week. I can't remember the specifics, but the degree of regression caused my heart to sink, since I feared Alice would not get back to where she had been. The second example is the problem of her insistence that she had been forced into prostitution. For three weeks, I made interpretations of everything I could think of. Nothing worked.

Finally, I asked her what a prostitute was. (Here we have the equivalent in psychosis of free association.) She told me, "It is when you sell your body and soul for food." "Oh," I said, "You had to give up your body and especially your soul, so your mother would take care of you." That was the end of her discussion about prostitution.

But that same incident is a good example of Rosen's inadequate attention to specifics. It is certainly clear to me now and has been for many years, that psychotics associate idiosyncratically, just like neurotics do. We all have different life experiences. Each boy has had somewhat different experience playing baseball or not playing baseball, as the case may be. The therapist cannot assume anything. Alice's prostitute problem is also, of course, a good example of how genital material can be only apparently genital.

Finally, the delusion that the state was what made her pregnant and various other birth theories lost conviction. She became foggy on and off. I have found this state in every patient of mine who has come close to being out of their psychosis. Rosen has interpreted that as a vision of the breast. But it seems to me more the same kind of unclear vision one might have just after waking up from a deep sleep.

She said the following with real affect: The content was that people were laughing at her insanity, and that she was so fat that she had lost her sex appeal. While saying it, she was close to tears. Even the dopiness (fog) didn't have the depth that it had had. She seems to be able to speak through it. This was the first appropriate affect she expressed and as you see the first real sexual concern.

I felt under the weather the next day and refused to take a walk with her. This precipitated a physical battle that ended only by my telling her I wasn't her mother. Interestingly, the battle was preceded by a barrage of abuse, which she would express only in Yiddish.

The next day I wrote, "Back to her usual self today. Some delusional material was expressed but without conviction. (The lack of conviction is most important in that it implies that patient no longer really believes it, but is probably only saying it by rote.)

The following day, she said she dreamt of gold bamboo, an outhouse, and her sister-in-law putting on lipstick and in a mink coat. The first two subjects were seen the day before in reality. (This dream is cause for celebration indeed. Rosen had said that psychotics don't dream because they are already dreaming. Or they may dream only of food.) In this dream, we see the day residue, and a dream like a neurotic might have. She said she woke feeling as if she had a yoke (read: millstone) around her neck. Part of the delusional material was that the birth had something to do with "being put through the mill." This is the neurotic version of that concept.

(It is most important that you recognize the significance of "as if." If one puts the phrase "as if" preceding most delusions, one would think the person was sane. This statement is also most significant since, during the psychosis, she often told us that she had been "put through the mill," which she later associated to the afterbirth. During my stay, this was never adequately interpreted.)

The next day she was clearer than the previous day and was embarrassed remembering her nudity on the first day she came. (She must have stripped on the first day, which I had forgotten.) Further notes describe her going back and forth between psychosis and sanity.

Finally, I remember her coming out of it altogether, and, on questioning, she was able to tell us just how women get pregnant and where babies come from.

What was important to me as far as my feeling of conviction of the method was that Alice had a very easily testable delusion and it was resolved. Further, in support of Rosen's theory that the psychosis is a dream, she had said quite spontaneously, "I feel like Rip Van Winkle. Tell me what has been going on in the world during the last five years." What I remember having to describe sadly were the McCarthy hearings.

Now the critics. Fortunately, in Rosen's third book, *Direct Psychoanalysis II* (11), there is a complete bibliography of literature about his work up to that time, entitled Appendix B. It may be difficult to believe now, but I gather from the literature that there was a great deal of excitement in psychiatric circles about Rosen's work in the 1950s and 1960s. Apparently, at the time I worked for him, the excitement was beginning. I would guess that the grants from the Rockefeller brothers and Doris Duke's Fund, apparently given in the late '60s helped spread the news. The grant was given apparently for the establishment of the Institute for Direct Analysis at Temple University Medical Center, which developed a research program.

I will begin with the earliest written criticism. In 1950, Rosen gave a speech at the New York Psychoanalytic Society, entitled "The Optimum Conditions for

Treatment of Psychosis unrelated to Diagnosis" (Archives, 17.) I am grateful to Dr. Jacob Arlow for having informed me of its existence, and Dr. Nellie Thompson for having dug it and a few other references out of their archives. There were several discussants, the most well known of whom was Phyllis Greenacre.

Rosen said, "The optimum conditions are that the patients be treated early in their illness, while they are still verbalizing and before other (organic) treatments are used." (I should insert here that Rosen was able to cure some patients who had had minimal ECT but the other patient in my house was apparently incurable due to the fact that she had had too much ECT, resulting in brain damage. For more on this subject, I refer you to the novel *Savage Sleep* about Rosen, by Millen Brand, which appears to me to be very little fiction and very much fact) (Brand, 18).

Under these conditions, Rosen says, the psychosis

> can be resolved in a matter of weeks-months at most. But classical analysis on completion gives immunity ... 27 cases were treated with direct analysis. Classical analysis followed in 22 cases. Of those 27, 3 were treated by someone other than me, so it does not depend on personal magic. These cases were not treated under optimal conditions. Some were regressed toward the end of the scale of verbalization. Two were given ECT. One case got insulin. An average of eleven shock treatments were given to those who received it within a few weeks' time
>
> *(Archives, 19)*

Rosen then presented a case of a patient who was eating her stool and chewing on urine-soaked sheets. Time does not permit me to present all of it, but one example is of an interchange with Rosen saying, "Don't worry. I won't let you starve." The patient, Mary, says: "Somebody did, anyway. Some cat. Well, I don't care. I stand by my religion." (I think the verbalizations can be relied on, since Rosen frequently had stenographers present while he worked.) The treatment took four weeks before the patient's release from the hospital. On this case, Rosen worked two hours every day.

Greenacre's response was to relate her experience at Johns Hopkins when she was a resident. She said that 85% of the cures by surgery of infected areas were successful, but after a few months all had to return to the hospital. I would characterize her response to Rosen as an attempt to be polite, but extremely skeptical, as was the general response, confirmed to me a few days ago by someone who knew Rosen socially.

Bertram Lewin felt confused, but years later became a supporter of Rosen's. Kubie was also skeptical, but applauded Rosen's getting into the patient's dream. De Saussures had seen Rosen's work and thought the most important thing Rosen did was symbolically gratify the patient. There were several other discussants, most of whom seemed most skeptical. My guess is that they were startled and, to the extent they believed what Rosen had done, they were envious. I cannot stress enough what an unheard of approach direct analysis was at the time. Perhaps only Schehehaye and Gertrude Schwing had even remotely similar approaches during this period. I gather that the view of those two women was that they were anomalies, and they were not taken seriously.

Another critic of that time, Bychowski, himself a specialist in schizophrenia, says, "The author avoids discussion of the theoretical implications assuming that the direct interpretation is his most potent therapeutic tool. To be sure, he must be given credit for a great deal of imagination and ingenious resourcefulness." But Bychowski worries this approach may make some patients worse, like mutism or stupor. (I must interject here that, in my experience, that concern is unfounded.) Bychowski also did not accept Rosen's view of the cause for psychotic regression, but concedes that "Rosen deserves recognition for his keen perception of the unconscious and his enthusiastic dedication to understanding and helping the psychotic" (20).

Flescher says that, "Rosen's therapeutic successes, it seems to me, are based on his tolerance for the negative transference reactions of his patients and on his ability to prevent their being frightened by his own reactive fears" (21). I am not sure about the last part of that statement, but in reference to the negative transference, let me relate the following incident: Alice was a very hostile patient and let me know in no uncertain terms what a poor opinion she had of me most of the time. My tolerance for her hostility will be discussed when I speak of Searles.

Leo Stone wrote a very thoughtful piece on Schwing and Rosen. He notes that consideration of the psychoanalysis of psychoses began with Abraham's papers of 1908 and 1911. It was Abraham who discovered that psychotics could make a transference (22). Stone describes Rosen as "naive, at times grandiloquent, at times humble, occasionally pathetic and moving, rarely even heroic. Shrewdness, humor, unvarnished roughness, rationalization, crude power, courage and many less obvious ingredients are co-mingled in this unusual book (*Direct Analysis*) (23). To which I say "Exactly."

Stone continues,

> The intentional assumption of a position within the psychoses was Rosen's first striking maneuver. By giving substantial and independent life to the creatures of the patient's narcissistic world, he provided what may well have been an indispensable bridge of transition to an object relationship in certain desperately ill patients.
>
> (Ibid., 24)

I consider this view to show the value of being able to understand and speak in language of concretization.

Stone would have preferred that Rosen had not assumed roles and patients given greater reality sense. He also complains that interpretations often have little immediate base in the material, and adds that Rosenfeld and Klein do pay more attention to the material. Here I think is an excellent example of Rosen's therapeutic error. I think Freud and Rosen are both almost always in error when they interpret *universal* meanings. Psychotics, like everyone else, have had unique lives, and one must therefore assume that their associations are unique, for example Alice's association to prostitution.

Stone puts his finger right on one of Rosen's unique contributions, when he points out that Fromm Reichmann advocates "an effort to keep in contact with the more adult remnants . . . avoiding the extreme indulging . . . which would establish him as an infant" (Ibid., 25).

Now let us look at perceptions in the late 1950s and 1960s after I had left Rosen's employ. One book that came out of that research was *Observations of Direct Analysis* by Morris Brody with forwards by Rosen and O. Spurgeon English (26). At the time, English was director of psychiatry at Temple Medical School. This research went on for approximately two years. From my reading, I believe that Brody, as well as others, tried very hard to be objective and, I believe, was successful.

Brody, other than describing the method as previously discussed, makes some interesting points. First, he reminds us of a fact that happens to be dear to my heart. "In what follows the words still do not enable the reader to hear the words as spoken" (27). I find this an important failing in all psychoanalytic literature. Both analyst and patient express so many varied emotions into their verbalizations that are not discussed in the literature and probably could not be adequately conveyed in any case. How ironic that this should be so, in a profession where the emotions are our primary interest! Yet, Brody is the first writer I have come across to mention this deficiency.

Secondly, Brody points out what I spoke of earlier and what many other critics did: namely the weak theoretical underpinnings. Brody says,

> The psychoanalyst would not consider Rosen's interventions as interpretations. They do not connect the patient's actual behavior to his infantile experiences. The psychoanalyst could call these interventions 'confrontations' and would doubt seriously that such confrontations could in any way educate the unconscious.

(As Rosen admits about the trick against the trick.) Rosen derives these confrontations from his own unconscious and frequently gives the patient little or no opportunity to verbalize. "It is not possible to say how accurately the confrontations correspond to the unconscious forbidden wishes of the patient" (Rosen, 28).

I must interpose here a speculation of mine regarding this research. There are many verbatim notes of Rosen's work with patients in this book. One thing is very clear to me when I read descriptions of this work. He was in a tremendous hurry to get the patient out of the psychosis. There was no such rush when I was there. He was getting patients out in weeks and even days. I assume this was to impress either the field or the grantors. Compared to what I saw, he did himself a great disservice by doing that. This work consisted much more of "the trick against the trick." Oral interpretations were just thrown at patients, willy nilly. There were no anal interpretations, and far too many Oedipal interpretations. (My private view is that Oedipal interpretations have no place in work with psychotics. As I stated earlier, even obviously sexual material should be interpreted either orally or anally. There is very little cathexis attached to sexual material in the psychotic. One may even view sexual material as a defense in psychotics. I think Rosen made the error here of confusing his patients with himself. Further, pre-Oedipal interpretations were not so popular in the days of his analysis, and apparently not with Nunberg.)

Brody also points out that the patient's "history was not important to Rosen. His approach is determined by his intuitive understanding of the problems with which the patient is confronted—an intuitive understanding which is more or less influenced by the patient's verbal productions and behaviour" (Direct Psychoanalysis II, 29). He also supports the observation that the patient is "fuzzy" when he comes out of the psychosis. It is like moments of sleep just before you awaken" (Ibid., 30.) Precisely that condition is what I described to you about Alice when she said she felt like Rip Van Winkle, though I think the word "groggy" might be more on target.

Albert Scheflen was also supported by the Rockefellers' grant to observe Rosen's work for three years. His book, *A Psychotherapy of Schizophrenia: Direct Analysis*, had a very positive preface by Lawrence Kubie, who applauds Rosen's courage in general, and specifically his courage in testing the patient's rejection of his delusion, by commanding him to go back to it. Scheflen, however, who is adamant in affirming his "objectivity," has an attitude of contempt and skepticism. I couldn't help wondering if he was not being more overtly so because he may have promised the grantor that he would be objective.

Speaking of objectivity, I now have to advise you that you may well question mine, when I speak of two more critics, Searles and Spotnitz. But I will do my best, while confessing to you that I have long been disapproving of both these gentlemen. Searles begins his review of Rosen's third book by admitting that "something alive is happening in this despair encrusted field" (Ibid., 31), but then says

> my negative reactions are so fundamental and so numerous that I scarcely know where to begin . . . Rosen's theoretical formulations—and I must assume, his treatment approach which is based on these—are greatly warped and weakened by his failure to see that hatred (referred to previously) has an essential role in healthy personality formation.
>
> *(Searles, 32)*

I saw no such hatred. Anger yes, hatred no. Nor, I hasten to add, did Jules Eisenbud, who says,

> There's one thing which impressed me about the work of Dr. Rosen during the time I have been privileged to observe it, and that is the fact that . . .

Dr. Rosen has absolutely no hostility toward the patient. This I think is a very important factor.

(Ibid., 33)

I leave it to you to arrive at your own inferences as to Searles' view of the necessity of therapists hating their psychotic patients.

Spotnitz and his group are well known in that period for their work with psychotics. In his 1961 review of Scheflen's book, he says that Rosen makes

> speedy contact to return the patient to the community as soon as possible. These goals are short-sighted in view of the psychological scarring which results in forcible suppression of an acute psychosis . . . He appears to be oblivious to the ego's role both in releasing aggression and in defending itself against the release of aggression.

He "does not investigate the possibility that the misbehavior may be just a symptom and that aggression may be the nuclear problem" (Eisenbud, 34).

In essence, my quarrel with both these gentlemen is that they seem to have no interest in what inspires the hostility in the patient (or the therapist), but only to want to focus on the hostility itself. I can see no potential for resolution in that approach. Further, from what I know about the work of both of them, they have in general, an approach which at best attempts to build up the healthy aspects of the patient's personality, rather than trying to lance the "rot." If one avoids the resolution of the major problem, that problem it seems to me, will inevitably undermine any other work one does.

There are many other thoughtful views published, notably those of O. Spurgeon English, Katherine McKinnon, George Devereux, and others, but space does not permit me to explore them.

1977 was the beginning of Rosen's apparent downfall, when a complaint was filed with the Pennsylvania Medical Board. On April 1983, nearly a dozen former patients alleged that Rosen, then 79 years old and living at least half the year in Boca Raton, Florida, subjected them to sexual abuse, physical beatings, improper restraint, and unsanitary conditions. Rosen admitted he left one psychiatric patient without proper continuing treatment and another in the care of therapists who were not properly supervised. As a result, Rosen's Pennsylvania license, but not his New York or Florida licenses, was revoked.

However, Dr. Daniel Bender told me that at the time of these proceedings, Rosen was in the hospital being treated for prostate cancer and had not given his permission for the agreement. When Rosen was discharged from the hospital, he went to the state capital and made an attempt to change the ruling. However, the legislator to whom he spoke pointed out that due to his age (80), the difficulties would hardly be worthwhile. Jeffrey Masson has written about Rosen's legal problems in more detail in his book, "Against Therapy," (35) but the chapter has serious internal inconsistencies, as well as the fact that Masson has general credibility problems.

Rosen died in March 1993, of cardiac problems, a week after his physician told him that continued work would endanger his health. The Institute for Direct Analysis continues under the co-chairmanship of Dr. Daniel Bender and Per Ostman. Looking at Rosen's work from the present perspective, one can ask, what is left of his legacy? I must turn to Europe for the answer to that question. The International Symposium for the Psychotherapy of Schizophrenia is thriving, at least in Europe. In general, much less medication is used in Europe, not to speak of less ECT. When I lectured in Sweden, I asked about whether they gave shock. The response I got was the same facial expression Alice gave the assistant therapist, when he pretended to have her delusion, i.e., trying to be polite, but clearly doubting my, or my country's, sanity.

There are some authors who have made contributions in the United States, though they find more appreciation in Europe. Among them are Bertram Karon (who studied with Rosen and has trained people), Giovacchini, Boyer, Robbins, and the Lidzs. I think it is possible that, in the coming century, this kind of work will find its way back.

My very unscientific sampling of lay people's attitudes suggests that they are becoming more skeptical of psychiatric drugs. Indeed, the whole medical profession is being influenced by the holistic movement. This "secret" of what is going on in Europe may finally be declassified here. More publicity may be given to the side effects of anti-psychotic drugs. More specifically, I think Rosen deserves great credit for his courage and his persistence, as he worked almost alone. Those are characteristics he shared with Freud and may well be applauded for. Masson tried to destroy them both. But perhaps, naively, I believe that great ideas cannot be buried forever.

There were numerous studies as to whether Rosen's cures were permanent. They varied so much, there is no point in going into them, especially as they were bound to change as Rosen learned more about the process. Certainly, analysis was necessary after the patient recovered.

I witnessed one dramatic example. Two women were pregnant while I was in Pennsylvania. One was the wife of one of the assistant therapists, a normal neurotic. The other was a recovered patient of Rosen's, who worked as an assistant therapist herself. The former had a difficult pregnancy, delivery, and a very cranky baby. The recovered patient worked until the day before she delivered, had an easy delivery, and a happy healthy baby.

Finally, I can say that working for Rosen was the most impressive educational experience I ever had. Not only did it guide my work with psychotics, but it made my work with neurotics much easier, since I had learned so much about the unconscious. To answer to the title question, I think Rosen was neither genius nor quack. But he was an extraordinarily talented, dedicated, and compassionate man.

References

1. Rosen, John. (1953). *Direct Analysis*, Grune & Stratton, New York, p. 6.
2. Rosen, John. (1962). *Direct Psychoanalytic Psychiatry*, Grune & Stratton, New York, pp. ix–x.
3. Rosen, John. (1953). *Direct Analysis*, Grune & Stratton, New York, p. 7.
4. Ibid.
5. Rosen, John. (1962). *Direct Psychoanalytic Psychiatry*, Grune & Stratton, New York, p. 60.
6. Ibid.
7. Rosen, John. (1953). *Direct Analysis*, Grune & Stratton, New York, pp. 98–99.
8. Ibid., pp. 146–148.
9. Rosen, John. (1974). Direct psychoanalysis: Theory and practice. In *Major Contributors to Modern Psychotherapy*, Roche Laboratories, Nutley, NJ, p. 18.
10. Freud, Sigmund. (1937). Constructions in analysis. In *The Standard Edition of the Complete Psychological Works of Sigmund Freud*, Vol. XXIII, Hogarth Press, London, p. 267.
11. Rosen, John. (1953). *Direct Analysis*, Grune & Stratton, New York, p. 32.
12. Federn, Paul. (1966). *Psychoanalytic Pioneers*, Basic Books, New York, p. 155.
13. Nunberg, Herman. (1961). *Practice and Theory of Psychoanalysis*, Vol. 1, International Universities Press, Madison, CT, p. 16.
14. Rosen, John. Direct psychoanalysis: Theory and practice. In *Major Contributors to Modern Psychotherapy*, Roche Laboratories, Nutley, NJ, p. 10.
15. Sullivan, Charles. (1964). Recent developments in "Direct Analysis." *Psychoanalytic Review*, 51(3).
16. Rosen, John. (1962). Bibliography. In *Direct Psychoanalytic Psychiatry*, Grune & Stratton, New York.
17. Rosen, John. *The optimum conditions for treatment of psychosis unrelated to diagnosis*. Archives of the New York Psychoanalytic Society.
18. Brand, Millen. (1968). *Savage Sleep*, Crown Publishers, New York.
19. Rosen, John. *The optimum conditions for treatment of psychosis unrelated to diagnosis*. Archives of the New York Psychoanalytic Society, p. 11.
20. Bychowski, G. (1954). Review of Rosen, J. N., "Direct Analysis." *Psychoanalytic Quarterly*, 23: 115.
21. Flescher, J. (1953). The 'primary constellation' in the structure and treatment of psychoses. *Psychoanalytic Review*, 40: 209.
22. Abraham, Karl. (1948/1908/1911). The psycho-sexual differences between hysteria and dementia praecox, and Notes on the psychoanalytic investigation and treatment of manic depressive insanity and allied conditions. In *Selected Papers of Karl Abraham*, Hogarth Press, London.
23. Stone, Leo. (1955). Two avenues of approach to the schizophrenic patient. *JAPA*, 3: 128.
24. Ibid., p. 135.
25. Ibid., p. 143.
26. Brody, M. (1959). *Observations on "Direct Analysis,"* Vantage Press, New York.
27. Ibid., p. 18.
28. Ibid., p. 20.
29. Ibid., p. 22.
30. Ibid., p. 34.
31. Searles, Harold. (1955). Book review, "Direct Psychoanalytic Psychiatry." *I. J. P.-A.*, 45: 597.

32. Ibid., p. 600.
33. Eisenbud, Jule. (1953). *Direct Analysis*, Grune & Stratton, New York, p. 84.
34. Spotnitz, Hyman. (1962). Book review: "A Psychotherapy of Schizophrenia." In A. E. Scheflen, *International Journal of Group Psychotherapy*, 12: 268.
35. Masson, Jeffrey. (1984). *Against Therapy*, Cameron Cage Press, Monroe, ME.

9

FIVE ERRORS IN FREUD'S STRUCTURAL THEORY AND THEIR CONSEQUENCES

I think it is incumbent on me to explain why I wrote this chapter at all. For many years, as I read Freud, I found myself saying every once in a while, "No, Siggy" (after reading him for so long, and having him be so much a part of my life I did not feel it was inappropriate to address him in a familiar way.) "I think you made a mistake there." Since I felt so close to him, I felt as if he should hear my thoughts and take them into consideration, but alas, the words in the book did not change. I complained "You ignored me" as if he were still alive and could hear me. But the fantasy was broken. I had to go my own way on some issues.

What never occurred to me until very recently was that all the errors I thought he made were structural. Further, they were all coincidentally obstacles to my technique. Or perhaps the technique was an outgrowth of my disagreements with him. Therefore, it seemed useful to bring all the disagreements together in one paper. Perhaps, I thought, that effort would make my new technique more comprehensible to someone unfamiliar with it.

I can well imagine that the reader, seeing the title of this chapter, might say, "Well if he made so many structural errors in the theory, one might as well throw the whole theory out." My response is, "No, that would be an error in itself, because there is too much of value in the original." I refer the reader back to my dedication, in which I say that I am a firm adherent of the belief in not throwing out the wheat with the chaff. Before Freud existed, who was there to even think of seeing that there were three distinct parts of the mind, let alone discovering the unconscious?

Nor should we be harsh with him for having made important errors. As I like to say, partly jokingly and partly seriously, he labored under two important handicaps. One was that he could be only one gender. That necessitated at least some lack of understanding of what it feels like to be a woman. I don't think having any number of women patients can quite compensate for that. (I will not go to into a discussion of the penis envy problem, because it would lead me too far afield.)

Secondly, there was no Freud to analyze him. How could he completely analyze his transference? How could he really completely observe his own resistances, since he was only one person and human?

Most importantly, we need to preserve the following concept: "The tension between the demands of the conscience (superego) and the actual performances of the ego is experienced as *guilt*" (p. 37, XIX, P) [1] (italics mine). It is my contention that the structural reason for schizophrenia is primarily the pathologically greater strength of the superego compared to the pathological weakness of the ego. If one accepts that premise, the rest of my approach to the treatment of schizophrenia follows.

Error #1: The Derivation of the Superego

Freud says, "The superego arises . . . from an identification with the father taken as a model" (XIX, 54) [2]. Actually, there are two errors in that statement. The first and less important is a cultural one. With the increasing freedom of women compared to the situation that obtained at the end of the nineteenth and beginning of the twentieth centuries, the superego may be derived from the mother, or even an older sibling. I gradually learned in my many years of practice that one could no longer take for granted the idea that the superego derived from the father, as expected in a patriarchal society. There are innumerable families at the present time in which the "boss" of the family is the mother, especially when the father is a passive man or the mother may make a substantial monetary contribution to the family. The derivation of the superego depends on who makes the rules and which parent is more threatening.

This brings us to the second error in that statement, which is far more troublesome. The superego, in fact, contains only the hostile attitudes of that figure. The knowledge of how to go to school, or tie one's shoes, goes into the ego, not the superego, unless it is accompanied by threats. It is pure objective knowledge. It is without a moral flavor. All of what is contained in the superego has the potentiality of giving its owner guilt, i.e., not doing one's homework, not doing the dishes as expected, or harboring hostile thoughts toward the superego parent. The latter would violate the edict "One should respect one's parents." I have found that, with children from Jewish Orthodox families, that rule takes precedence, without exception, over truth-telling.

Unless one makes the distinction between the parent's hostility toward the child and his or her other attitudes toward the child, one does not isolate the guilt. If that distinction is not made, then weakening the superego and strengthening the ego is very difficult, indeed, I believe impossible. One must remember that the development of the superego begins when the child is very small, even, according to Klein, in infancy (Klein, *The Psycho-analysis of Children*, p. 179) [3]. Freud suggests that it is later, that it doesn't begin until five or six.

Indeed, Klein's opinion may be derived from the fact that her little patients became ill unusually early. I would suggest that the difference between Klein's and Freud's opinion as to the age of the formation of the superego is due to the fact that her patients were much sicker than his. Her little patients developed superegos so early that their egos had barely begun to form. The superego, always an enemy to the ego, acted as an obstacle to the growth of the ego. Because the ego was so weak at that age, the superego had a much greater advantage in its destructive ability than an adult's superego. Thus, the children couldn't wait until they were five to become overtly ill. Consequently, I suggest that Freud and Klein were both right in their observations of their particular patients.

To return to the source of the superego, the rules by which the superego controls do not depend on the culture, either international or domestic, but only by the rules and ensuing hostility corning from the ruling parent. It is that necessary ingredient that is one of the factors that makes it possible for me to talk to the superego. Both my patient and I experience those conversations as if I were talking to a person.

Error #2: The Superego Is Dumb

This may be Freud's most important error, in that it so efficiently prevents him from battling the superego. In discussing the "muteness" of the superego, he appears to be resigned to defeat.

> In the end we come to see that we are dealing with what may be called a 'moral' factor, a sense of guilt, which is finding its satisfaction in the illness and refuses to give up the punishment of suffering. We shall be right in regarding this disheartening (italics mine) explanation as final. But as far as the patient is concerned this sense of guilt is dumb: it does not tell him he is guilty; he does not feel guilty; he feels ill. This sense of guilt expresses itself only as a resistance to recovery, which it is extremely difficult to overcome. It is also particularly difficult to convince the patient that this motive lies behind this continuing to be ill; he holds fast to the more obvious explanation that treatment by analysis is not the right remedy for his case.
>
> *(XIX, [4])*

The footnote on the same page underscores Freud's lack of hope: "The battle with the obstacle of an unconscious sense of guilt is not made easy for the analyst. *Nothing can be done against it directly*" (italics mine), "and nothing indirectly but the slow procedure of unmasking its unconscious repressed roots, and of thus changing it to a conscious sense of guilt" (XIX, [5]).

I have never been able to understand why Freud did not understand this problem with the superego (which he earlier calls a "negative therapeutic reaction") (XIX, [6]) as a part of the patient's illness. It's as if one considered the pneumococcal bacteria as only an obstacle to recovery from pneumonia, and not the primary cause itself.

The beginning of my use of the technique of talking to the superego was inspired by a very overtly non-schizophrenic anxious patient, who complained more than once of a "gray voice: (not a hallucination). I found that the messages it gave her made me quite angry with it, no doubt exacerbated by the patient's suffering and very small size. (I think now that her small size may have represented to me unconsciously the small size of her ego. I presume that my anger at it was in response to what I felt was bullying by the superego of this petite young woman.) I dealt with *my* sense of helplessness by expressing *my* anger directly at it. Unfortunately, I can't remember the specifics of sessions 40 years ago, little realizing at the time how significant it would turn out to be.

However, I do have some random notes that come from experiences a few years after this patient. I began asking the conscience (superego) what it had to say about a particular subject and what the brain (ego) had to say about that subject. Then, it became apparent to me that a third party had to be introduced: me. I saw that attitudes toward me became a factor in these conversations. I soon learned that, when I really damaged or frightened the superego, it could tell me that it hated me. I realized that was cause for celebration, because it meant I had hurt it, and therefore weakened it. The result was that the ego became stronger, very often in surprising ways. One very shy patient, to my amazement, suddenly became extremely social.

At this point I feel it necessary to digress. All too often, I hear stories that patients of other analysts tell me of how frightened, rejecting or resisting in other ways, their analysts were, about the patient's hostility toward them. I confess that when I hear these stories, I want to exclaim, "Haven't they ever heard of a negative transference? The interpretation of that can be the most productive part of the analysis." Someone should be saying, "If an analyst can't take the hostility of the patient, how can he or she be an analyst? If a physician can't stand the sight of blood, is he fit to be in clinical work?"

I will now return to conversations with the superego, or lack thereof. One patient wouldn't respond to his superego when it spoke to him. He tried to ignore it. I could say to such a patient, "If someone is pointing a gun at you, will ignoring it protect you?" Unfortunately, therapists who do supportive work with schizophrenics often recommend that patients ignore the voices they hear, and messages from the superego. Quite the contrary, I believe that ignoring the superego gives it an opportunity to do more mischief behind the patient's back. As the saying goes, "Sunlight is the best disinfectant." This view became so obvious to me that I made it a firm rule to say to all my patients: "Never ignore your conscience. That's dangerous. It would be too easy for it to make trouble for you. Pay attention to what your conscience says, but listening, doesn't mean you have to *obey* it. Listen, so you can get a clue as to how it will try to hurt you in the future." Ignoring the conscience makes a fertile field for paranoia.

Another ploy is for the superego to respond as if it were the ego. Examining it will expose the deceit. Freud himself fell victim to that ploy. He says, "When one speaks hopefully to them (patients) or expresses satisfaction with the progress of the treatment, they show signs of discontent and their condition invariably becomes worse" [6] (XIX, 49). Freud did not recognize that that was the superego speaking, not the ego (see also my chapter "Identification with the Superego") [7]. The analyst has to be on the alert not to be taken in. All condemnatory, hostile criticism, ridiculing, etc. remarks come only from the superego, not the ego. Both patient and analyst must learn to pay diligent attention.

Clearly, being able to speak to the superego diminishes confusion for both patient and analyst. We don't need to be curbed by the "slow . . . unmasking (of the) unconscious repressed roots" that Freud speaks of (XIX, [7]). Indeed, the important concept that this technique has illuminated is that, though much of the superego may be unconscious, it is surprisingly easy to make it conscious. One must remember that the *patient* is listening as I speak to his superego. The result is that much less patience on the part of both patient and analyst is required, resulting in less discouraging, speedier work.

Error #3: We Have That Higher Nature, the Superego

Freud was disturbed by the reaction of those about him, who complained that he discussed only the lower side of man. But then he says,

> So long as we had to concern ourselves with the study of what is repressed in mental life, there was no need for us to share in any agitated apprehensions as to the whereabouts of the higher side of man. But now that we have embarked upon the analysis of the ego, we can give an answer to all those whose moral sense has been shocked and who have complained that there must surely be a higher nature in man: 'Very true' we can say, 'and here we have that higher nature, in this . . . [the] superego, the representative of our relation to our parents. When we were little children we knew these higher natures, we admired them and feared them; and later took them into ourselves.'
>
> *(XIX, 36)*

But the guileless Freud fell right into the trap. My hundreds of conversations with superegos have shown me that the reverse is true. Far from being a "higher nature," the superego is, if anything, the lower side of nature. It tells the truth, only when it can no longer escape a persistent ego. It tricks the patient (and very often the analyst to some extent as well), manipulates, leads the patient into traps, etc. It purports to have the patient's interest at heart, but acts only in its own interest, i.e., makes certain, to the extent that it can, that its strength is not diminished, keeping the ego as weak as possible, and continues its blackmailing of the patient with promises of "I will never leave you." It always tells or implies to the patient, "I know the honorable thing to do. Just listen and obey me. I will steer you correctly." It purports to be the voice of morality, as stated earlier, but can be depended on to lead the patient to his destruction, as much as it can get away with.

Part of the reason it took me so long to be certain of its deviousness was that I found it difficult to believe that there were no exceptions to this rule. I kept thinking, "Surely, this can't always be true and true for every patient." But, indeed, I found it always to be true. There were times when I thought, "No, I was wrong. I have found an exception," but further scrutiny forced me to the conclusion that there were no exceptions. I could absolutely depend on the superego's duplicity.

Indeed, now I can say, "If it has nothing to hide, why is it not more open?" Remember, dear reader, this is the voice that so often tells the schizophrenic, "You really should kill yourself. That would be best for everybody." The superego is the clever parasite that will cling to the patient, until the patient's ego has it fully exposed. Finally, when its back is to the wall, it has to confess, "O.K., I really do hate Jane (its hostess) but try to understand, I have to live too." Then it bursts like a bubble. Its standing as a fantasy is revealed.

A question then can be raised as to why "I will never leave you" is so effective and is always the last weapon for the superego to use. I believe it is because there is always an implicit threat in the parent's disapproval, the threat of desertion, certainly a threat of loss of love. Consequently, the "glue" that holds the parent to the child is seen as not dependable. That is the most effective threat that can be used on a child. When the patient can say "What's stopping you? There is the door. The sooner the better," and the child leaves, then the battle is over. But by then, the ego feels substantive and anxiety is minimal.

I think Freud would be very surprised at the outcome of such a conversation, since he had fallen victim to the belief that the superego was the "higher" part of man, which promised never to leave the patient. Freud was clearly not aware that the superego was composed only of that part of the governing parent that was *hostile* to the child. He also erred in that he believed that only his patients were subject to psychological conflicts, not their parents.

Error #4, The Death Instinct

The concept of the death instinct is not, strictly speaking, part of Freud's structural theory, but, in my view, he made an error by not making the connection to the structural theory. The beginning of his error, I believe, starts in the following statement, "there remained in me a kind of conviction, for which I was not as yet able to find **reasons** (emphasis mine), that the instinct could not all be of the same kind" (XXI, [8]). This led to: "I drew the conclusion that, besides the instinct to preserve living substance and to join it into ever larger units, there must exist another contrary instinct seeking to dissolve those units and to bring them back to their primeval, inorganic state" (Ibid., [9]).

Unfortunately, having seen the phenomenon of conflict, he drew the conclusion that it was an instinct, not the energy from the superego, that was in opposition to the life affirming instincts. At this point, I must assert that other than the life-preservative and sexual instincts, I see no necessity for postulating any other instinct, nor constitutional explanations for psychological phenomena. It seems to me that other instincts or constitutional explanations are asserted only when the proponent of those phenomena cannot explain them in any other way. I believe that the constitutional explanation is a cop out. Further, if the excuse for a phenomenon is either that it is instinctual or constitutional, it denotes that there is no hope for the patient's improvement. I am not ready to concede that. However,

> [t]o the end of his life, Freud continued to maintain doubts of about the death instinct. In a letter to Marie Bonapart, June 17, 1937, he wrote: 'Please do not overestimate my remarks about the destructive instinct. They were only tossed off and should be carefully thought over if you propose to use them publicly' (from *The Life and World of Sigmund Freud*, Vol III., Basic Books)
>
> *(Jones, 1955, p. 465)*

But there is no necessity for postulating an instinct to explain sadism. Its source can be explained by the life-preservative instinct, coming from two different sources. The first is part of the biological instinct itself. It is demonstrated in the form of protection when attacked. The evidence for this is obvious in the whole of the biological world. An animal that is hungry will attack another animal that it can eat. The object of the attack will defend itself. The result is not arbitrary sadism but self-preservative on the part of both animals.

The second source is psychological, originating from the ego (psychological identity), which fights off the parasitic superego, in order not to lose strength and keep the superego from gaining strength. The superego, on the other hand, using whatever strength it has, depending on the seriousness of the patient's illness, will attack in response to defend its life.[1] (I do recall the hebephrenic who took the Rorschach using the phrase "the space between life and death." Since, there is, in fact, no "space between life and death," we can understand the drive to attack the threat to life.)

Freud says, "I believe that the fear of death is something that occurs between the ego and the superego" (Freud, XIX). Interestingly, he says, "It would be possible to picture the id" (and consequently the ego) "as under the domination of the **mute** (emphasis mine) but powerful death instincts, which desire to be at peace and (promoted by the pleasure principle) to put Eros, the mischief-maker to rest: but perhaps that might be to undervalue the part played by Eros" (Freud, XIX [17]).

I find that paragraph interesting on two counts. One is that he calls the "death instinct" mute, without a previous foundation, but it is how he has previously described the superego. Secondly, he calls Eros the mischief-maker, but admits he may be in error. I would suggest that he cannot see the connection between the superego and his hypothesis of a death instinct, because he is caught in the myth of the superego's "supermorality" (Freud, XIX).

It seems to me that he also commits a scientific error in logic. Although organic beings end in death, this doesn't mean that there is an instinct that causes it to arrive in that state. I subscribe to the usual explanation of death. Decay will suffice.

But Freud, ever the man of integrity and science, says himself,

> It may be asked whether and how far I am myself convinced of the truth of the hypotheses that have been set out in these pages. My answer would be that I am not convinced myself and I do not seek to persuade other people to believe in them.
>
> *(Freud, XVIII [14])*

So, we can see a possibility of a happy ending. "Cs is characterized by the peculiarity that in it (in contrast to what happens in the other psychical systems) excitatory processes do not leave behind any permanent change in its elements but **expire** (emphasis mine) in the phenomenon of being conscious" (XVIII, [15]). That is something that is very possible to achieve if the analyst and patient attack the mischief-making of the superego.

Error #5: Reality Testing

In "Group Psychology and the Analysis of the Ego" (XVIII, [16]), Freud ascribes the ability to do reality testing to the "ego ideal" (superego). He later corrects himself in the "Ego and the Superego: (XIX, [17]). He says, "a differentiation within the ego, which may be called the 'ego ideal' or 'superego' have been stated elsewhere. They still hold good." But he adds a footnote, "Except that I seem to have been mistaken in ascribing the function of 'reality testing' to this superego— a point which needs correction" (n. Ibid., [18]).

It is a very important error, the implications of which Freud appeared not to notice. The superego knows the reality, which is why it is useless to argue with it, as patients often do, as if the "error" were not purposeful. At the beginning of my using my technique, I fell into the same error. After a while, I learned to expose its lies, ridicule it, or ask it what it is afraid of. The superego tells only lies to the patient (and the analyst) until its back is to the wall. However, all the lies that the superego tells can be undone by the ego and the analyst. Once the patient's superego is weak enough, the energy attached to the superego goes into the ego. An excellent example of that is Kathleen's observation, "I don't need my conscience to tell me what is right, I can figure that out for myself and do a better job than it does."

Addendum

Frequently, Freud writes as if the ego-ideal and the superego were the same, and sometimes as if they were separate identities. He was so inconsistent that I haven't dealt with the concept at all, since I thought it would only confuse matters. If the reader wishes to further explore the concept of the ego-ideal, I recommend Janine Chassequet-Smirgel's excellent book *The Ego- Ideal* (Ibid., 19).

So, what conclusions can we draw from these corrections? First, as I said in the dedication, what is important to me is separating the wheat from the chaff. Freud's structural theory is enormously important work. Improvements do not make it less valuable.

I think I can speculate fairly accurately that it was his emotional reaction. He was certainly not a narcissistic man. It may be said that, in an emotional sense, science was his religion. He was willing to accept wherever the truth led him. Nor did he believe that he had said the last word on anything; "this is how things appear to us now, in the present state of our knowledge: future research and reflection will no doubt bring further light" (XXI, [20]). As a result, I believe he would be pleased with the offer of my improvements, as he was by the contributions of Sabina Spielrein, for example (XII, [21]).

Note

1 (see Rorschach Chapter 22) (10)

References

1. Freud, Sigmund. The ego and the id. (1923). In *The Standard Edition of the Complete Psychological Works of Sigmund Freud*, Vol. XIX, Hogarth Press, London, p. 37.
2. Ibid., p. 54.
3. Klein, Melanie. (1932). *The Psycho-Analysis of Children*, Hogarth Press, London, p. 179.
4. Freud, Sigmund. (1923). The ego and the id. In *The Standard Edition of the Complete Psychological Works of Sigmund Freud*, Vol. XIX, Hogarth Press, London, pp. 49–50.
5. Ibid., p. 50.
6. Ibid., p. 49.
7. Ibid., p. 50.
8. Freud, Sigmund. (1976). Civilization and its discontents. In *The Standard Edition of the Complete Psychological Works of Sigmund Freud*, Vol. XXI, Hogarth Press, London, p. 118.
9. Ibid., p. 36.
10. Rorschach, Chapter 22, this book.
11. Freud, Sigmund. (1923). The ego and the id. In *The Standard Edition of the Complete Psychological Works of Sigmund Freud*, Vol. XIX, Hogarth Press, London, p. 58.
12. Ibid., p. 59.
13. Ibid., p. 54.
14. Freud, Sigmund. Beyond the pleasure principle. (1920). In *The Standard Edition of the Complete Psychological Works of Sigmund Freud*, Vol. XVIII, Hogarth Press, London, p. 59.
15. Ibid., p. 25.

16. Freud, Sigmund. (1921) Group psychology and the analysis of the ego. In *The Standard Edition of the Complete Psychological Works of Sigmund Freud*, Vol. XVIII, Hogarth Press, London, p. 114.
17. Freud, Sigmund. The ego and the superego. In *The Standard Edition of the Complete Psychological Works of Sigmund Freud*, Vol. XIX, Hogarth Press, London, p. 28.
18. Ibid., p. 28, n. #2.
19. Chasseguet-Smirgel, Janine. (1985). *The Ego-Ideal*, Free Association Books, London, 1985.
20. Freud, Sigmund. Civilization and its discontents. In *The Standard Edition of the Complete Psychological Works of Sigmund Freud*, Vol. XXI, Hogarth Press, London, p. 122.
21. Freud, Sigmund. Postscript. In *The Standard Edition of the Complete Psychological Works of Sigmund Freud*, Vol. XII, Hogarth Press, London, p. 80, n. #2.
22. Jones, E. (1918). *Hate and Anal Eroticism in the Obsessional Neurosis*, Papers on Psycho-Analysis, 2nd Edition, William Wood, New York, p. 465.

FIGURE 10.1 Roz Chast/The New Yorker Collection/The Cartoon Bank. Reprinted with permission

10
COMMUNICATING WITH THE SCHIZOPHRENIC SUPEREGO

I am most grateful to John Kerr and Helen Gediman for their excellent suggestions. Without them this paper would not be as comprehensible as it is.

The world of schizophrenia is a world of chaos, certainly to the patient and to the student of schizophrenia. Early in his career, Freud was pessimistic about the possibilities of psychoanalytic intervention in this condition. But later in his life, in *An Outline of Psychoanalysis*, he held out hope for comprehension and amelioration of schizophrenia. Freud says, in "An Outline of Psychoanalysis"

> A dream, then is a psychosis, with all the absurdities, delusions, and illusions of a psychosis . . . and we learn from it that even so deep-going and alteration of mental life as this can be undone and give place to the normal function. It is too bold, then, to hope it must also be possible to submit the dreaded spontaneous illnesses of mental life to our influence and bring about their cure?
>
> *(1940, p. 172)*

In this article, I approach the problem of schizophrenia by making practical use of an important tool that Freud has given us, namely, the concept of the id, the ego, and the superego. With his description of psychic structure and the dynamics among the parts, I contend that Freud has given us a framework to begin to decipher an important aspect of the problem. Put simply, in his portrait of the internal relations between the ego and the superego, Freud has given us a means to understand the "method of madness."

(Originally published in *the Journal of the American Academy of Psychoanalysis*, 24(e), 709–736, 1997. Reprinted with permission of Guilford Press)

To avoid misunderstanding, an initial clarification is in order. The concept of the superego, as described in the totality of Freud's writing, and as I am using it here must be distinguished from the ego ideal. I have found it easier, and more practical, rather than trying to disentangle one from the other on the basis of metapsychological considerations, to distinguish them from the affects that are induced. That is, if the patient feels guilt, the problem is the superego. If the patient feels shame, the problem is the ego ideal. In this respect, my approach to the problem resembles in some ways the approach of Piers and Singer (1953). I was aided in coming to this view through my work with a particular patient. It became clear that the superego was introjected from one parent, whereas the ego ideal was an introject from a much older sibling. I will not discuss the ego ideal in this paper.

Freud describes the superego as the heir to Oedipus. But in working with schizophrenics, we can see that guilt begins much earlier. Other writers have traced the emotion of guilt to earlier libidinal stages, such as the anal stage and what Ferenczi (1927/1950) calls its accompanying "sphincter morality." Melanie Klein traced guilt even further back to the vicissitudes of the oral stage. She made it quite clear that she believed the superego begins at the "end of the first year and the beginning of the second year of life," though she noted that feelings of guilt arising in this stage "receive reinforcement through anal frustrations undergone during the training in cleanliness" (Klein, 1928/1948, p. 202). Note that, like Ferenczi, she also supports the connection between the superego and the anal phase, when the child is potentially set into conflict with the external, at times punitive, authority.

In terms of psychic structure, I do not find it helpful to view the superego as part of the ego as Freud (1923) does. I see the ego as evolving from the id, but I see the superego as a foreign introject. Indeed, I have frequently found it useful to clarify the concept of an introject to my patients. I point out the difficulty physicians have of transplanting a foreign organ, like the heart or kidney. I say that human beings cannot normally assimilate foreign bodies as the cells of each human being have their own identity.

Similarly, people can internalize the admonitions of an unloving and punitive authority only by a kind of psychic equivalent to the sort of immunotherapy used to stifle the body's reactions in transplant operations. Just such a suppression (normally verbalized as "shut up") of the mind's natural coping methods in the face of a foreign introject is a key cause of the generalized ego weakness we see in schizophrenia.

Another confusion that commonly arises about the superego, which Sandler (1960/1987) points out, derives from Freud's view that the superego is the locus for the self-critical function. In recent years, as my conversations with superegos have continued, it has become clear to me that there are two kinds of self-criticisms.

One is self-criticism by the ego (Levin, 1965). The ego may say to a patient who is considering buying a dress, "That dress is a becoming color, but the waist is cut too low for your figure. Perhaps another size might look better, or it might be worthwhile to have it altered." But the superego in appraising the situation would have a qualitatively different response, such as: "Your waist is way too high. You have such a misshapen figure. You might as well take that dress. You will never find anything better. Besides, it is self-indulgent to waste more of your time trying to look better."

As we can see, these two self-perceptions are diametrically opposed. Self-perception by the ego leads to an adaptive modification of the impulse. Self-perception by the superego leads to a suppression of the impulse—and to guilt. I will delve more deeply into the distinction later on, when I present what I call "conversations with the superego." But before leaving this dress-buying example, I would like to point out that this imaginary incident is typical of a patient who bemoans her lack of ability to "fit in," here demonstrated literally, rather than trying to find a dress or situation that will fit her.

In portraying the superego as an essentially punitive introject, I am taking my warrant from Freud. In *New Introductory Lectures on Psychoanalysis*, Freud (1932, p. 60), in regard to obsessive-compulsive disorders, says "a clinical picture ... throws a striking light on the severity of this agency (superego) and indeed its cruelty." In relation to schizophrenia, I have found this to be an understatement. To me "vicious" would be more accurate as I learned during the course of my conversations with various superegos. Indeed, the technique that I describe shortly aims at exposing the degree of the hostility of the superego in an experientially vivid way to the patient.

I have been using this technique for some 37 years, yet I still continue to be surprised at the manipulativeness, deceptiveness, conniving ways of the schizophrenic superego. I found that almost the only time it doesn't lie, is when its back is to the wall, so to speak, at which time it gets very angry at me. It wishes only to preserve itself and control the patient, even if this means the patient's death. Indeed, at times it behaves as if it were even able to survive the patient's physical death, for example, when it urges the patient to commit suicide.

As a theoretical aside, let me say that I think that this hostility toward the ego is the true source for what Klein perceived as the death instinct. To be sure, Klein (1933/1948) herself was well aware that the child feels persecuted by its superego, but she denies that what comes from the parent(s) can fully account for it.

I have two difficulties with Klein's view. The first is that I don't have a problem tracing the hostility back to particular parent(s) and their behavior, subtle or overt. Since I have begun having conversations with superegos, I find this to be very true. Second, I find her view unnecessarily pessimistic. If the child's hostility toward him or herself is indeed instinctual, the therapist can do nothing to alter it in its essentials. Klein affirms this view when she says, "analysis can never entirely do away with the sadistic nucleus of the super-ego" (1933, p. 275). I agree that we can't change the nature of the superego so that it is no longer sadistic. However, if the child's hostility toward him or herself is due to the parents and, subsequently, to the activity of the superego, we need, theoretically at least, only the therapist and the ego of the patient to influence or extinguish it.

I can imagine the shock, the response of "What?!" or "Is this woman mad?" when I speak of "extinguishing the superego." Several colleagues have said to me, "But without a conscience, one would do dreadfully immoral things. One would kill people, rob them, and so on, without a qualm." I have found this a frequent threat from superegos themselves. The superego does not hesitate to point out to the patient what a total moral wretch, unworthy of love or redemption, he would be were it not for the superego's presence. But, conversely, all the superego voices I have heard have promised not only to take care of the patient, but to make him or her *superior* to everyone else. When checking with the ego, however, both concepts turn out to be lies.

Case Example

For example, one patient (Carolyn), had a superego, which, when it was not telling her how evil she was, told her she had what Carolyn and I called "God in my pocket." Carolyn used to feel that she could always get people to take care of her, no matter what scrapes (mostly financial) she got into. Indeed, when she first came for treatment, I feared she was a psychopath. Her view was that God looked out for her and her alone, and therefore, she was superior. Besides, she said, she had had a hard childhood, so she deserved a special dispensation from others.

You may well ask, if the superego does not indeed give the ego valid moral values, what prevents a person with little or no guilt from becoming a psychopath? First, we know that psychopaths do, in fact, have some guilt. But what they lack is *identification* with others. Further, clinical observation confirms that as the superego weakens, patients become kinder and more loving to others. If one's attitude is, "I am bad, so the world must hate me," love is not likely to ensue. But if one feels, "I am a nice person, which must be obvious to most people," there is no reason not to feel warmth toward a world from which one expects warmth. Carolyn, for example, since her superego has substantially weakened, has lately acquired the ability to kiss people who are not from her family, an unheard of behavior for her and one not discussed in treatment until after the fact. Freud is most revealing on this subject:

> The more virtuous a man is, the more severe and distrustful is its behaviour, so that ultimately, it is precisely those people who have carried saintliness furthest who reproach themselves with the worst sinfulness. This means that virtue forfeits some part of its promised reward; the docile and continent ego does not enjoy the trust of its mentor, and strives in vain, it would seem, to acquire it. The objection will at once be made that these difficulties are artificial ones, and it will be said that a stricter and more vigilant conscience is precisely the hallmark of a moral man. Moreover, when saints call themselves sinners, they are not so wrong, considering temptations to instinctual satisfaction to which they are exposed in a specially high degree-since it is well known, temptations are merely increased by constant frustration,

whereas an occasional satisfaction of them causes them to diminish, at least for the time being.

(Freud, 1929)

In fact, my suggestion that it might be desirable to extinguish the superego is mentioned by Freud himself:

The uncomplaining resignation with which ... people often put up with their hard fate is most remarkable, but also revealing. In warding off this resistance, we are obliged to restrict ourselves to making it conscious and attempting to bring about the slow *demolition* of the hostile super-ego.

(Freud, 1938)

You may well argue, "That is the hostile or tyrannical superego. What about a beneficent superego?" Here I pointedly disagree with what Schafer (1960) and others have attempted to argue. (For a full exegesis of my disagreement with Schafer's "The Loving and Beloved Superego in Freud's Structural Theory" [1960], see my chapter "Awakening the Schizophrenic Dreamer" [Levin, 1987].) Communicating with the superego has led me to the conclusion that there is no such thing as a beneficent superego. What I have discovered is that, when the ego is obedient to the superego, the superego is merely silent, or it makes no further demands. That is to say, a "benevolent" superego is simply one that has stopped persecuting the patient for the moment. In schizophrenia, the superego is insatiable in its demands. You might say, "Well, in nonpsychotic patients we can sometimes see evidence of an internal voice saying 'You did a good job. I am proud of you.'" But in all my conversations with the superego, I have never heard anything positive, with the exception of "I will take care of you" (without any evidence of the promise), and "You will be better than everyone else" (morally). I have never heard anything like the approval of "You did a good job," merely silence when the patient has bowed to the superego. Further, I will remind the reader that the voice of the ego is rational.

My supporting evidence is based on my clinical experience: If one probes deeply enough, one discovers that the superego is never truly rational. It took me a long time to be really certain of that, because at times the superego does *appear* to be rational. But if one investigates, one will find that behind that apparent rationality, there is, in fact, a scheme to damage the patient and ensure the superego's own survival and power. But let me postpone further discussion of this until I have shared some of my clinical experience.

In discussing obsessional neurosis, Freud (1925, p. 118) says,

The over-acute conflict between id and super-ego which has dominated the illness from the beginning may assume such extensive proportions that the ego, unable to carry out its office of mediator, can undertake nothing which is not drawn into the sphere of that conflict.

How much more must this be true in psychosis. But taken from the vantage point of intervention, Freud puts one hand behind his back, so to speak, by declaring, "as far as the patient is concerned this sense of guilt is dumb . . . This sense of guilt expresses itself only as a resistance to recovery which is extremely difficult to overcome" (Freud, 1923). What I have found with my patients is that, in fact, the superego is not dumb, though at times it refuses to speak. But it fears, so to speak, both literally and figuratively the light of day. For example, Carolyn's superego quite literally used to threaten her with blindness, until I suggested that her superego was frightened of what she would see.

By now some readers may be ready to remark that I speak of superegos as though I were on a first-name basis with them. Indeed, in a manner of speaking, I *am* on a first-name basis with the superegos of schizophrenic patients. That is to say, I talk about them (referring to them as "consciences") to the patients as though they were present in the room. Frequently, I go further and talk directly *to* the superego. And most of the time, the superego answers back, often in ways that both the patient and I find revealing. This procedure evolved spontaneously in my work with severely disturbed patients and as I have found it useful, I have stayed with it for purely practical reasons. But as I reflected back on my experience, I have been led to certain theoretical considerations by way of justification.

Clearly, when Freud writes of the id, ego, and superego as though they were independent agencies, each with its own aims, he is taking, in the first instance, a certain literary license. What makes his portrait of the different agencies attractive, however, is precisely the fact that most people see their consciences as having a life of their own. Adlai Stevenson once remarked that "the conscience, in many people's experience, is that part which feels terrible when everything else feels just great" (1965). Yet, for most people, this personification remains a metaphor or figure of speech.

The matter is quite different when the superego's autonomy goes beyond metaphor and becomes a continuing part of psychic experience. Here we are in a realm where it is proper to speak of "introjects." Interestingly, when Fairbairn (1944/1952) first offered his revised portrait of psychic structure in schizoid patients as comprised introjects and split-off fragments of the ego, he responded to criticism that he was introducing "demons" back into psychoanalysis, by pointing out that his view of the autonomy of the introject corresponded to classic views of the autonomy of the superego.

Precisely so, in my opinion: The superego is an introject. But this does not spare us the problem of how to conceptualize the matter. After all, we really do not want to allow demons back into our consulting rooms. Perhaps the clearest statement on this issue is Schafer's (1968) analysis in *Aspects of Internalization*. There Schafer argues that the introject must be viewed as a fantasy. And just as some fantasies are more vivid and absorbing than others, the experience of the inner voice or presence of another, such as is entailed in the experience of an introject, can be more or less compelling. Schafer specifically goes on to link the degree of vividness of the fantasy to the ego in a way directly relevant to the present discussion. He argues that a fantasy or daydream becomes more involving to the degree to which one suspends one's self-awareness as the thinker. With the experience of an introject, he suggests, the suspension of self-awareness has become habitual so that the fantasy of another presence within is experienced as more or less real, at least for the moment, rather than as a fantasy perceived as such.

This corresponds in rough outlines to my view of the superego in schizophrenic and borderline schizophrenic conditions. Strictly speaking, the superego is a fantasy, but it is not experienced as such, that is, as a creation of the patient's own mind. To be sure, the index of reality that the patient attributes to the fantasy-introject will vary depending on the acuteness of the psychosis. In the examples that follow, the patients are not actively hallucinating during the session; some degree of contact with reality is preserved.

In essence, what I am proposing by way of "talking with the superego" is a practical complement to Schafer's description. From a theoretical standpoint one could say that the patient's absorption in his or her fantasy interactions with the introjected superego, with an accompanying habitual lack of self-reflection vis-a-vis the fantasy, constitutes an important source of ego weakness. Practically, however, what one finds is that this very relation is embodied in the content of the fantasy, that is, the superego actively discourages the patient from thinking autonomously or from reflecting on what the superego is about. Just this must be challenged by the therapist.

The reader may still object that by talking to the superego one is treating the fantasy as real. In fact, the procedure I am about to describe does constitute a form of enacted or dramatized fantasy, strictly speaking. Rather than fostering the continued fantasy relation to the superego, however, the therapeutic enactment, as it occurs in the interpersonal space between therapist and patient, helps the patient to become aware, usually for the first time, of the truly fantastic nature of the whole business. Further, because the "messages" it is getting are not valid, they need not be taken seriously.

When the patient finds the voice of his or her superego, he or she is beginning to share his or her experience of it with me. Prior to that, it was his/her secret, but one that was taken for granted: The patient is a "bad" person, and his or her conscience is doing its best to set the patient on the "right track." Supposedly, if the patient can only do that well enough, "trying to be good," eventually he or she will be out of danger.

But the reality is that when the superego first begins to speak to me, it will be vulnerable to my attack, whereas before it could beat the patient into submission. The superego is a phony, but it must never be spoken about to the patient as if it were a fantasy. This would be equivalent to trying to argue with a delusion. Hundreds of years of trying to treat schizophrenics with "rationality" have proved how useless that is.

In fact, it is worse than useless because the patient "knows" it to be a reality (having heard a real voice in his or her head), and will only be antagonized by the therapist's refusal to see it that way. Additionally, if the therapist insists it is all fantasy, it is the therapist who is wrong, not the patient, in the following way: If one interprets a dream, one discovers much about the reality of that patient. If nothing else, one discovers the reality of a wish. As Freud says, "there is not only *method* in madness, as the poet has already perceived, but also a fragment of *historical truth*" (Freud, 1937). It is wisest to leave it to the patient to discover in what way he or she has fooled him or herself, or allowed him or herself to be fooled by the superego. (Embarrassment usually follows.) Only *the patient* can discover exactly where that trick or lie took place. The patient will eventually recognize that the superego was erected on a fantasy, in the same way that a desert traveler may finally recognize that the "oasis" he or she saw was a mirage. We will see an example of that in the last conversation with Carolyn.

So now let me give some examples of conversations with superegos that I have had. It happens that my memory is not as good as I would like, so that I take pretty extensive notes during sessions. But it is very hard to write and speak at the same time. The result is that my notes are better about what my patients say, then what I say. (Taping with paranoid patients would be, I feel, too disturbing to the therapy, though I have sometimes done it.) Suffice it to say that in these conversations I don't take a neutral stand. I am direct and sometimes even harsh when speaking to the superego.

All three of the patients I present are in their early forties. All three are very bright. Bathsheba had 11 therapists before me. She had attempted suicide several times. She believed that she would go to Heaven and sit on the left side of God, while Jesus sat on the right side of God (a most interesting delusion, as she came from an Orthodox Jewish family). She had had such hysterical rages that the police frequently had to be called. Well read, she diagnosed herself as psychotic. Because of her brilliance, she was always able to work despite her illness.

Samantha was able to work for only a few months in her life. She had also attempted suicide several times. She could also threaten violence and had been violent several times. Her associations were so loose, and her verbalizations were so concretistic that a diagnosis of schizophrenia could be made in 5 minutes.

Carolyn had a psychotic break just before she came to me. She frequently believed that her food was poisoned by coworkers and neighbors, if she left it unattended, and would throw it out when she came back. At one time, she believed that someone had urinated in her shampoo bottle. She entertained a private delusion since adolescence that she had "God in my pocket," meaning that God would keep her, but only her, out of trouble. In daily life, this delusion was infrequently threatened seriously because she easily manipulated others into giving her what she wanted.

Of course, all three of these patients had many more symptoms, but these are the most prominent. In effect, they have all been ill since adolescence. Now to the dialogues.

Case Examples

The instructions to the patient are merely "Say what your conscience says." Patients catch on quite quickly.

Bathsheba

Bathsheba had been with me a year when this conversation took place. By this time, she was much improved, considerably less depressed and suicidal than when she came. But note how vicious the superego still is.

Bathsheba:	I have to make my mother happy.
I:	You must feel she wants to kill you. (My comment refers to a previous dream of Bathsheba's.)
Bathsheba's superego:	I feel Val (therapist) is mentally sick. Val doesn't believe in the perfection of motherhood (laughs).
I:	Why are you laughing?
Bathsheba:	I always laugh when I get angry. The voice does that.
I to superego:	What happens if you take her seriously?
Bathsheba:	It says, "You're a silly, terrible girl."
I to superego:	What if she is right about something? What if she takes herself seriously?
Bathsheba's superego:	I'll lose authority. I'll rot in a grave. My daughter loves me. She's a good daughter. All the doctors in the world can't take her away from me. She has no right to her feelings.

In this example, after the first two sentences, we see an illustration of the superego recapitulating the essentially destructive attitude of the mother; in this respect, it is a relatively unusual example of the superego very closely modeled on the parent directly. Prior to the following conversation, Bathsheba has just met the man who will become her future husband.

Bathsheba:	I'm so scared of it (the relationship). The world is coming to an end. I'm afraid someone will kill me. (Grabbing her abdomen, as if the worst is about to happen), "I'll cry."
I to superego:	You want to kill her.
Bathsheba:	It will kill me. It is my fault. I provoked it.
I to her superego:	How did she provoke you?
Superego to me:	It wasn't her boyfriend's fault. ("It" refers to the threat of the superego to kill Bathsheba.) She deserves to be hurt. She provoked it.

I to superego:	How? I don't believe you. You just made it up.
Superego to me:	I wash my hands of it. I'm innocent. (A sure sign of mischief, as no one accused it of anything.)
I to superego:	You said something before about her being too pretty. (Bathsheba is beautiful.)
Superego to me:	She is bad because she has a body. Because she should have been a boy.
I to superego:	You are jealous of her because she has a body.
Superego to me:	That is disgusting. (Really angry at me which means I have hit the mark.) I don't want her telling you things. (Here is an example of fear of exposure.) I don't want her to have a husband. She'll shake with terror. (Neglecting to say that *it* is the one who will frighten her. This is a very frequent ploy of superegos. They point to some unknown external threat to the patient, as if they were protecting the patient. But, in fact, it is the superego itself that will cause the damage. For example, "You will feel guilty" as if, it itself, were not the originator of the guilt.)
I to superego:	She doesn't have to be afraid. You can't do anything.
Superego to me:	I don't want her to have a new boyfriend. I don't want her to use sex to attract him.
Bathsheba:	He's a tennis player. Fourth in his age group.
Superego:	I could beat him with one hand behind my back.
Bathsheba:	My conscience is really scared because my new boyfriend likes Judaism. (Note the progress here in that first, it is the superego rather than Bathsheba that is frightened and second, Judaism is a conflictual issue for Bathsheba.)
Superego:	I like the old boyfriend. He gave her a hard time. He made her suffer. It's good for her. I'll make her feel guilty. (By this stage, the superego is admitting that it causes guilt. It is still trying to intimidate her, but the tone is one of empty threats.)

We can learn several things from this conversation. First, we can see clearly without being concerned with subtleties how much the superego wants to damage the patient. Second, we see that we can threaten the superego. Third, we can see the irrational braggadocio, "I can beat the new boyfriend (in tennis) with one hand tied behind my back." Fourth, we see the superego's denial of responsibility and the attempt to shift all the blame on the patient. This is the usual stance of superegos, which results in both guilt and grandiosity, because it implies that the patient has so much power. This patient feels guilty about her beauty and happiness, and that is why she can't enjoy her relationship. Finally, and most important, we can see the net result in terms of affect.

Communicating with the Superego 129

Now I will present another conversation about the new boyfriend. Bathsheba's parents, who were out of town, are returning and she asks me if she should tell them about her new boyfriend.

I to superego:	Why are you afraid of her parents knowing about her new boyfriend?
Superego:	(silence.)
Bathsheba:	I know what it's afraid of, but I am worried about their reaction.
Superego to me:	If they know, then it's real. Then I am history. (Bathsheba laughs) Then I got no role. (To Bathsheba) I'll make you doubt yourself.
I to superego:	You add to *my* conviction.
Superego to me:	I like her to think she is an orphan. Then she has no power. So, she still hides. So she cuts out pieces of herself and doesn't have it together. Her connections are deep. A lot has to be discovered. She wants to throw away her upbringing. (Reference at the very least to the fundamentalist religion with which she was raised.)
I to superego:	(sarcastically) What has gotten into you, that you are telling the truth? You are right. By not telling them, she gives them power.
Superego to me:	She is very scared of her parents.
I to superego:	If she tells the truth, she won't be scared of them, and mostly she won't be scared of you. (Bathsheba very often withholds the truth.)
Superego to me:	It is foolish of her to go out on her own. She needs so many doctors. (Bathsheba has several psychosomatic complaints. But it is also a reference to all the mental health professionals she has consulted before me.)
I to superego:	What is more dangerous and corrupting than you?
Superego:	(Goes on and on in the same vein, an example of the obsessiveness that these patients experience.)
I to Bathsheba:	*You* answer. I'm getting bored with answering it. (I am bored. But additionally, I feel confident that at this point she can handle it herself, and needs to have the "exercise" in doing so.)
Bathsheba to superego:	You're crazy. I can't believe I let you influence me. I must have been an idiot to listen to you. I'm finally using my intelligence, thanks to this nice lady. I'm taking you to the laundry. You made me sick. You took a healthy person and made me sick and then you complain I am sick.

In this dialogue, we see how the superego supports her fear of her parents. It also admits how threatened it is, if she tells the truth and is courageous. And I realize that to some extent I have underestimated the strength of her ego.

Samantha

Samantha covers her pain with bravado and hostility, but never cries. Prior to the following conversation, this issue has been occupying us recently when the following exchange occurs.

I to superego: You don't want her to cry.
Superego to me: If she cries she will open her eyes and I will fall out of them.

This last statement is not meant as something desirable but as a threat of abandonment, which is the trump card of all superegos. In general, one discovers that the superego mixes the threat that facing reality will be too painful, with covert, tantalizing promises to stay with the patient always. Fairbairn appears to be describing something similar when he says, "On the one hand, it (an unsatisfying object) frustrates; and on the other hand it tempts and allures" (Fairbairn, 1944/1952).

In the following conversation with Samantha, a wide spectrum is evident from primary process material to healthy ego material. I think you will find it interesting to see how Samantha goes back and forth as she struggles with her isolation problems.

Samantha to me: I was reading about feminism and patriarchies. I should have been perfect. You expect it.
I to Samantha: Your conscience expects it.
Samantha to me: You felt it's O.K. to get well. (As if just remembering.) My parents were brutalized and I should be able to cure them, as well as myself. (Samantha has expressed guilt before about being so fortunate as to have me as an analyst, whereas her parents didn't. She has steadfastly ignored the fact that her parents didn't want therapy.)
I to Samantha: That is very grandiose.
Samantha to me: I can't make a flawless emergence from mental illness. I keep wanting everyone with me.
I to Samantha: If you do come out of it alone, then what? (That is, she'll be the only healthy one in her family.)
Samantha to me: I feel guilt.
I to superego: What trick are you trying to pull?
Superego to me: She will leave them to die in the fire.

Communicating with the Superego   131

I to superego:	Why are you telling her all this bullshit? (Though on reconsideration, this might better have been interpreted as a wish immediately.)
Samantha to superego:	(Barrage of hostility.)
Samantha to me:	If I feel good, I'll be punished for getting well. I can't see the forest for the trees.
I to Samantha:	That's what happens if you keep your eyes shut. (This is a symbolic reference to the ego, which I know she will understand.)
Samantha to me:	If I believe in women, then I don't live for my father. I live for myself. I would take care of my wishes. My conscience says I will never find a job because I am fat and I smoke and I can't stop.
I to superego:	What would happen if she got well?
Superego to me:	Everyone would laugh. She has no talent. (In school, she was greatly praised for her writing talent.)
I to superego:	Why are you so afraid of her love?
Superego to me:	*I exist for death, not life.* (Is there better proof that there is no death "instinct"?)
I to Samantha:	(Attempting to get her to use her ego.) What do you say to it?
Samantha to superego:	You have no right. You are a leech.
Superego to Samantha:	I am an implant of your parents. It would heighten their unhappiness if you got better. (I believed that at the time, but later discovered by her mother's reaction to her improvement that this was a lie. Her mother was indifferent.)
I to Samantha:	But that is what you *want*, for them to be unhappy.
Samantha to me:	Give me a chance to see it. When I was little, I had a nightmare that my mother was dead. The therapist said that was what I wished. I'm a good girl.
I to Samantha:	Your idea of being a good girl is to lie about your wishes.
Samantha to me:	I have a continuous wish to kill my father. I am sure they wanted to kill me.
I to Samantha:	So why are you surprised that you want to kill them?
Samantha to me:	Whey they die, I will cry because they weren't what I wanted them to be. (To superego) I want them to die. Stop trying to make me into a stained-glass window. (This is a primary process way of saying "saintly.")
I to Samantha:	How do you feel?
Samantha to me:	Relief. I don't have to pretend to myself that things aren't what they are. You are too darned good at what you do. I want you to die. I want to slap your face. (Said with no

I to Samantha: affect.) I like having my conscience. It makes me superior. (It is that feeling that makes superegos *addictive*.) I didn't see its corruption.
I to Samantha: Does that make you feel superior?
Samantha to me: No, if I get rid of it, I will have freedom. I was a cracked bell. I'm not free to *do* what I want, but I would be free to *be* what I want. I'm not free to hit you over the head with the Liberty Bell (Samantha acts out frequently) and you aren't either. So, we control ourselves, so we don't get a headache. It's natural to have anger, but we have to agree not to hit each other, so we will be safe.
I to Samantha: (Astonished at such a clear statement of her ego, which she certainly didn't get from me, but could only have come from a diminishment of the superego.) What does your conscience say to that?
Superego to us: ch, ch, ch, (spitting sounds)
Samantha to me: Let it spit. I feel you see me as naked.
I to Samantha: What is wrong with that?
Samantha to me: I like it but I'm not ashamed. (Sounding surprised.)

We learn from this about Samantha's guilt in reference to getting better without her parents' getting better, and her certainty of how unhappy her mother (with whom she has a symbiotic relationship) will be if Samantha gets well, although I later realized this is Samantha's wish. Also, we see her hostility toward me for having accomplished whatever I have been able to do, which comes from my threat to her grandiosity.

But in the end, we see how the ego is suddenly enabled to come to the fore with apparently completely unrelated material. I have seen this happen innumerable times, that is, I've seen the unpredictability of what the ego does when it is freed. Do not be misled by Samantha's apparent altruism of wanting to cure her parents. It is a screen for the anxiety and pain of being alone, both in the sense of being separate, and in the sense of being the only one in her family who would not be ill.

Carolyn

Carolyn can get a job that is a big step up from the one she has now. The following is a conversation about that. Here I should mention that I have previously discussed Carolyn's "brain" (ego) with her in terms of its rationality.

I to superego: What is bothering you about this job?
Superego to me: Carolyn will not get this job.
I to superego: Don't you wish! What are you scared of?

Communicating with the Superego

Superego to me: If she gets this job, she will be able to see you twice a week and I don't want that.
I to superego: You don't *have* to like it. (In a voice that says I am happy that it doesn't.)
Carolyn to me: I feel so guilty. I am hiding it. My conscience won't let me get this job. After I saw you last time, I felt sadness, looking at it (conscience) disintegrate. It is making me feel that my father (the parent whose introject became her superego) had a hard life.
I to Carolyn: Your conscience is not literally your father. Your father is dead. (This needs to be said to remind patients that if the superego disintegrates, they are not killing the parent, but as discussed previously, I never say the superego is a fantasy [Schafer, 1968].)
Superego to me: I am making Carolyn feel responsible for everyone.
I to superego: How do you convince her of such grandiosity?

From this followed a discussion of why Carolyn hides her pain. The defense against her pain turned out to be part of her grandiosity, that is, others had pain, but not her. In a later session, she reported how important it was to her that I had pointed out that, in fact, her conscience was not literally her father. She says in her own succinct way, "My conscience is part of me and I can have power over it. I didn't have power over my father." The importance of *stating* this differentiation is not just new for Carolyn but for me as well. One can let a superego disintegrate without guilt and have only healthy consequences. Killing a father would not solve any psychological problems, and of course, would have dire consequences.

She reported after that session that the "real me" has come out and since then she has been much more affectionate with people and less hostile with me also. Additionally, she says "I can see the difference between consequences and punishment, (a problem for many schizophrenic patients). I feel like the world is my oyster." I am pleased to hear this, as it means to me that some normal feelings of omnipotence have replaced some grandiosity (Levin, 1986).

During the following session,
Carolyn says: I want to need you as long as possible.
I to Carolyn: You aren't questioning that?
Carolyn to me: My conscience says, "I want to be here as long as possible."
I to superego: What is the problem today? You are really trying to make a fool of Carolyn.
Superego to me: I need you for that. (Sarcastically.)
I to Carolyn: (Somewhat confused at how ego syntonic this is.) This monkeying around is dangerous, because you are not disturbed by what you are doing.
Carolyn to me: I didn't like when you said last session, "You are getting healthy." At the party over the weekend, I was a real hit. (Other than

being with her family, Carolyn has an almost nonexistent social life.) It was the real me and I had a good time. I don't know what I was afraid of. My conscience says I will be empty and get a black hole again. (This is a reference to a previously resolved problem [Levin, 1996].)

I to superego: It is amazing that you would try that again. (Carolyn hasn't had a black hole in 2 years.)

Carolyn to me: I know, but I knew it wasn't true. (In fact, it did not return.) As my eyes open up, I see the past differently. I see how isolated and lonely I was.

I to Carolyn: I would think that would make you *more* eager to get rid of your conscience, not less. I would think you would want to make sure it doesn't happen anymore.

Superego to me: She can't handle the pain of the past.

I to superego: All the more reason to get rid of you. Is it Carolyn or you that can't handle the pain of the past?

Carolyn to me: It is saying it loves me. My father did make me a sweet-sixteen party, it said to me. But I said to it, "Most fathers do that. That isn't that special." But I want to keep my conscience. I am afraid of being *alone*. I want it to keep me company.

I to Carolyn: *It* is what keeps you alone. You haven't had girlfriends and only one boyfriend since you were 18, when your brother died.

Carolyn to me: Yes, I went like this (arm extended in a pushing-away motion) to people. I did it because my conscience moved in. (This is not to say that the superego was not there before, but merely that it greatly increased its strength because of the conflicting emotions that Carolyn had about her brother's death.) It made me feel responsible for his death. (In her previous 12-year therapy, the major focus of her treatment was her brother's death, an occurrence rarely mentioned now.)

I to Carolyn: And you bought it.

Carolyn to me: I thought I would replace my brother in my parent's affections. I thought I could make them happy. I'm less grandiose these days. Before I felt I had to do everything for my nephew (aged 5, to whom she is very attached), that no one else could. Now I see all the other people who can do things for him too.

I to superego: You don't want her to know how alone she has been, *because* of you, not in *spite* of you. (To Carolyn) I was impressed that you kissed a few people lately.

Carolyn to me: It is nice to be with the girls in the office. My paranoia is down. They aren't like me, but they aren't out to get me either. It's wonderful to reach out to people. It's the best feeling in the world.

There are many lessons to be learned from these conversations with Carolyn. First, we see how Carolyn's superego doesn't want her to get a new and better job, both because of the satisfaction she will get from it and because it will enable her to come to therapy twice a week. If that happened, it would mean that it would be even more exposed and vulnerable to attack by me, as it well knows, not to be speak of Carolyn.

Second, it clarifies the way in which she has defended herself against exposing her pain. Having "God in her pocket" supposedly protected her from pain. Instead of exposing her pain, she used to go on the attack in the most self-destructive ways, which she does much less often now. The superego kept her grandiosity in place by denying her pain. Pain was also hidden by her "black hole," an experience of terror that she got when she blocked the experience of her own wishes.

Third, we can see by her mention of the "real me," that the ego is gaining strength. By contrast her superego supports the dubious project of showing a false self to the world—and to herself. The weakening of the superego permits the ego to show itself, and is experienced as "coming out of prison." This gives her an opportunity to have the ego make choices.

Fourth, "I don't know what I was afraid of" is a most interesting remark, but one that doesn't surprise me. As the superego diminishes, the patient forgets what it was about, in the same way we forget at least part of our dreams. But she has no need to remember it, as the ego has replaced the superego in that area. We see how determined and desperate the superego is by threatening her with a problem, the "black hole," which she hadn't had in two years. But her ego is still not strong enough to say, "That's silly. It can't come back."

Fifth, she has spontaneously begun to see how lonely she has been. This shows greater ego strength than she had previously had. It also gives me an opportunity to point out the superego's role in keeping her isolated. The promise (and fact) of the superego to "keep her company" is the most seductive tool it has. Every superego I have studied promises that, in almost the same words. With the superego constantly present, the patient feels she is never alone. Never mind that it punishes, destroys, misleads, and so on. It never leaves her. That fact constitutes the greatest resistance to any patient's letting the superego go. It offers absolute insurance against loneliness, but never advises the patient that the means for doing this is keeping relationships with real people at a minimum and as shallow as possible.

In the session, Carolyn's superego attempts to seduce her by saying it loves her. It brings up one of the few positive things her father did for her. But by this time, the ego is strong enough, so she can see that compared to how destructive the superego is, the sweet-sixteen party is unimportant.

As a result of the weakening of her superego, as Carolyn notes herself, both her grandiosity and paranoia are lessening. We see her pleasure in it when she says, "It's the best feeling in the world."

I have no illusions that Carolyn is finally done with her superego. It will fight last-ditch battles. It is returning in the transference. But the goal, so to speak, has been sighted. She has tasted the healthy life, so that it is no longer some vague dream. I sometimes think that mental health is like ice cream. No one can convey to someone else how wonderful it is, especially to someone who has been very ill. One can't know until one has tasted it. Apparently, it cannot be imagined with any accuracy. I often think our work would be much easier, if that were not true. But I do try my best to give tastes of it, when I see the opportunity, in order to give my patients some hope, when the opportunity presents itself and they are feeling particularly hopeless.

Transference and Countertransference

I am going to address the subjects of anality, identity and the superego, superego manipulations, the seductiveness of the superego, handling the negative transference of the schizophrenic and the personality of the analyst, etc. So, in this article, I will say little about the transference or the countertransference.

In reference to the transference, during the period when I am having dialogues with the superego, I say relatively little to the patient about it as in the example of Samantha above. I only warn the patient occasionally during the course of treatment, that "there will come a time when you will hate me. It will be very difficult, but when it is worked through, you will derive great benefit from it."

I take this approach for practical reasons. Since I am taking such a non-neutral stand, the transference becomes diluted. During the period when I am doing dialogues with the superego, I am being the patient's benign protector from the "enemy." Clearly, this would cause the transference to be muddled and attempts at interpretation would only cause confusion.

However, my experience has been that later, when the superego is already in a weakened condition, the chaos is reduced, the patient is functioning more like a neurotic, and the feeling of *sturm und drang* has passed, the negative transference comes to full flower. Of course, it is stronger than a neurotic transference would be and the paranoia is a little stronger. The ego is still so weak that the patient finds it more difficult than a neurotic to believe that it is just a transference. This is a very difficult period for both me and the patient. The treatment may founder at this point, either because of my own lack of skill, or because the hostility and painful reality are too difficult for the patient to bear. But I handle it as I would anyone else's negative transference.

As far as the countertransference goes, I approach the patient with complete respect for her concretistic thinking. I do not challenge it, but rather look for the lack of logic *within* the system. For example, I might say to a superego, "I love it when you hate me. That means I am scaring you and you won't be able to hurt Jane so much."

In order to take this approach, I must feel an emotional conviction that I am doing hand-to-hand combat with the "enemy." At least the quality—though not the quantity—of the emotion is there. On rare occasions, when I discover that a superego has been tricking me in a way that I had not suspected, I do not become angry, and may say something like, "You (expletive deleted). You are trying to drive her crazy with your lies. Who the (expletive deleted) do you think you are?" I am not on my best ladylike behavior in such a situation. But such an outburst serves two practical functions: it allows me to express my hostility, and shows the patient that it is not just an intellectual exercise formed. However, I would warn a possible practitioner of this method to be very sparing of such outbursts, or the patient may suspect you of being insincere.

Though it is not perfect, the best analogy I can give for this technique is to assume the role of the normal protective mother. This is seen not only in normal human beings, but in animals as well. The mothers goes to any extent to protect her young, even at the risk of her own life. I saw an emotional response in myself when the petite patient told me about her "gray voice". Interestingly, at that time I did not intellectualize. I just responded angrily because it was trying to hurt my patient. My feeling is that I am trying to rescue my patient from the pain and terror (too often ignored by analysts with these patients) of the abyss with which the superego is threatening her. When the intervention is successful, and the patient demonstrates an understanding of what trick the superego is up to, I experience relief and pleasure. Again, this is expressed minimally. I take care not to express the full extent of my excitement, for fear of interfering with the patient's full emotional appreciation of what has happened. I don't want to take it away from her.

One may argue that this is not truly psychoanalysis. It violates neutrality too much. Freud says, "The voice of the intellect is a soft one, but it does not rest till it has gained a hearing. Finally, after a countless succession of rebuffs, it succeeds. This is one of the few points on which one may be optimistic about the future of mankind, but it is in itself a point of no small importance" (Freud, 1927b.) These conversations are designed to help that voice get louder, so that, if the reader would not agree that this is psychoanalysis, it is a technique that hopefully will make psychoanalysis possible.

I would also argue that it is psychoanalysis in that I am facing the reality of the fact that the schizophrenic patient experiences herself as constantly in danger of loss of identity. She is frequently in fear that the next moment may bring death. In this situation, *she* is being realistic, in the sense that the superego is very frequently threatening to overwhelm the ego. This is experienced as loss of identity, which is the psychological equivalent of death as in the case of Kathleen, below. If I do not accept that, then it is *I* who am being unrealistic. My patient needs more than an interpretation to "save her life." She needs me to battle at her side.

The Advantages of Handling Guilt With This Technique

The question may be raised as to what advantage this technique has over ordinary interpretation of guilt. Without this technique, the patient may merely express her feelings as, "I feel I am bad," or "I feel guilty about this piece of behavior or that feeling." Or worse, and more likely in schizophrenia, she "knows" she is "bad" and is certain that that "badness" is obvious to the analyst. The rationale is, "If I weren't so bad, I wouldn't have gotten sick and your job is to take the badness out of me." But generally, when patients talk *about* their guilt, it is expressed much more mildly than when the superego expresses it directly and both patient and analyst get a misleading picture of it.

Without the suggested technique, the analyst would ordinarily be working on increasing ego strength. But the superego itself, hiding away in the dark recesses of the mind (how often I have seen its terror of the light!), is free to continue its mischief without either patient or analyst knowing exactly how it is doing it. The superego's "rationale" remains vague. The patient and analyst struggle with forces that neither can clearly define. They can muddle along for a long time, struggling with what exactly this accusation is based on. When the superego "speaks" (after being pushed for a while), what may emerge is, "You are bad for telling the truth." Obviously, this puts a very different light on the accusation. The ego, no matter how weak, will have difficulty in accepting the idea that truth-telling is immoral. From this, we can see that communicating directly with the superego is, at the very least, a time saver, because we know what weapons the superego is using.

However, saving months or years is often the least of it. All of my patients let me know very soon after their arrival that nothing can be done for them, and politely imply, with veiled contempt, that *I* am mad to think I can help them. Because I start to communicate with their superegos very soon after treatment commences, often with dramatic results, I can frequently prevent premature termination.

Secondly, when the superego is forced to admit that its accusation of "badness" is based on such "crimes" as truth-telling, or sometimes even loving, it loses much of its strength. When the ego sees that the accusation has no merit, and therefore need not be taken seriously, the psychic energy of the superego is automatically reduced and goes directly into the ego. This strength gives the patient greater confidence in her own intellectual ability. She can behave in the external world with greater certainty that her behavior is self-preservative. Her anxiety is greatly reduced. Her feeling of "I know what I am doing" is increased.

Summary

The procedure reported here, which I have called "conversations with superegos," raises a number of important questions, both about ordinary versus psychopathological psychic structure, and about technique.

First, let us consider the issue of psychic structure. I have argued that the superego is a hostile agency within the mind whose operations are essentially inimical to the patient's growth and well-being. (As an element of psychic structure, the superego can be distinguished from the ego ideal on the basis of the associated affect, that is, guilt rather than shame. Similarly, it is possible that the superego may be constructed on the basis of identifications that are different than those that may form the basis of the ego ideal.)

Further, I have argued that the superego is neither a force for true moral development nor a platform for the voice of the patient's "better" nature, (although it purports to be until challenged). A structure that lies, manipulates, threatens, and appears to be motivated in the end solely by its own continued existence, must certainly be considered suspect as an authority on morality. On the contrary, I see true morality originating in the patient's ego, because in that structure lies the ability to identify with others.

One could object, however, that this way of viewing the matter is an artifact of working with a particular patient population. That is to say, it might be the case that in psychotic and borderline psychotic conditions, the superego does function this way, whereas in healthy or neurotic conditions it does not. In a similar vein, it could be argued that a pattern of development that was sufficiently skewed so as to result in psychosis would be more than likely to have been peopled by hostile, punitive, and essentially destructive identification figures, such as could form the basis for a pathological superego, whereas in normal or neurotic development this might not be the case.

I would disagree on the following basis: I believe that the course of development is laid out by nature; that is, events like the separation-individuation phase, the oral, anal, phallic, and Oedipal phases occur in all of us. It is what *happens* in the course of that development that will lead either to normalcy or various degrees of pathology. For example, we all project. But it is whether we project an expectation that the next person we meet is a decent, civilized human being or a monster out to destroy us that causes us happiness or pain.

That said, my own view of the matter is that the general principal holds for conditions other than the patients reported here, with the difference being one of degree. Where identification figures are essentially benign and foster the development of the self, then their strictures, whether moral or merely practical, would be likely to become assimilated into the ego, without the telltale restriction of reflection and autonomy together with the accompanying guilt that characterize the superego's activity, in which case, we are not talking about superegos at all. What distinguishes psychotic and neurotic development, in my view, is not the issue of whether superego operations are benign or not, but the degree to which the ego is compromised with the resulting formation of fantasy-introjects. I have found, as if it were a principle of physics, that the stronger the ego, the weaker the superego and vice versa. And when some energy of the superego is released, it appears to go directly into the ego without my intervention, though I sometimes ask the "brain's" opinion.

The second issue concerns technique. In psychosis, the voice of the superego is very loud, so much so that there are times when I have had to shout to be heard. On the other hand, my patients report that the voice of the ego may be so quiet that the patient hasn't heard it at all, or hears it as a whisper. Quite clearly, in my conversations with superegos, I adopt a role of advocacy that is quite far from what one would consider a properly "neutral" stance. I treat the superego as though it were an actual presence in the room, finding it interestingly (by patients' suggestions) in area left of the shoulder. (I have no explanation for that, except that in my office, it is furthest from me.) I gradually make clear to the patient that the superego is the enemy that is causing the confusion. (Of course, it is a long time before the patient has had enough experience in these conversations to believe me.) I openly declare war on the superego, by accusing it in various ways of not having the patient's interests at heart, lying, being cruel, and so on. I ridicule it, insult it, challenge it to expose itself, rejoice in its anger at me, and so on. One could not consider such techniques analytic in the usual sense, although the transference and resistance are handled in the usual psychoanalytic way.

In defense of my procedure, let me make a few points. First, I have been regularly startled by what the superegos of my patients have to say for themselves, so to speak. In any science, the more data one can observe, the more likely the scientist is to have a higher degree of success. The microscope, the telescope, and magnetic resonance imaging are all obvious examples of that principle. That is why I frequently instruct my patients not to report what the superego says in the third person, but to speak what the superego says directly, so that we can get the most exact data possible. In addition, the better one knows one's enemy, the more vulnerable. the enemy becomes.

Second, on the basis of my experience, these conversations have regularly led to clinical improvement. Further and very importantly, they have led to greater patient comfort. Anxiety is reduced because chaos is reduced and a general goal is laid out. As I get to know that patient's superego better, the goal gets more specific and the patient knows it, as we can see in Carolyn's last conversation. All this gives the patient the feeling that, at least in general, I know what I am doing. And if I don't know specifically how to solve a problem, I know where to look to find the answer. This is most important, as patients assume in general that their illness is just as inscrutable to an analyst as it is to them. But they can see by my attitude that I am not floundering or dumping all the work on a barely discernible ego. This, I believe, approximates Winnicott's concept of the person as container.

I would like to make a third point in terms of my approach. Uppermost in my mind is the patient's variety and degree of discomfort. Relieving that, either directly or indirectly, is my motivation. I am not viewing the patient as an embodiment of psychopathology, like hallucinations, delusions, thought disorders, and so on. I am aware of those things, but my focus in on the patient's pain and what pathology could be causing it. In other words, I look at the patient empathically, not objectively. (I don't think one has to be a self-psychologist to do that.) To whatever extent I have succeeded in adding to knowledge in this area, I believe that has been an essential factor.

In conclusion, what I try to do is expose the irrationality of the patient's faith in the superego, which has caused him or her so much guilt and terror. Through that process, one hopes the patient will gradually learn to place trust in her or his own ego, thus weakening the former and strengthening the latter.

Let me now describe Kathleen's experience with my conversations with her superego. When she first came to me, she was convinced that there was no hope for her, and said to me with great disdain, as if I were trying to make a fool of her, "You *know* there is no hope." A year later, with a much weakened superego, she announced that far from being contemptuous of me for being hopeful for her, not only did she realize that she had improved considerably, but was convinced she would get quite well.

When I asked this paranoid patient, who used to be certain that all observations about her were meant to hurt her, how she felt about my conversations with her superego, she said laughingly, as if she enjoyed my "blaspheming," "You treat it with such contempt. I like it. It's nice that you are on *my side."* Kathleen is another *patient who tells me she is finding what she calls the "real me."*

Addendum: Recently, Charles Brenner (1994) proposed the idea that psychoanalysis should discard the structural theory and substitute the sole concept of compromise formation. My feeling is that if the field of psychoanalysis were to accept this idea, far from simplifying our work, it would become more complicated. This is especially true in work with schizophrenics, because (a) we would have even fewer tools with which to reduce the chaotic feelings of the schizophrenic (not to mention the confusion of the analyst) and (b) we would be less able to deal with the enormous degree of guilt from which the patient suffers.

Because of the concretistic thinking of the schizophrenic, the structural theory is as illuminated as if it were lit in neon. The schizophrenic gives us a glaring idea of what it is like to have so small an ego (secondary process). Equally clear is the manifestation of the id bursting through with scatological language. And who can quarrel with the idea that it is the superego that is constantly threatening the patient with terrible punishments for the least "infraction" of the "rules"?

In working with schizophrenics, I find the structural theory almost tangible. Further, in this kind of work, I find the term "compromise formation" quite misleading when the patient is most ill. Rather, it seems more accurate to describe the conflict as a fight for life and identity, and that the question is rather, will the outcome be submission or victory?

References

1. Brenner, C. (1994). The mind as conflict and compromise formation. *J. Clin. Psychoanal.*, 3: 473–487.
2. Fairbairn, W.R.D. (1952). Endopsychic structure considered in terms of object relationships. In *Psychoanalytic Studies of the Personality*, Routledge and Kegan Paul, London, p. 111. (Original work published in 1944)
3. Ferenczi, S. (1950). Psychoanalysis of sexual habits. In *Further Contributions of the Theory and Technique of Psychoanalysis*, Hogarth, London, pp. 259–297. (Original work published in 1927)
4. Freud, S. (1923). The ego and the id. In *The Standard Edition of the Complete Psychological Works of Sigmund Freud*, Vol. 10, Hogarth Press, London, pp. 28, 50.

5. Freud, S. (1925). Inhibitions, symptoms and anxiety. In *The Standard Edition of the Complete Psychological Works of Sigmund Freud*, Vol. 21, Hogarth Press, London, p. 118.
6. Freud, S. (1929). Civilization and its discontents. In *The Standard Edition of the Complete Psychological Works of Sigmund Freud*, Vol. 21, Hogarth Press, London, pp. 125–126.
7. Freud, S. (1932). New introductory lectures on psycho-analysis. In *The Standard Edition of the Complete Psychological Works of Sigmund Freud*, Vol. 21, Hogarth Press, London, p. 60.
8. Freud, S. (1937). Constructions in analysis. In *The Standard Edition of the Complete Psychological Works of Sigmund Freud*, Vol. 23, Hogarth Press, London, p. 267.
9. Freud, S. (1938). An outline of psychoanalysis. In *The Standard Edition of the Complete Psychological Works of Sigmund Freud*, Vol. 23, Hogarth Press, London, p. 180.
10. Klein, M. (1948). Early stages of the Oedipus conflict. In *Contributions to Psychoanalysis*, Hogarth, London, p. 202. (Original work published in 1928)
11. Klein, M. (1948). The early development of the conscience in the child. In *Contributions to Psychoanalysis*, Hogarth, London, p. 275.
12. Levin, R. (1965). *The self-critical function of the ego*. Unpublished manuscript.
13. Levin, R. (1986). Infantile omnipotence and grandiosity. *Psychoanal. Rev.*, 73: 57–76.
14. Levin, R. (1987). Awakening the schizophrenic dreamer. *Issues in Ego Psycho.*, 10: 52–64.
15. Levin, R. (1996). "Black hole" phenomena: Deficit or defense? *J. Clin. Psychoanal.*, 5: 175–190.
16. Piers, G., and Singer, M. (1953). *Shame and Guilt*, Charles Thomas, Springfield, IL, p. 11.
17. Sandler, J. (1987). The concept of the superego. In *From Safety to Superego*, Guilford, New York, p. 25.
18. Schafer, R. (1960). The loving and beloved superego in Freud's structural theory. *Psychoanal. Study Child*, 15: 172–186.
19. Schafer, R. (1968). *Aspects of Internationalization*, International Universities Press, New York.
20. Stevenson, A. (1965). *The Stevenson Wit and Wisdom*, Ed. P. Steiner, Pyramid Books, New York.

11
COMMUNICATING WITH THE SCHIZOPHRENIC SUPEREGO REVISITED
A New Technique

I would like to express my gratitude to Helma Wolitzer for asking me a very good question, which added immeasurably to the value of the paper. She asked, "How do you recognize the voice of the superego?"

> In the narcissistic neuroses [psychoses] the resistance is unconquerable; at the most, we are able to cast an inquisitive glance over the top of the wall and spy out what is going on on the other side of it. *Our technical methods must accordingly be replaced by others;* and we do not know yet whether we shall succeed in finding a substitute.
>
> *(Freud, 1917, p. 423; italics added)*

The theory upon which this work is based is the idea that psychosis is a waking dream (Bion, 1962; Esquirol cited by Lothane, 1982, and Rosen, 1953) and that the patient can be "awakened" by having her "dream" interpreted.

In the previous article (Levin, 1996a), I described a technique to facilitate how analyst and patient might find their way in what often seems the morass of schizophrenia. This technique would be equally pertinent to patients suffering from psychotic depression, and to borderlines. For purposes of brevity, I will refer merely to patients with schizophrenia. Since the publication of that article, I have spoken to people who have used this technique but who have had many questions as to how it can be most effectively used. I myself have since resolved some minor questions that have come to the fore in relation to my own patients—as well as questions from colleagues that I had not anticipated in the first paper, or which would not yet have arisen.

I will begin by reminding the reader of Freud's original assumptions about the superego, and then will go on to discuss his later contributions to our understanding of it. Please note that the approach and technique followed in this article do not apply to those patients with benevolent superego communications.

Freud's Assumptions about the Superego

Fortunately, Freud (1923/ 1927) caught himself in an error concerning the veracity of the superego: "I seem to have been mistaken in ascribing the function of "reality testing" to this super- ego" (p. 28). However, I fear he did not carry his correction far enough. The results of his failure to do so will be discussed later, but at this point I would like to insert what may be an explanation of why this happened. Eissler (1971) quotes a letter from Freud to Hollos, a colleague of Ferenczi, who wanted Freud to interest himself in the world of the insane. Freud's response to this request, in short, was "I do not like these patients . . . I am annoyed with them . . . I feel them to be so far distant from me and from everything human" (Eissler, 1971, p. 319). My discovery of this phrase answered questions that I have had for years about Freud's lack of interest in severely ill patients. Despite his passionate interest in the unconscious, he was so repelled by psychotic patients that the knowledge that exploration of their unconscious would have elicited was not available to him.

As we all know, Freud (1923/1927) believed that the superego was the heir to the Oedipus complex. Later authors—most noted of whom was Melanie Klein—disputed the idea that the superego could have evolved so late in the child's life. Loath as many analysts are to dispute Freud overtly, I think most are inclined to believe that the superego's evolution came at least two or three years earlier than Freud believed, even though they may not agree with Klein's speculation that it begins prior to the first year. My assertion is that the superego's evolution was not only the heir to the Oedipus complex and that Freud erred in believing that it was; this is to me an example of a misjudgment that resulted in his feeling of repulsion toward the very ill. I believe that had he been willing to investigate their unconscious material, he would not have made that error. The same may be said about his assumption regarding what he calls "the higher nature of man" (Ibid., p. 36). The "tyrannical superego" is now a well-accepted concept in psychoanalysis. The very label clearly implies that, far from being "higher," it may very well be destructive and immoral.

However, the "tension between the demands of conscience and the actual performances of the ego is experienced as a sense of guilt" (Ibid., p. 37). I doubt there would be many who would dispute the feeling of discomfort that comes with guilt. My question is, how much guilt is necessary to preserve civilization and good mental health? That question was explored directly and indirectly throughout the predecessor of this article and will continue to be explored in this article. I must confess that there is one question related to this for which I have no answer and about which I have wondered for years. I do not know whether the answer will reveal much or little, but it continues to trouble me. That question is, Why does every latency child know that guilt comes from one's conscience, and why do adults—at least the ones in my practice—all seem to have forgotten that concept? In this article, the terms "superego" and "conscience" are used synonymously.

Freud declares that "the mature ego remains subject to its [the superego's] domination. As the child was once under a compulsion to obey its parents, so the ego submits to the categorical imperative of its super-ego" (Ibid., p. 48). To me the important question is, how much domination? When we have a problem—even in neurosis—concerning the tyrannical superego, how much more is it a problem in the serious illnesses?

In this regard, let us consider as an example only one function of the ego, namely, reality testing. Since, as we have seen, Freud admitted being in error in attributing that function to the superego, we must ascribe it to the ego. But if the superego dominates the ego, is not the exercise of that function hindered?

Another area in which that domination is evidenced is in the analysis of neurotics. In *The Ego and the Id*, Freud (1923/1927) vividly describes the "negative therapeutic reaction" which he ascribes to the patient's feeling of guilt (p. 49). But in so doing, he—without meaning to—misses an opportunity. He says this sense of guilt is "dumb" (Ibid., p. 50). Later he insists on it by saying, "Nothing can be done against it directly, and nothing indirectly, but the slow procedure of unmasking its unconscious repressed roots and of thus changing it to a conscious sense of guilt" (Ibid., p. 50). Perhaps with neurotics, this is true.

However, in the severe emotional illnesses, "dumbness" becomes at least "implications" or "hints." That fact has made it possible for the analyst not to be restrained by a "slow procedure," but to attack the superego directly. Freud is concerned later in that footnote about the "analyst [playing] the part of prophet, saviour and redeemer" (Ibid., p. 50). I feel that this risk is small when compared to the tremendous pain and despair of the patient. When someone is in a burning building, it is not very important whether it is a firefighter or a passing pedestrian who saves the victim. Additionally, one can solve any resulting problem later when working on the transference neurosis. Freud brings up this possibility himself:

> In certain forms of obsessional neurosis, the sense of guilt is *over-noisy* but cannot justify itself to the ego. [When this happens in treatment, I handle it by speaking at a high decibel, but without hostility—I refuse to be drowned out.] Consequently, the patient rebels against the imputation of guilt and seeks the physician's support in repudiating it. It would be folly to acquiesce in this, for to do so would have no effect . . . It is possible to discover the repressed impulses which are really at the bottom of the sense of guilt.
>
> *(p. 51)*

I submit that the one does not obviate the possibility of the other, at least not in serious illnesses. The patient suffering from a serious illness whose outcome is believed to be in grave doubt by both patient and analyst need not be left alone floundering about in an ocean of creatures reminiscent of a Bosch painting (see book cover).

Freud raises the question:

> How is it that the super-ego manifests itself essentially as a sense of guilt? If we turn to melancholia first, we find that the excessively strong super-ego which has obtained a hold upon consciousness rages against the ego with merciless violence, as if it had taken possession of the whole of the sadism available in the person concerned.
>
> *(p. 53)*

He answers his question by saying, "What is now holding sway in the super-ego is, as it were, a pure culture of the death instinct, and in fact it often enough succeeds in driving the ego into death" (p. 53). I ask why he has changed his explanation of the development of the superego. Earlier, it came about through identification. Now, he postulates an instinct. This is not a mere academic or intellectual question. The first explanation permits at least a theoretical possibility of cure. But how much of an effect can the analyst have on an instinct? Are we to throw up our hands in the face of severe depression and serious threats of suicide? Those who postulate a "chemical imbalance" would be delighted to hear that. My view is that the death-instinct explanation is useless and prevents constructive work.

Strachey (1934) says that Freud felt that the "ultimate factor in the therapeutic action of a psychoanalyst was the suggestion on the part of the analyst acting on the patient's ego in such a way as to make it more tolerant of the libidinal trends" (p. 133). Strachey himself says "it would seem highly probable that the superego should play an important part, direct or indirect, in the setting-up and maintaining of the repressions and resistances the *demolition of which has been the chief aim of analysis*" (p. 133, italics mine). Strachey also says that "Alexander launched his theory that the principal aim of all psycho-analytic therapy must be the complete demolition of the superego and the assumption of its function of the ego" (p. 134). That is my aim.

But Strachey thinks that is going too far. "It seems probable that its [the superego's] abolition, even if it were practical politics, would involve the abolition of a large number of highly desirable mental activities" (p. 135). Unfortunately, Strachey does not say what he thinks they are, so I am not prepared to agree or disagree when working with neurotics.

Bergler's Views on the Superego

Edmund Bergler (1952) makes several points that are relevant to how I deal with the superego. One important idea he had is that the character of the superego "once established cannot be abandoned or modernized" (p. 16). This is important to notice since patients frequently wish to do just that. They are unhappy at the idea of losing what appears to be their "friend." My view is that pieces of it must either be dissolved or kept, but that the "personality" of the superego cannot be amended. Indeed, we frequently see this same attempt on the part of the patient to change the personality of his parents. For example, a patient may say, "If I could only make my mother understand how much she hurts me, she wouldn't say what she does." The reality unfortunately may very often be the reverse, since a very strong and cruel superego indicates that the parent *wishes* either consciously or unconsciously to hurt her child.

Bergler supports Freud's correction that the superego does not do reality testing. He says that it has a "cavalier disregard for reality and will not accept the usual excuses, some of which may be justifiable" (p. 19). In relation to that, it is important to point out that these patients do not experience compassion either for their efforts or for their pain. (For further material on this subject and ideas that are very similar to mine, see Theodore Rubin's 1975 book *Compassion and Self-Hate.*) Bergler speaks of the superego's "exclusive interest in torturing the ego . . . It camouflages its cruelty by accepting the cultural standards of the specific environment" (p. 19). Evidence for this in the clinical realm is that patients are constantly lecturing me on what "society" says. I have learned that whenever the word "society" is used, it is the superego in disguise purporting to be society's advocate. Of course, each patient's view of what "society" says is idiosyncratic. What is surprising is how firmly that view is held and how certain each patient is that she is being quite objective in maintaining that belief.

Bergler underscores Freud's comment concerning the composition of the superego view: "The superego seems to have made a one-sided choice and to have picked out only the parents' strictness and severity, their prohibiting and punitive function, whereas their loving care seems not to have been taken over and maintained" (Freud, 1923/1927, p. 62). I would like to elaborate on that idea by using a metaphor: that which cannot be "digested" (i.e., internalized into the ego) becomes the superego. I tell my patients that the superego ideas are ones that they have neither digested nor been able to spew out. They cannot be "digested" both because they are false and because they are destructive to the patient; they do not match the patient's "DNA" personality. But the patient also has difficulty spewing them out because she is threatened with isolation if she does so. This is expressed in the superego's reassurance, "I will never leave you." Another metaphor I use is that the problem is the same as a transfusion between blood groups: an "A" type cannot accept "B" blood because the patient will become very ill if she receives blood of a type that is *foreign* to him. This *foreignness* may be the reason that children so often believe they were kidnapped from their real parents and put into a family not their own.

In terms of the technique I am presenting, perhaps the most important lesson we can learn from Freud and Bergler is the derivative of their discovery that we cannot depend on the superego for reality testing. In fact, many years of the study of the superego have gradually led me to the conclusion that the reverse is true: the superego *always* lies. Bion (1962) encapsulates that idea by saying, "It is an envious assertion of moral superiority without any morals" (p. 97). Indeed, I feel it incumbent upon me to stress the idea to the reader that I was extremely resistant to this idea. My attitude was, "Well surely it must *sometimes* tell the truth." In spite of my resistance, however, this turned out not to be true. The only situation where there was an exception to this rule was when both the patient and I, after a great deal of work ridiculing and unmasking had weakened the superego sufficiently that it could not wiggle out of the situation: it would finally admit its hostility toward its host.

The analogy that comes to mind now is akin to those television shows where the police badger a suspect until he finally admits he is the one who committed the murder; or perhaps it is Perry Mason, who finally cuts off every retreat so that the murderer *must* confess. This may appear to be simplistic, but it truly works out this way. Sometimes, however, there is a further problem. It may happen that the patient does not believe or take seriously what has just come out of her own mouth. Here the therapist must be the one to hang on to the" confession" and to do the working through until the patient truly believes she has been betrayed.

Identity and Grandiosity

I ask the reader to accept the premise that in schizophrenia—or even in severe depression—the constant concern of the patient is a feeling of the threat of death (see Hurvich, 2003). This concern is experienced in a psychological rather than in a biological sense. It is a fear of loss of self. Surprisingly, this threat creates even more anxiety than the biological fear of death. The biological fear is what enables soldiers to go into very dangerous situations; but when the patient fully experiences fear of *psychological* death, he or she will go into a panic, perhaps even some kind of paralysis. We see the literal form of this in catatonia.

Paul Williams, in a presentation of January 25, 2003, spoke of a "foreign body." I believe he was referring to the same experience I spoke of earlier. The "foreignness" is—to varying degrees—a threat to the integrity of the self, and therefore produces anxiety. Williams spoke of a patient who heard the voice of a " Director" in her head. Williams said, "I made the mistake of thinking that the 'Director' was malevolent." I submit he was right the first time. I believe that what happens is that the same parent who is at the core of the superego may also teach the child useful and ego-enhancing things such as how to tie his shoes, the definitions of words, or a song that will be meaningful to the child. That knowledge can be digested. However, when that same parent demands constantly that the child give up pieces of herself in order to be a copy of the parent, or constantly disparages the child's creative self-expression, those concepts will become part of the superego (see also Jackson and Williams).

How does this become a threat to the identity? Strangely enough, it comes about at least partially through the child's grandiosity. If a parent makes threats— "If you don't behave yourself, you are going to your room" or "I will leave you

Communicating with the Superego Revisited

home the next time I go out" or "That is the silliest idea I ever heard"—the child feels that she can afford to *give up* the offending behavior (or even thought and emotion) in order not to have to suffer aloneness. These are decisions, though, of a small child who is not old enough to realize that this constant renunciation of pieces of herself will lead to an extremely diminished self. That which a three-year-old believes she can afford to do without, in order to keep herself more comfortable, the adult will recognize as extortion and threat of extinction.

Jane, a patient of mine, constantly gave in to her mother's demands that she not express any feelings at all, or at least that she express only the feelings her mother told her to have. In order to protect him from her mother's anger, Jane never told her father about this state of affairs. She hoped that in return her father would protect her, though he very seldom did so. I pointed out to Jane that she had paid an enormous price—her whole emotional being—for this tiny bit of hoped-for protection. She had renounced so much of herself that later in life she had to be institutionalized; she had behaved as if she could afford deprivation. In treatment, she began to realize she had driven herself to emotional pauperdom for no good reason.

Another patient, Deirdre, found her grandiosity on her own. She wrote in her journal,

> My mother—I see now for the first time—had an image of herself as the Madonna/beatific nurturer . . . Part of her being a Madonna was telling me, "There is nothing like a daughter" [as opposed to a son] and making me feel special in her eyes. [Deirdre felt that it was her responsibility to keep her constantly complaining mother happy.] A certain *elitism* was implied, and I bought it.

It takes a great deal of work on the part of the analyst to get to the point where the grandiosity begins to show. But it is the *linchpin* of the superego. As long as it remains unquestioned, the superego will hang on. The grandiosity is a reward for being obedient to the superego and not questioning the guilt that the superego sends to the patient. However much the patient complains about all the pain he or she endures in complying with the demands of the superego—the constant anxiety of the superego threats, the refusal to defend himself or herself against the insults and contempt of others (much less to attack others for their hostility)—the specialness that the superego promises keeps it all in place. The grandiosity, however, is largely unconscious. That being so, the question is: How do we get to the linchpin?

The Usefulness of Talking to the Superego

Since the grandiosity is so unconscious, must we wait for dreams or slips of the tongue for it to reveal itself? Fortunately, it is not necessary to do so because although the grandiosity is hidden, a very large part of the superego of the seriously disturbed patient is *not*.

Many years ago a patient—who ironically was *not* very seriously disturbed—told me that she heard a "gray voice" in her head. Since I still remember that incident, it had obviously struck me as significant, though I certainly had no idea at that time that the finding could be useful in solving problems of schizophrenics. The result is that I am unable to remember how I gradually came to the idea of speaking to the superego as a method of both understanding it and decreasing its energy. What became clear, however, is that the superego is much more conscious than we, as analysts, had thought.

The discovery that evolved from speaking to the superego is that doing so can gradually decrease its energy. When its energy is decreased sufficiently, the grandiosity of the particular patient will make its appearance to both analyst and patient. The issue is what *kind* of conversations I will have with the patient's superego that will effectively reduce its energy. How best to do that—and seeing how much could be done—is what took so many years for me to learn.

When I speak of talking to the superego, I should make clear that my side of the conversation is either to investigate its position, or to oppose it. Further, when I oppose it, I am either exposing its hostility or retaliating against it for the harm it does to my patient. I have been doing it for so many years that by now it is intuitive, on my part to explore ways to weaken it.

Leston Havens (1986) writes of this view when he speaks of "treatment of such small paranoia psychoses is, first, empathy with pain and then an alliance against the object. A friend can quickly be made by kicking the offending object for the original person" (p. 126). He quotes Fritz Perls: "The therapist places himself on the side of the forbidden wish" (p. 129).

One advantage of the way in which I respond to the superego is that it obviates the difficulty of communicating empathy, because it proves it. I not only make empathic statements, I prove my position by attacking the superego. I believe this has a stronger emotional impact in a shorter length of time. Indeed, I believe that one of the major advantages of my technique is that it is more efficient, that is, it literally takes Jess time to accomplish the hoped-for goal. The same may be said for the psychodrama technique of Moreno, a technique that has the advantage of emotionally exposing the problem, though it does not guarantee that there is a therapist—an experienced authority—to go to bat for the patient (Watkins, 1999).

★ ★ ★

One day after publication of this paper, Dr. Marvin Skolnick called me. He said,

> I tried it on my patient and it worked. I had a patient for a number of years. She calls me when she is upset, and she is very frequently upset. I heard her father's voice. I talked back to it and even began using his name. It expanded the space in a significant way. It broke the impasse. We are objectifying it. It attacks me. I answered it. The patient did not want to give it up for fear of

loss of identity. Now, it is letting out the true self. I became the bad object. But I am also her. I let myself be angry at the superego. She said, "Now I know that you really feel what it is like to be me."

I was interested in this experience because Dr. Skolnick was the first person I knew who had used it, beside me. It reassured me that this was not a personal idiosyncratic experience.

The Nature of the Superego

Using this technique depended on the nature of the superego: I needed to find out what each superego's tools were for attacking any particular patient, where its vulnerabilities lay, etc. Gradually, I realized that I must see the concept of introjection quite concretely. The sicker the patient, the more this is true. The clinician who tries this technique will find that the patient's concept of him or her is *concrete*. For best communication, the analyst must view it the same way.

It is fashionable in some analytic circles to try to force the patient to speak and think on the secondary-process level. To that my response is: Do children grow because we pull their hair up or stretch them on a rack? No. We give them good, nutritious food, hopefully allowing them to eat as much as they would like, and let nature take over. When we try to help a seriously ill patient grow, we look for the *obstacle* that prevents that growth and try to remove it. That obstacle is the superego: it has too much energy because it has deprived the ego of the energy that naturally belongs to it. When that energy is released because of our having weakened the superego and eventually exposed the grandiosity, the patient can grow normally. In other words, the principle on which I operate is to try to remove the obstacle that prevents growth, while recognizing the concreteness of the patient's experience and speaking that language. I do not say to a patient, "I will not speak to you until you are willing to speak *my* language." I say, in effect, "I will speak *your* language until you are awake enough to speak *mine*."

One of the characteristics of patients who are very ill is their intense loneliness. A most revealing disquisition by Frieda Fromm-Reichmann (1990) was published posthumously, followed by several colleagues' comments. To me, what was most important in her and their discussion was the difference between the loneliness of the schizophrenic and the loneliness of others less disturbed; Fromm-Reichmann makes this distinction. Although Mendelson (1990), Mohacsy (1990), Satran (1990), and Hegeman (1990) comment on her paper and seem to feel empathy for it, only Hegeman makes the distinction.

Unlike the other commentators, Hegeman (1990) insists—as do I—that the schizophrenic loneliness is not a question of greater loneliness on a continuum. It has a "frightening and uncanny character ... an incapacity for connectedness and thus a missing of others which is so profound that the other, even in its absence, is not understood or felt as such" (p. 365). She reasons the cause of the loneliness as over-exposure to reality and premature giving-up of fantasy. I found that statement most interesting, since I thought that that was one of the symptoms in what used to be called schizophrenic children. But I have maintained for many years that the ultimate cause is the mother's hatred of the child, and her overt denial of that hatred.

Ann-Louise Silver (1990) also notes that Fromm-Reichmann's description of the loneliness of the schizophrenic is "non-constructive and disintegrative" and comments that the loneliness of the very ill patient cannot talk about it—it is "too terrifying and brings hopelessness" (p. 44)—but then goes on to discuss the expected loneliness of Fromm-Reichmann because of her own growing deafness. I am quite sure that the loneliness did not entail the panic that the severely ill patient endures. An analogy I often make about that loneliness is the following: Suppose you are suddenly placed on an island from which you cannot escape. No one understands your language and cannot learn it—nor you theirs. Nor do you have any hope of someone who understands your language ever landing on this island. I think this situation is what schizophrenic loneliness is like.

A patient has to have a minimal degree of comfort in order to be able to absorb anything from the outside world. If she finds someone who is able to "speak her language"—that is, not tell her that there are no voices when she hears them, or not tell her she is not in danger of being poisoned when she feels poisoned—she will not feel as lonely or anxious as she would with someone who insists on speaking in secondary-process language. The analyst must shift her thinking so that she can accept the idea that in some way there truly *are* voices which she (the analyst) cannot hear and that the patient is being poisoned in some way the analyst does not yet understand (Freud, 1937/1940).

Discovering the nature of the superego took many years. I needed to discover which characteristics were true of one patient's particular superego, and which were *generally* true. Some of the points I will make here have been discussed in the previous article and earlier; but as so much of this material is new, I believe it bears repeating.

1. *All* schizophrenic superegos lie. One can easily make the mistake of thinking that any particular superego is ignorant or foolish or sick itself. If one makes that mistake, one will both waste time and mislead the patient. The superego is intent on keeping its "home" and torturing the patient as much as it can. The latter ensures the former. It knows the truth very well, but it does not want the patient's ego to know it.
2. *All* schizophrenic superegos want to kill the ego. The superego wants a patient to feel as guilty as it can make him or her feel. It wants to disable him or her as much as it can. Sometimes, of course, it does drive the patient to suicide—as if it could survive the patient's death. In my experience, this is the only error it makes. It is this phenomenon that I believe Freud mistook for a death instinct.

3. *All* schizophrenic superegos—when they are challenged sufficiently and are, as I say, with their backs to the wall—will finally admit the truth: that is, they hate the patient and want to kill her or—in the case of a patient who is less sick-damage her.
4. *All* schizophrenic superegos promise always to take care of the owner—a particularly insidious promise. When the superego speaks of "taking care" of the patient, it means it in the sense in which the Mafia would "take care" of one. Interestingly, in *Macbeth* Shakespeare uses that same kind of logic. In Act IV, Scene 1, the second apparition tells Macbeth, "for none of woman born shall harm Macbeth" (Shakespeare, p. 874). Macbeth takes the statement literally and says, "Then live Macduff: what need I fear of thee?" However, we later discover that Macduff was "untimely ripped" from his mother's womb. The third apparition says, "Macbeth shall never vanquished be until Great Birnam wood to high Dunsinane hill shall come against him." Macbeth makes the same error as he had before and says, "That will never be: Who can impress the forest; bid the tree unfix his earth-bound root?" Later, Malcolm has his soldiers cut down a bough of the trees of Birnam wood "and bear it before him: thereby shall we shadow the numbers of our host, and make discovery err in report of us" (p. 881). Thus, the witches behave like superegos: by punning, they lie to him. The analyst, when considering statements from the superego, must constantly be on guard against this kind of deliberately misleading statement, and remember that we frequently make puns in our dreams.

Particular superegos, of course, vary. Some are silent at times, thus leaving both the analyst and the patient unenlightened. All have particular patterns of speech. Some are prone to particular areas of attack, such as constantly telling the patient how stupid she is.

We can see the paranoia of some patients when we speak to superegos and find that what they accuse the patient of is something for which they themselves blame others. For example, the patient looks at a man on the subway and feels that he is laughing at the patient or accusing him of being lazy, etc. In fact, it is the superego that is doing that; however, wanting to appear to be the patient's friend and not be blamed or have its "cover" spoiled, it convinces the patient that it is the man on the subway who is demonstrating this hostile behavior. Such a maneuver can result in the patient's attacking the subway rider, either verbally or physically. Certainly, if there is a great deal of such trickery by the superego, the patient will feel that the whole world is hostile.

Speaking of paranoia, Leston Havens (1986) makes a most interesting point that, in a clinical situation, can confuse the analyst: "Oddly, paranoid people tend to be ingenuous and forgiving. (This has also been my experience.) That may be one reason they become clinically paranoid, having trusted too far and been double crossed" (p. 134). I have found that the paranoia is easy to spot, but the overly naive area in a particular patient can too easily melt into the rest of the personality and cause the patient to come to grief. On the surface, it may look like masochism (Levin, 1998). Is there such a thing as a non-hostile schizophrenic superego?

Is there such a thing as a superego that is not experienced as a blood-sucking vampire or parasite? (I learned those labels from my patients as they began to learn the nature of their superegos.) My answer is: not in the severely ill patient. I will not speak for other patients. Of course the next question is, If superegos are useless as moral guides, what can the patient use in their stead? I will quote the answer to that question, which Kathleen, in my previous article, discovered to her surprise: "I don't need a conscience to make those decisions for me. I'm perfectly capable of deciding for myself what is right and what is wrong, and do it better." I must confess that I was rather surprised at the simplicity of that statement; but after pondering it for some time, I decided she was right. The ego is rational and speaks rationally, unlike the superego: it truly has the patient's interests at heart; it contains the patient's identity; it does not lie to the patient—and, it can reason. As I frequently say to my patients: even if the ego does make a mistake, it happens rarely. If one relies on one's superego, it will always give bad advice, even if it sometimes appears to be correct on the surface.

Guide for the Analyst to Talk to the Superego

When one accepts the premise that the superego is trying to serve its own needs, one needs to respond either overtly or covertly with the question, "What does it hope to gain from making this particular attack on the patient?" For example, the superego may say to the patient prior to a job interview, "You'll never get that job. They will instantly see you are incompetent." If the patient is relatively new to me but has already found her superego and knows I will speak to it, I can ask the superego overtly, "What do you hope to gain by undermining Joan?" It may very well respond by saying, "I don't want to undermine her. I'm just saving her from disappointment." I can say, "You are a liar. You know perfectly well that she can do that job. You are just afraid she will find out how competent she is and really believe it, and then you will not be able to control her as well."

Note that I do not waste my breath arguing about Joan's competence. The superego knows perfectly well that she is competent. I never (or try never to) go on the defensive; I simply attack. This serves to decrease the patient's isolation. Every patient with whom I use this technique tells me how important it is to have someone on their side. From that standpoint alone, my talking to the superego serves the function of decreasing isolation while giving support to the patient in her endless battle to prevent damage and "death" to her identity.

After a while, I encourage the patient to talk to her superego herself. The patient generally makes the error of simply denying the accusations or of merely defending herself. I tell her this is only a holding action and that it will not advance her cause. She must learn to attack: a shield is insufficient—a lance or sword is also required. To whatever extent the patient can accomplish this she decreases her isolation, feels more empowered, and frequently gains further insight into her condition. Also, she can feel that she is in session whenever she wishes to be, to some extent, without my having to be there. (In addition, in an effort to decrease her anxiety I give her a small doll named after me soon after she comes into treatment.) The failure to accuse the superego, rather than simply defend herself, is interesting. It appears to take a very long time for the patient to do that. It seems to me much more an emotional than an intellectual obstacle. My guess is that the patient is just too afraid to do it when she is alone; however, I have not explored that sufficiently to say for certain.

I do also encourage the patient to be aurally sensitive and to distinguish the tone of the superego from the voice of the "brain" (as I refer to the ego when I am speaking to the patient). I want her to be on the alert as much as possible so that as soon as she hears that "instrument," she will be on guard.

How to Recognize the Voice of the Superego

1. The content always has a moral injunction which implies or overtly states "You should" "You should not" or "You should have" or "You should not have," or "That is (would be) right (or wrong)." These are references to behavior or speech, as if there were only one correct way to speak or behave. The idea of "relative morality" is unacceptable to the superego, in the same way that the Christian Right finds relative morality abhorrent.
2. The superego promises always to take care of and never abandon the patient. (The ego, in contrast, never does that; the ego's attitude is that it is being taken for granted by the patient, in much the same way that he or she takes it for granted that his or her hand will not fall off.)
3. The superego insists that it can always control the patient, threatens him with guilt, and causes him irrational anxiety. (Sometimes the cause for the anxiety may look rational, but the superego acts as if the consequence will be "the end of the world." The reality is that it will not. For example: a run in one's stocking is annoying, but it is not the end of the world.)
4. The superego also implies that all negative conditions are irreversible—that is, "You are stupid:—implying that they can never be otherwise. The ego, however, causes anxiety of realistic consequences; for example, if one is about to be hit by a car, one can move quickly to get out of the way and possibly save oneself.
5. The superego pretends to be a friend, but in fact it is destructive:"Don't try to gain (any achievement).You will only get hurt." In fact, the superego fears that the patient may be successful. One important fact that the patient can discover is that she can make the superego afraid—not just the other way around.
6. The superego will increase its dislike of the therapist as it sees the patient improving.

7. The superego attempts as much as possible to make the patient dependent on it and to isolate it from other people—for example, from one's spouse, friends, and therapist.
8. The superego lies, tricks, and manipulates.
9. The superego's criticism is always destructive—not constructive—unlike that of the ego.

Dos and Don'ts When Speaking to the Superego

1. Use your hostility. Here is an opportunity to vent your frustration with the patient. Additionally, if you are really concretizing, you will be angry at the introject for trying to harm your patient. You can speak loudly. You can swear. You can use vulgar language. (In addition to the other benefits mentioned, you will delight the patient when he or she sees and hears you behave in this disrespectful manner to what is—to him or her—the awe-inspiring, sacred superego. It is as if one were able to say to Queen Elizabeth, "Liz, baby, you wear ridiculous hats.")
2. Never look directly at the patient when speaking to the superego. For some reason, I find myself looking to my patient's right. I do not know whether that is significant. One must be certain that the patient does not think the therapist is being so hostile to her—only to her superego.
3. The superego may tell the patient not to listen to me—or that I am lying or crazy. The therapist must advise the patient that this is one of its lies and that it is becoming afraid of the therapist.
4. When the superego says it hates me, I know I have done something very therapeutic; otherwise, it would not be so hostile. One can explain precisely this to the patient, who is likely to be frightened for the therapist when he first hears that. When this happens, I demonstrate my delight very overtly with a big smile and with joy in my voice. The time to worry is when the superego likes the analyst. It may mean that the analyst has fallen into some sort of trap.
5. The superego threatens that if the patient does a particular piece of behavior, she will feel guilty. On the surface, it may appear to the patient that the superego is protecting her from that guilt. However, one must remember that it is only the superego itself that can make the patient feel guilty, so remind the patient that the correct phrasing of that statement should be, "If you do that, I will make you feel guilty." The superego, however, is most unlikely to say this since it would show it (the superego) as responsible for being the "bad" one. An appropriate response for the analyst could be, "Are you going to try to make her feel guilty? Okay. Then by all means, she should do it because then she can truly say she hurt you."
6. Patients must be warned that one can never "kill" a superego though they frequently express a wish to do so. "Killing" implies it has reality. It is a fantasy,

so it can only dissolve. Trying to kill it will lead only to frustration. Concreteness does not make reality. The superego, no matter how concrete it feels, is still only an introject.
7. If the patient says or does enough things that would ordinarily make him or her feel guilty and does so in a defiant—not sneaky—way, the guilt will begin to subside because the superego will see that it has lost the ability to intimidate the patient in that area. Further, the patient's ego will grow with the freedom to do the previously forbidden behavior. One trap the therapist must avoid is that of becoming intimidated by the (patient's) superego's extremely fierce attack when the patient does something new. Warn the patient that this may happen, and advise him that it means he has truly hurt the superego—that is, otherwise, it would not be reacting so ferociously. This is a victory—not a defeat. The fact that the patient can do a previously forbidden behavior means that the superego has, to that extent, lost control. For the superego to lose control means that it is that much closer to dissolution. It is very much a matter of economics: the stronger the ego, the weaker the superego.

Clinical Material

The following are examples of how this technique was used by me and another colleague.

Clinical Presentation

Penny is a young woman in her early twenties who had been on a heavy antipsychotic drug when she came to me and who had gained 65 pounds as a result. At the time of the following interchange—six months later—she is off the antipsychotic and is taking a mild antidepressant.

She is losing weight very nicely and I discover she is beautiful. At the time of the exchange, her grandmother's friend's daughter from Arizona is staying with her. The guest is also quite disturbed but generally over-controlled, and Penny is feeling responsible for her and is overwhelmed by it.

Penny: The job that Daphne wanted is unavailable and she is glad, and she said that maybe she should go home. My reaction was that I was mad because she wouldn't give me a date about when she would go. I have to be a perfect person [the *sine qua non* of a superego statement]. That is why I felt I shouldn't push her to go. I reacted the opposite to how I feel. I do that sometimes. It scared me . . . What will happen to me if she leaves? I fear it will be a negative change.
Therapist: What kind of negative change would it be?
Penny: I can be independent, and therapy would be based on what I feel instead of talking about Daphne all the time. [She has been doing that since Daphne came to live with Penny and her mother.]

The following is my actual spoken dialogue with her superego. Therapist-C represents me, talking to the superego. C-Therapist represents the superego talking to me. Please note that I solicit from the patient what her superego seems to her to be saying in response to my question. This technique, soliciting the response of the patient's superego, is generally followed throughout in this clinical approach.

Therapist-C: What are you trying to do with her?
C-Therapist: She will be in psychosis if Daphne leaves.
Therapist-C: What kind of bullshit is that? [Vulgar language is used purposefully to shock and to show anger. It is deliberately aimed at showing disrespect to the superego in order to contrast it with the patient's expected fawning and frightened feeling toward it. The patient is intimidated by the superego. One thing I want to show is that not only am I not frightened by it, but on the contrary I am contemptuous of it. All of my patients have assumed that it is unthinkable. It would be as if a religious Catholic were to spit on the altar.]
Therapist-C: You want Daphne to stay.
C-Therapist: It would be better for her brain.

To my surprise, Penny says:

Penny: My mental health will be better if Daphne leaves—and you are a liar. [I should specify that Penny sometimes amazes me with her quickness of insight.]
Therapist-C: You hate me, don't you?
C-Therapist: Yes, because you make her better and I can control her mind and make her ill, and you interfere with that.
Therapist-C: You are grandiose to think you can do that to her. [Said with contempt.]
Penny shows she understands by saying,
Penny: Speaking of grandiosity, I feel I made John [apparently a manic-depressive whom Penny went with for some time) suicidal.

Having presented this snippet of my work with Penny, I would in addition like to present what was for me a pleasant surprise. I thought that if my theory about this technique is correct, I should also be able to be successful with auditory hallucinations. Penny came to me complaining of voices and severe anxiety attacks. Two weeks after she began treatment with me, I decided to try to talk to her voices if she gave me the opportunity. The apparent precipitating factor for her psychosis, which had begun two years prior, was a physical beating by James.

Therapist: You have a choice. You can talk more about the beating, as you said you wanted to last time, or we can focus on the voices.
Penny: The voice. It said, "I'm going to hurt you."

Communicating with the Superego Revisited

Therapist-C: What are you up to? [Having made it clear that I am talking to the voice.]
C-Therapist: She tries to ignore me, but you keep talking to me.
Therapist-C: Why are you trying to hurt her?
C-Therapist: I don't like her, and she's done wrong.
Therapist- C: You did something wrong.
C-Therapist: It's what James did.
Therapist-C: You are James. [While it is clear by how Penny is talking that James—and not the original superego—is the voice, I talk to it, trying to get it out of the way so that I can talk to the original superego. In this particular situation, it is clear that the James image has attached itself to the superego.]

It is made quite complicated by the fact that the mother has the usual kind of personality that patients who become schizophrenics have, that is, superficially devoted to their children but unconsciously extremely hostile to them. Additionally, Penny's father was an emotionally abusive man, and the marriage broke up when Penny was two. At any rate, all these hostile figures have apparently joined up together and become the superego; it is my job to tease them apart.]

C- Therapist: James said that he does that to a lot of girls. [Here we see it slightly separating from the original superego, but I want to make certain I make him frightened of me.]
Therapist-C: You were scared of falling in love with her.
C-Therapist: I know I did wrong.
Penny: I think I hear that because I've been murdered. [This is a wonderful description of what the superego attempts to do to the ego.] It's a big change.
Therapist: [Quite startled.] You think you died?
Penny: I'm relieved. I'm not the only one who hears it, but it's also psychotic.
Therapist: How do you feel about my talking to it?
Penny: It makes me feel good. Like I was being helped. No one ever did that before. [Penny underwent many kinds of therapy when she was a child, presumably for behavior problems.] I felt I did something wrong. [There is the guilt that the superego foists on the ego.]
Therapist: How did you feel when I blamed it? You thought you were responsible for what he did.
Penny: I see myself as a dummy that I didn't see it coming.
Therapist: By taking responsibility, you were killing yourself.
Penny: I can't believe he is that way. [She had prided herself on being a good judge of character.]
Therapist: You wanted to believe he was someone wonderful. It's hard for you to accept that he was a phony.

Penny: I have a greater expectation of myself. It's hard to believe he was such an asshole. When you were talking to my conscience, I thought I was crazy or you were crazy. I feel you are helping me.

One month later, I am able to talk to the voice as the original superego, that is, the mother.

Penny: I am doing well, but was afraid I would be a lone. About the voices. I think it was that I was so anxious that I started hearing things. I'm going from nine milligrams to four milligrams of anti-psychotic. In one month, I will be off it. I don't feel a difference. I feel I will be very scared.
Therapist-C: Wouldn't you love it if she were to feel anxious after dropping the drugs?
C-Therapist: I can get her anxious. It's not that hard for it to come back.
Penny: I have anxiety even with a family member.
Therapist-C: You want her to lose people.

Following this, she tells me exactly how she was assaulted. She said, "It's so gross, I feared you wouldn't see me anymore." By the time she is completely off the antipsychotic, it is two months from the time I first talked to her voices and she no longer hears them. She does occasionally hear murmurs, but she is unable to distinguish what they say. They do not seem to trouble her, however, and I have no insight into their meaning.

Six months later, Penny and I have the following short exchange:

Penny: My conscience says to me, "You disgust me."
Therapist-C: What bothers you about her being beautiful?
C-Therapist: The more beautiful she is, the more she will get assaulted.
Therapist-C: You get jealous. You can't stand it.
C-Therapist: I don't like it when she is confident. [I always try to consider that the reality is the opposite feeling of what the superego complains of. Here I pushed the superego into a corner and it is forced to admit its joy in Penny's anxiety.]

By way of contrast, I had another patient who heard voices. I discovered this six months after I started seeing him. I spoke to those voices, and one week later he reported to me that he hadn't heard them all week. But when I made the mistake of agreeing that they were voices, he fled. His father had committed suicide as a result of his own schizophrenia, and my patient was just his age when he was seeing me. My emotional response to both patients is that while I am not surprised that the problem was responsive to this technique, I am surprised at how quickly they (the voices) were disposed of.

Dialogue by a Colleague and His Patient

The following is a presentation by Marvin Hurvich, Ph.D. [The following text has been approved for publication by Dr. Hurvich. -*Ed.*]

> I consulted with Revella Levin about a patient I have been seeing for 25 years who, though she had made significant and tangible progress over the years, was dominated by a hostile introject. A brief description of the patient is followed by a series of exchanges illustrating my response to the patient which was based on Levin's approach to such material.

Hurvich: This is a 48-year-old female patient with borderline personality organization who functions near the psychotic border. She has made a number of suicidal attempts, which were often followed by psychotic episodes. She is in an ongoing struggle to retain her sanity, but the pull toward death and psychosis is strong. The patient experiences a "Black Force," an inner presence that dominates and controls her. This introject threatens death if the subject tries to grow psychically, have good relationships, cooperate with the therapist, or take pride in any achievement or personal characteristic.

> It's like a ghost that lives inside me and appears at certain times. It takes over and tells me what to do. And if I don't comply, it forces me, and then it says, 'I won, I'm stronger than you.' So much of the time it completely rules me, occupies my mind and body, and destroys my will. When the FORCE tells me I can't do something, I can't. When I try to do something for myself, it rises up and pushes me back down again. It drains my energy. Like another me, I have dialogues with it. It has a grip on me and is trying to squeeze me until I break. I'm not safe any place. The FORCE can invade every cell of my being and I can't get him out. I'll never escape. The FORCE has trained me to obey or keep silent, and I'm scared. [Of what?] That I'll lose control and hit you and pull the books off of your shelves." [I suggest here I would not leave that fear undisturbed. I would first have established whether it was she or the FORCE who would hit Hurvich. If it were she, I would ask why she would hit Hurvich instead of hitting the FORCE. If it were the FORCE, I would point out how powerless it would be to carry out that threat since it has no body—which gets a laugh.] "It's like a cyclone feeling—that spinning feeling that was in that early dream I told you about.

Here is a sampling of the patient's statements, and my Levin-influenced responses:

Patient: It forces me . . .
Therapist: It can't force you if you fight back.
Patient: I can't stand up to it.

Therapist: Yes, you can. It wants you to believe that lie. [Comment by Levin: My compliments to Hurvich that he caught the lie so soon.]
Patient: I can't. It's too strong!
Therapist: I'll fight alongside you. [Then I turn to the side as though talking to the FORCE.] You're afraid that K. will get strong, and that makes you weaker: you're in trouble.
Patient: I'll lose control and hit you and pull all the books off your shelf.
Therapist: Is that the FORCE, or is it you? [Comment by Levin: Here Hurvich does ask the patient who will do it, but does not demand an answer.]
Patient: If the FORCE went away, I'd be toast.
Therapist: No, you'd be fine. [Comment by Levin: Here Hurvich fell into the trap so easily fallen into by both therapist and patient: a denial of the fact only gives momentary relief and does not offer an effective blow. I would have added something like, "It wants you to believe that lie" or "It would be toast."]
Patient: I have no capacity to get upset and angry. I'd be without power, defenseless.
Therapist: You need your anger to stay alive—your anger, not its anger! Your anger will save your life. [Comment by Levin: Bravo. At one stroke, Hurvich strikes a blow which can potentially deprive the superego of the power of its hate and offer the power to the patient. I hope he will pursue that line in future sessions. And note: the patient got the message.]
Patient: It holds all my anger.
Therapist: We have to get it to release your anger.
Patient: It takes care of me.
Therapist: It's like the Mafia takes care of you.
Patient: It's my negative friend.
Therapist: It's not your friend at all.
Patient: I must keep him inside to protect others.
Therapist: I am not afraid of the FORCE: you can let it out.
(End of Hurich presentation)

This can be an introduction to further conversation directly to the superego.

I should repeat that very often after a successful blow, the superego will attack the patient more viciously than before because its survival is threatened. Unless the patient is warned about this, she may get discouraged. This is what Hurvich's patient complains about. The patient must be told that the fact that the conscience is acting up so much is proof that it has been wounded-a reason to rejoice, not to be discouraged.

A more difficult patient is one who identifies with the superego. In that situation the patient is constantly confused as to which she is and which the superego is, thus making it much more difficult for both therapist and patient. I have two such patients now, and I believe I have the solution. I will write about this problem later.

A factor that I have implied but that may be directly stated is that the superego has a variety of tricks, manipulations, threats, etc. Of course, each superego has a different repertoire, so that each patient becomes a different "teacher." This variety is one of the reasons that it took me so long to evolve a comprehensive theory. Stemming from this is my discovery that the therapist must fulfill one requirement: he or she must have an emotional concept of what an enemy is. Some people are quite naïve in the sense that they have difficulty in believing that others intend to do them harm, at least on a one-to-one basis (Levin, 1998). Such a therapist may not be capable of doing this kind of work successfully. The therapist must understand that the use of this technique requires an emotional-not merely an intellectual-attitude; it is a fierce and unrelenting battle. As Eissler (1971) says, "The therapist's own emotionality has to become the carrier of the therapeutic action" (p. 225). Certainly, when working with schizophrenics the therapist must know in the back of his or her mind that the patient has experienced a life-long panic as to whether or not the next moment might bring the death of her identity (Hurvich, 2003).

In various ways, some therapists have recently been commenting to me (see Chapter 17) that they have been or are now "burned out" (Levin, 2000). One therapist hit the nail on the head, I thought, when she said, "When you have no impact, you get burned out." I hope you will agree with me that this technique makes it less likely that such an eventuality will occur.

I remind the reader of the patient the late Marvin Scolnick told me about: he had a patient who persistently called him at home (to his great frustration) and he used my technique. He found that it worked perfectly, and the patient did stop calling him. I must credit him with the idea that this technique is useful when the therapy or the therapist is stuck and cannot get out of the quagmire. That thought had not occurred to me until I reviewed my experiences and realized how many times I had used it in just such a situation automatically.

To you who are interested in trying this technique on your difficult patients, I think I can safely promise you, at the very least, an exciting intellectual adventure. We can, of course, continue to treat psychotics solely with drugs and allow them to suffer all the attendant psychological and extra-pyramidal side effects of those drugs-and further, not to interfere with their hopelessness. (I have had so many patients come to me with terrible unhappiness at being told, "I will have to be on drugs for the rest of my life." They understand that this means they are not only incurable but are condemned.)

The fact of the matter is that there are various approaches that can help patients, of which mine is just one. These approaches are being used in Canada, Western Europe, and South America and are beginning to be used in Eastern Europe. These therapists are actually trying to listen to patients and to understand them. Do we not have a responsibility when a patient comes to us for help to do the best we can? Yes, it will take more work on our part, both intellectually and emotionally. But is that a sufficient reason to throw all the relevant books out and pull out the prescription pad?

Summary

The technique of the analyst speaking to the superego was inspired by my discovery that the superego was far closer to consciousness than I or the psychoanalytic world in general had thought. When patients began to tell me what their superegos were saying to them, I felt that their superegos were not just attacking them, but attacking me, and I could not resist attacking back. This was on the grounds that I felt it would undermine the relationship if the superego attacked me and I did not attack back, that is, I would look helpless to my patients. Further, I saw how therapeutic it was for both my patient and for me to have such immediacy. At the same time, I saw, of course, that Freud was in error, as I noted earlier when he said that the sense of guilt was "dumb." Indeed, it can speak-sometimes quite loudly. (see Chapter 9)

As I continued to search out the superegos of my patients, I discovered that the patient could find the "voice" fairly easily. At times, the patient might complain that I was crazy to want to have such dialogues, but as we continued to do it and as the patient saw how empowering such interaction was, the complaints discontinued and changed increasingly into delight.

This discovery makes it much easier to free the amount of energy the superego possesses. This in turn makes it possible for the freed energy to be acquired by the ego so that the patient can gain greater control over his or her life.

As I discovered that the superego was more available than I had previously thought, I began to develop the technique that enabled me to help the patient gain greater control over the superego, and as a result help the ego grow. The greater energy that the ego could gain from this process enabled the patient to deal with her problems with greater rationality and gain a firmer sense of identity. She came to be less at the mercy of her superego.

This second article endeavors to point out pitfalls that the therapist may fall into and describes more fully the nature of the superego, so that the therapist can aid in more efficient drainage of energy from the superego. Because of other therapists' attempts to use this technique, I have learned better how to help others use it. It also enabled me to discover that hallucinations can be dissolved psychotherapeutically. Naturally, delusions can be more easily decoded through this method. I am making no claim for its usefulness for neurotics since I do not have experience using it for other than schizophrenics, borderlines, and severely depressed patients.

Having used this technique gradually more and more with schizophrenics for the past 20 years, I feel quite knowledgeable about it. It is my hope that others will find it useful, too, and to that end I am making myself available as a resource for therapists who are interested in using it.

In the course of editing this book, I remembered a patient I had near the beginning of my career. I will name her Louise. I have no notes on her but I do remember the following facts about her. She was about 25, the oldest of five children. The family was devoutly Catholic. All the children attended parochial schools. Louise had a steady clerical job.

I only remember the feelings that I had, i.e. the therapy was going well. But there was one important obstacle. She implied that in her adolescence, she had had a psychotic episode. But no amount of my urging would get her to tell me about it.

After a while she left me. Clearly she was not making substantial progress. Then, some time later, she returned, but then shortly after left again.

As I was editing this book, I recalled her to a small degree. Now I realized that if I had known about my technique of communicating with the schizophrenic superego then, I could have solved the problem. When she came back to me, I got a small hint that she had received a "message," i.e., that her fears *protected* her. That as long as she didn't talk about them, she would be safe. And she believed the message. Her therapy was clearly a failure, despite the fact that she gave me a second chance.

If I were seeing her now, I would have recognized that that was the superego talking, and I would have attacked it as a liar, wanting to control Louise and making a fool of her. Without that knowledge, I was "weaponless." After she left me for the second time, I never saw her again. And I suppose she is on some kind of drugs.

Now I see how much more helpless I would have been, had I not begun talking to the superegos.

References

1. Bergler, E. (1952). *The Superego: The Key to the Theory and Therapy of Neurosis*, Grune and Stratton, New York.
2. Bion, W.R. (1962). *Learning From Experience*, Jason Aronson, London.
3. Eissler, K. (1971). *Talent and Genius*, Quadrangle Books, New York.
4. Freud, S. (1916/1917). General theory of neuroses. In *The Standard Edition of the Complete Psychological Works of Sigmund Freud*, Vol. 16, Hogarth Press, London.
5. Freud, S. (1927). The ego and the id. In J. Strachey (Ed. and Trans.), *The Standard Edition of the Complete Psychological Works of Sigmund Freud*, Vol. 19, Hogarth Press, London. (Original work published in 1923)
6. Freud, S. (1933). The new introductory lectures. In J. Strachey (Ed. and Trans.), *The Standard Edition of the Complete Psychological Works of Sigmund Freud*, Vol. 22, Hogarth Press, London. (Original work published in 1932)
7. Freud, S. (1940). Constructions in analysis. In J. Strachey (Ed. and Trans.), *The Standard Edition of the Complete Psychological Works of Sigmund Freud*, Vol. 19, Hogarth Press, London. (Original work published in 1937)
8. Fromm-Reichmann, F. (1990). Loneliness. *Contemporary Psychoanalysis*, 26: 305–329.
9. Havens, L. (1986). *Making Contact*, Harvard University Press, Cambridge, MA.
10. Hegeman, E. (1990). The paradox of loneliness: A comment on Fromm-Reichmann's "loneliness." *Contemporary Psychoanalysis*, 26: 361–366.
11. Hurvich, M.S. (2003). The place of annihilation anxieties in psychoanalytic theory. *JAPA*, 579–616.
12. Levin, R. (1996a). Communicating with the schizophrenic superego. *Journal of the American Academy of Psychoanalysis*, 24, Winter: 709–736.

13. Levin, R. (1996b). "Black hole" phenomena: Deficit or defense? A case report. *Journal of Clinical Psychoanalysis*, 5(1).
14. Levin, R. (1998). Faith, paranoia and trust in the psychoanalytic relationship. *Journal of the American Academy of Psychoanalysis*, 26, Winter: 553–573.
15. Levin, R. (2004). *The burnt out therapist, presented to ISPS*. Unpublished, Chicago, IL.
16. Lothane, Z. (1982). The psychopathology of hallucinations—a methodological analysis. *British Journal of Medical Psychology*, 55: 335–348.
17. Mendelson, M.D. (1990). Reflections on loneliness. *Contemporary Psychoanalysis*, 26: 330–355.
18. Mohacsy, I. (1990). Solitude in a changing society: A discussion of Fromm-Reichmann's "loneliness." *Contemporary Psychoanalysis*, 26: 360–363.
19. Perls, F. (1973). *The Gestalt Approach and Eyewitness Therapy*, Science and Behavior Books, Palo Alto, CA.
20. Rosen, J. (1953). *Direct Analysis*, Grune and Stratton, New York.
21. Rubin, T. (1975). *Compassion and Self-Hate*, Simon and Schuster, New York.
22. Satran, G. (1990). A note on Fromm-Reichmann's "loneliness." *Contemporary Psychoanalysis*, 26: 367–369.
23. Shakespeare, W. (2003). *The Complete Works*, Barnes & Noble, New York and China.
24. Silver, A.S. (1990). Frieda Fromm-Reichmann, loneliness and deafness. *International Forum on Psychoanalysis*, 15: 39–45.
25. Strachey, J. (1934). The nature of the therapeutic action of psychoanalysis. *International Journal of Psychoanalysis*, 15: 127–159.
26. Watkins, P. (1999). *Psychodrama*, SAGE Publications, London.
27. Watkins, P. (2003). Speech given on January 25, 2003, American Academy of Psychoanalysis.
28. Jackson, Murray and Paul Williams (1994). *Unimaginable Storms*, Karnac Books, London.

12

IDENTIFICATION WITH THE SCHIZOPHRENIC SUPEREGO

Carolyn, to whom I have referred in previous papers, was extraordinarily resistant. The work was going very slowly. People in our field often tell us how important it is to have a therapeutic alliance. Indeed, I have often read in work by well-known authors that, without a therapeutic alliance, therapy cannot be done. To Carolyn, that concept was as foreign as snow in July. For at least half the time, therapeutic war would have been a more apt description. Without exaggeration, I can safely say that in the nine years I have been treating her, she has threatened to leave at least 100 or 150 times. In earlier times, at least once a month, she would not appear for a session for which she knew she would have to pay. Any session, in which I was more than usually insightful would be followed by a session that was mostly spent with her attempts to manipulate me, trick me, ignore me, lie to me and resist in any way, she could. In effect, no good deed of mine went unpunished. On November 1997, the following interchange took place:

I: Are you frightened of being alone?
C: Yes, it's creepy being alone. It's like being in another world.
I: Who are you without?
C: My mother and my guilt. Yes, I'm without my mother but I'd like being alone if I **were** my mother.
I: (startled) If you are your mother, then where is Carolyn? (At this point I have the insight that she is literally identified with her mother and she is not Carolyn when she is hostile.)
C: Then I am her. I hate her. I don't want to be her. I could let her go, if I knew where to put her (looking genuinely puzzled as to where, literally, to put her mother). What do I say? If I was her, she'd love me. Same thing with Johnny

(her dead brother about whom she has obsessed for 18 years when she first came to see me.) I'd keep him alive.
I: You're Johnny too?
C: I'm not Johnny. He is too hard to be.

This was how I discovered that a patient could literally revoke her own identity and assume that of her parent, thereby—as I learned later more clearly—convincing herself that she could "force" her mother to love her. But by doing so, she takes on all the superego's motives in trying to keep the patient ill and fighting off all the therapist's interventions. Worse yet, the more potent my interventions were, the more severely did Carolyn attempt to punish me.

Some seven months previous, the following exchange took place:

C: My guilt is scary.
I: What is your conscience saying?
Conscience: We don't want them (parents) to die.
I: (astonished because I still had not grasped the extent of the identification) You and your conscience have the same wish?
C: That is horrifying. Conscience wants me dead. I want to die. I have to separate myself from my conscience.

I believe that it was because of Carolyn's secrecy that I was so slow to gather the full impact of the identification. I must also confess that I didn't know what do about it, except to keep chipping away at it. However, the discovery of this identification explained a great deal of my difficulty with this patient. As came out recently, she trusted her conscience when it said that if she spoke the truth of her childhood, she would go crazy. I was the enemy. The superego was the friend. This was quite unlike my other patients who would quickly begin to recognize how much their superego wished them ill, wanted to control them etc. Later in the session, she expresses her identification by saying "I like being sick and keeping secrets." Previously such a statement as "I like being sick" would leave me totally confused. In my view schizophrenics, however irrational their thinking may appear to be, always want to get well. Near the end of the session, Carolyn said, "I'm ready to leave. Conscience says we have to leave." Partly to be therapeutic and partly to let my hostility out, I said to the superego, "You can go and Carolyn can stay." She stayed.

I will present several exchanges starting from 1998.

C: I'd have been better off without you. Did that hurt you?
I: For what crime do you want to punish me? (I was always looking for the answer to that question.)
C: For having helped me. (After this session, she left a message on my machine saying she was leaving therapy, in a tone of voice that she always uses, as if it were the first time she had ever said that).

The following is a long speech in which one can see how she switches from identifying with the superego and being herself. She begins as herself:

> If my mother (Mildred) stays, I will die. If she goes, I will find me and the good things, and be a more compassionate person. I would be alive, so why don't I send her away? Maybe I could have her on the outside of me. She would still be my mother. Maybe I can move her out of me and still have her. I can still have my longing and wishes.[1]

Now see how she switches over to the superego:

> "If I become the real me, I'll throw out my wishes. You don't want me to have my wishes."

Now back again to being Carolyn:

> "When it's me, I 'm smart. When I'm her, I'm stupid. When I'm her, I'm drugged."

The "drugged" state is equivalent to what she calls being in a "fog," when she looks a bit stuporous and clearly identifies with the superego, as if in a hypnotic state. This has been a problem since the beginning of treatment. I was sure she could get out of the fog if she wanted to with a snap of her fingers, but I didn't know her motivation for staying in it, so I didn't have the tools to resolve the problem. When she is in that state, I have to repeat things as few times for her to hear me and she was unable to think, truly like someone in a deep sleep.

A later exchange:

Carolyn:	I don't like being in therapy (a frequent complaint, as in "I don't like your therapy" and "I don't want to be sick, so I will stop coming to therapy [sic]")
I to conscience:	You are having a hard time keeping Carolyn sick, aren't you?
Carolyn:	(Brightens up) Actually she is having a hard time keeping me sick. I shouldn't give it away.
I:	But you show no anger. You let her have her way.
C:	I was amazed that recently, I felt safe without her. For so long I felt and believed my parents, that I needed them. I thought "I'll pretend to be dumb, so they'll love me. But without her, I'm happier, whole, safe in my own harbor."

That is Carolyn speaking. But of course, it is only temporary. In fact, I think this period is when I felt she had stopped being Mildred, but I took a week or so off and when I returned, she was back again to being Mildred. No amount of questioning availed me. No matter how happy she was being Carolyn (and she admitted being very happy), she would not tell me why she regressed and why she would not budge again.

Through most of her therapy, she believed that she had what she called "God in my pocket." This God was supposed to protect her and her alone from pain. To an extent it actually worked in that she was very good at manipulating people into doing what she wanted them to do. For example, even though she was frequently fired, she was a wonder at getting jobs. She was also very good at manipulating me, because I did all the work. (Of course, as I frequently pointed out to her, that it made it go slower, since I had less access to the material.) If she did come up with an insight, she treated it with extraordinary lack of importance. As she once pointed out, "you get more excited about my insights than I do." (Only recently did I discover that all this time, her superego, was telling her that her insights were unimportant, as soon as she spoke them.) In the latter part of '98:

C: God and I are stronger than you. I wanted to get back at you. I feel like going home. I want conscience to take over. I can't bear that you, a mortal, can win over my God.
I: What are you doing about it?
Carolyn's conscience says "we are a team," (there is the non-therapeutic alliance).

A frequent complaint:

C: You think you're right about everything. (said with great bitterness.)
I: Yes, I am most of the time. I have your brain. You gave yours away, so you think I have it. Why do you promote Mildred?
C: I thought that was the only way to have power. (Deirdre, a patient I will soon discuss later on, said that "Protecting conscience is the only way to get along in the world.")

Somehow I discovered that Mildred stands in front of Carolyn in her mind's eye. I said "You are embarrassed that I'll see Carolyn and not Mildred." In terms of technique, it is important to be aware of that when I am attacking Mildred. If not, the patient will experience me as attacking her. I could even tell Mildred to get away from being in front of her.

I: How does that make you feel?
C: You and I are a team? (quite spontaneously and a surprise to me) It makes me feel vulnerable and naked.

Now we come to the problem of trying to explain why this identification happened. But first let me tell you about Deirdre. She is in her middle forties as is Carolyn. But she is not as ill. She has no delusion that I am aware of. But she came to me very depressed, and wanting to go off medication. Like Carolyn, she has had 20 years of therapy, but with various therapists, unlike Carolyn, who only had one other therapist. Carolyn has been with me for 9 years, while Deirdre has been with me for only one and half years. Both patient complain that their mothers hated them because their daughters were not like them. This view carne up in different ways and I finally realized that they were both saying the same thing.

Deirdre came into the world with her umbilical cord around her neck. Her mother and her minister father were both convinced that she was brain damaged, at least partly due to the suggestion of the intern who was involved in the case. But like Carolyn, Deirdre's early life was apparently free of identification with their superegos. Indeed, Deirdre relates with obvious glee how she and a few boys played in the vacant lot next door. She was the leader of the gang. She recently related to me how they had a "pee pot" that they all used when they couldn't be bothered going to the bathroom and indulged in other such mischief.

But Deirdre's mother could not allow her to have anything of her own, including her own taste in home furnishings or clothes. Deirdre finally ended up playing in her closet, because her mother took her garden away from her. Indeed, she is a very good example of another factor that is involved in this problem. Although she is quite bright, even she has difficulty differentiating her own thoughts from those ideas that come from her superego. I find I need to point out each aspect of the difference patiently, as if she were stupid. In my previous paper, I have pointed out the different sound that the superego voice has for each patient, but she still has difficulty distinguishing the voice of her superego from her own.

The following are some examples of how Deirdre identifies herself with her mother/superego. In January of this year, she reported a phone conversation with her father, in which he was more responsive than usual. Comparing him with her already dead mother, she said, "She would swallow me up." This should be treated as being experienced concretely not metaphorically. Otherwise, the patient will not feel truly understood nor have sufficient emotional courage to attack the problem.

In February, the following conversation with her superego took place, regarding her getting a new job, which she badly needs.

Conscience: She is a sleeper.
I to con.: What is a sleeper?
Con.: A sleeper is a really good movie that no one knows about. Deirdre doesn't need to know that.
I: Wow! What do you think of that, that is you don't need to know that?
D: It shows how totally dishonest it is. It is a liar. The truth is that it feels "I don't want her to know that."
I: It said that as if it were in your interest, not its interest for you not to know that. (Here is an example of how the superego encourages the

	host to believe that their interests are identical, not opposing, so that the patient aids in her own destruction.)
D:	It is a symptom of the problem. It is in power. Its demands are voracious. The gall, the horror (very angry) that attitude of superiority.
D to Con.:	You say Deirdre as a weak link squashed down. It is a dance, when it should be a battle. Before I thought all the negativity was me.
I:	Yes, when you were being your mother. (3)

In March, she said, as if she were a therapist, "If there is a barrier between a child and a parent and there is no relationship between the two, a child will die. Remember I told you, that when I was young (late teens), I wondered if I existed. I felt like I had abandoned my corpse." (In fact, the year before, she told me "I have to eradicate myself in order to survive.")

In this session, I encouraged her hostility so that in the following session, she said," I know my mother felt she was entitled to own me." Later, she said, "After the session I saw my mother's presence stepping away from me. It was very faint but really important. The implication was that I was possessed, sort of dead."

With both patients, I had just been chipping away, but wished I could find a shorter route, a device in the same way I had found one in the previously mentioned "Black Hole" paper. And then Carolyn gave me a clue. About a month ago, she let me know that her dead brother, Johnny, had loved her. In all the years I had worked with her, she had never given me an inkling of that. But it was at the time of his death that Carolyn formed the delusion that she had God in her pocket. My discovery that Johnny loved her and bringing to her consciousness the same fact, brought us an alliance most of the time. We were going forward at an excellent pace when the following happened.

C:	I wished my mother would have held me. When Dobson (her dentist on whom she has a crush) touches me, it's warm. My mother was so much not the mother I wanted, either intellectually or emotionally. I became her to see what it was like to be her, to see how she saw the world, to be close to her, because she was so foreign to me. Now I am more connected to the human race.
I:	It is very interesting that you are so happy because you always fought off the human race.
C:	I feel connected to the warmth and joy of others, like Roseann at work with whom I have a real relationship.
I:	And if your mother is foreign to you, what is the result?
C:	She and I are strangers. Now I see her as receding and you are coming toward me. (Previously we saw Deirdre describe a similar receding of her mother.)
C:	I feel healthier, sane, more separate. Why is that so? Suddenly I don't know her. I know myself better.

Then I recalled that both patients complained in essence that their mothers hated them because the daughters were different from themselves. This view came up in different ways and I finally realized that they were both saying the same thing. They both sounded depressed and frustrated when they expressed that feeling and it finally came to me, that that experience was what caused the identification with the superego. Now I feel I have at least a handle on the problem. The mothers could not accept how different their daughters were from themselves, so they simply denied their children's identities. The children, finding it impossible to get close to their mothers or have them recognize who they were, felt they had no other course but to reject their own identities and completely identify with their mothers. They experienced it as a matter of survival.

Here, although I am usually skeptical of genetic explanations, I feel it is appropriate to hypothesize one. I think there are genes for aesthetic tastes. I am using the word "aesthetic" in a very broad sense, i. e., anything one likes or doesn't like, which not only includes arts, but the sense of taste, weather, an interest in politics etc. I think the daughters were experienced by their mothers, as foreign, and so, held them as far away from themselves as they could. But the children found this so intolerable that they closed the gap by denying their own genetic proclivities and trying to adopt their mothers' tastes.

I found the denouement striking. Carolyn is now seeing her mother as foreign, rather than herself. This gives her an opportunity to rejoin the human race whose caring she always demanded but rejected, because she felt she did not deserve it unless her mother loved her first. Deirdre is now seeing her identity as that of an artist, but is not yet ready to see her mother as foreign.

In closing, I would like to refer the reader to Franco de Masi's article "Intimidation at the Helm: Superego and Hallucinations in the Analytic Treatment of Psychosis." De Masi's approach appears to be quite similar to mine, although he does not suggest a specific technique. However, de Masi may give the reader another perspective on the same problem, which may provide some cohesion and insight.

Note

1 This is a reference to the beginning of her therapy and her insistence on throwing out wishes that couldn't be fulfilled (see Chapter 6).

References

1. Levin, Revella. (1996). Communicating with the schizophrenic superego. *The Journal of the American Academy of Psychoanalysis*, 24(4), Winter.
2. Levin, Revella. (1996). 'Black Hole' phenomena: Deficit or defense? *Journal of Clinical Psychoanalysis*, 5(1).
3. de Masi, Franco. (1997). Intimidation at the helm: Superego and hallucinations in the analytic treatment of a psychosis. *The International Journal of Psycho-Analysis*, 78(Part 3), June.

13

"OUT, DAMNED SPOT! OUT, I SAY"; OR, KARL ABRAHAM REVISITED

The connection between the superego, guilt, and anality has been either in the center or the periphery of my attention the whole of my professional life, provoked by the material presented by the six-year old schizophrenic with whom I spent a summer supposedly babysitting. Following working with him, I did therapy with a post-partum psychotic woman who also presented this same combination of anal material. Some of what I have learned about the combination seems quite obvious. But some seems rather complex. I will begin with what seems self-evident, in the hope that it will shed light on the more complex.

Benedict Carey (NY Times 9/12/06) describes a study that showed that "People who washed their hands (literally) after contemplating an unethical act were less troubled by their thoughts than those who didn't." An author of the research, Chen-Bo Zhong, from the University of Toronto, says "The association between moral and physical purity has been taken for granted for so long that it was startling that no one has ever shown empirical evidence of it. The researchers call this urge to clean up the 'Macbeth effect.'"

My experience with patients in a related area was surprising to me. While any child knows that it is the conscience that makes one feel guilty, repeatedly I have found that adult patients seem somehow to have split that knowledge off from consciousness. I would ask patients what it was in their mind that made them feel guilty, and consistently they looked bewildered, confused etc., as if it were a great mystery. "Do you remember Jiminy Cricket?" I would ask. "Oh, yes," they responded, but again, seemed not to have made the connection.

Indeed, the splitting seems so consistent in so many patients that I have speculated that somehow the superego itself finds some way of keeping the patient in ignorance. I wonder if this is not the more true as the person grows older, and, as a result, the unconscious is more repressed. It is the only piece of knowledge that I know of, where children are more aware than adults.

Shengold puts it well when he quotes Freud as saying, "Onset of the organization of the superego begins with 'parental influence ... which is the precursor of the superego, the ego's activities by prohibitions and punishments, and encourages or compels the setting up of repression" (Freud, 1940, p. 185). These partly internalized parental prohibitions and rewards center around toilet training: the transformation of narcissism into object relationship and then into character and superego takes place in relation to what Ferenczi (1925) called "sphincter morality."

The anal and urethral identification with the parents ... appears to build up in the child's mind a sort of physiological forerunner of the ... superego ... a severe sphincter morality is set up which can only be contravened at the cost of bitter self-reproaches and punished by the conscience (p. 267).

Shengold believes that the child's toilet training has been accomplished both out of love and out of fear, but given the conflict between the id's desire not to be controlled and the demand of the parent, I cannot agree that it comes purely from love.

Though Freud had much to say about anality, it is the much-neglected Karl Abraham, I believe, who is the more vivid, pertinent, and useful. I think we have lost a great deal due to his early demise. And we must begin, despite all the jokes about it, with toilet training. It is, after all, the first time when the child, not the parent, is in control. In all the prior situations, between infant and parent, it is the latter who is the physically stronger, and controls the child's body. Dressing, lifting, going out or staying home, nose wiping, hair combing, withholding, or offering food or toys are decisions made by the parent, and at her whim. But when or where to deposit excrement are in control of the child. And when the mother first begins to discuss toilets, that difference comes into stark relief. I urge you to think of the alternative: Can a mother squeeze urine out of a little penis, much less a girl's bladder? Can she reach in and pull feces out of a little intestine? No, not only is the child powerful, but it occurs to me, for the first time, the parent can be helpless.

Abraham says, "in many cases, he (the baby) will refuse a demand or request made to him but will of his own free choice make a person a handsome present" (p. 377). In psychological terms, one can almost see man's progression from authoritarianism to democracy in the contrast. In that sense, because excreting is by virtue of his own wish, it is the primitive beginning of an identity.

But the view of that gift is in sharp contrast between mother and child. Abraham says,

> The child's primitive method of evacuation brings the entire surface of its buttocks and lower extremities in contact with urine and feces. The contact seems unpleasant, even repulsive, to adults, whose repressions have removed them from the infantile reaction to these processes. They cannot appreciate the sources of pleasure on which the libido of the infant can draw, in whom the stream of warm urine on the skin and contact with the warm mass of feces produce pleasurable feelings.

(p. 372)

It is the transition of the child's feelings from "Oh, this feels so good. What possible difference can it make to Mommy where and when I put it?" to "I must take my pants down first and I must do it in the toilet, not when I feel like it."

It is very hard to put oneself back in the mind of a one- or two-year-old child. To him there are only two values, pleasure and non-pleasure. By identification one can imagine that when mother objects to the mere pleasure of evacuation whenever the child wishes, a child may "diagnose" mother as strange because she doesn't understand how pleasurable it is. Then, if mother gets angrier, she is "diagnosed" as "mean," "cruel," and "vicious" or "stupid."

Still, as Abraham says,

> The majority of children adapt themselves sooner or later to these demands. In favorable cases, the child succeeds in making a virtue of necessity, as it were: in other words, in identifying itself with the requirements of its educators and being proud of its attainment. The primary injury to its narcissism, is thus compensated and its original feeling of self-satisfaction is replaced by gratification in its achievement in **being good** (emphasis mine) in its parent's praise.
>
> *(p. 373)*

Yes, but there is the rub. We often see in the newspaper journalist's inquiries into the childhood of murderers. To the consistent surprise of all, neighbors say "He was so good, so nice, so polite as a child." Neighbors find it difficult to believe that this man could have committed a crime and readers find it difficult to believe he could have been so "good."

If the child cannot defend himself against too great an injury to his narcissism, the superego can get intolerably strong, the ego never gets strong enough and the result is the break in adolescence.

As Abraham says,

> All children are not equally successful in this respect. Particular attention should be drawn here to the fact that there are certain over-compensations behind which is hidden that obstinate holding fast to the primitive right of self-determination which occasionally breaks out violently later. I have in mind those children who are remarkable for the 'goodness,' polite manners, and obedience but who base their underlying rebellious impulses on the grounds that they have been **forced into submission** (emphasis mine) since infancy.
>
> *(p. 373)*

Anality and Schizophrenia

One may well question why I am putting so much emphasis on anality in a book on the treatment of schizophrenia. The short answer is that all my patients so frequently talked about dirt. They spoke of it so frequently that, no matter what the subject under consideration was, I was constantly being yanked back, like one would yank a dog on a leash, to a discussion of dirt or its synonyms. When I first began treating these patients, the "yanking" that took place, was unexpected but consistent. After a while, I learned not to be surprised.

Abraham quotes a patient's dream fragment,

> he dreamed that he had to expel the universe out of his anus. The idea of the omnipotence of defecation is very clearly expressed in his dream. It recalls the myths of the Creation, in which a human being is produced from earth or clay, i.e., from a substance similar to excrement . . . here we find expressed the more primitive idea of the omnipotence of the products of the bowel.
>
> *(p. 320–321)*

As I have written elsewhere, the experience of infantile omnipotence is necessary for the healthy foundation of the personality. Interference with its evolution will cause a break in the structure. A period of infantile omnipotence without any major interference is a natural, necessary stage in healthy growth.

In the previous section, the phrases "possible helplessness of the mother" and "being forced into submission" presented themselves. The toilet training phase can become a tug of war, if the mother is, for whatever reason, too adamant in her demands. Certainly, this can be expressed in many different ways. Does she scream? Does she grit her teeth in a persistent, controlled, hostile voice? Is she physically brutal? Does she evince the idea that she is being deliberately injured by the child's reluctance? All these are idiosyncratic variations for each patient that the therapist must discover for himself.

Of course, you will say—what patient can remember that far back? People's characters don't change that much. The screaming, controlled hostility etc. will doubtless carry over into the child's adolescence, which your patient will most likely remember. If the mother dies too early, one will have to deduce, which is, of course, more difficult. But I believe that with a thorough grounding in theory, the therapist should be able to do a creditable job. However, I do believe it is necessary, as Abraham says, quoting Ferenczi, "we can understand this man's (a patient's) eccentric behavior as an anal character-formation, and therefore as a precursor of paranoia" (p. 391). Speaking of which, I should not neglect to state a fact that is rarely mentioned, namely, that obsessive-compulsive behavior is almost always a characteristic of the schizophrenic. It is that factor which makes me wary, in the case of an apparent obsessive-compulsive. I always wonder whether or not schizophrenia may be hiding under the apparent neurosis or may come in the future.

Definitions and What I Believe to Be Some Errors in Freud

First, it should be understood that I am using the word *anality* as a symbol for everything (urine, feces, speech, ideas, creativity, etc.) that emanates or is expelled from the patient. In this sense, it is contrasted with all that the patient ingests or which others wish him to ingest. In that sense, I am speaking of it in the terms that a physics professor might use it. I am speaking of it in the sense of direction, not organ.

Secondly, I must take issue with Freud about one statement he has made, so that the following will be more understandable. In his discussion of happiness, Freud shows his lack of clinical experience with schizophrenics by stating the following. "The man who sees his pursuit of happiness come to nothing in later years can still find consolation in the yield of pleasure of chronic intoxication or he can embark on the desperate attempt at rebellion seen in a psychosis" (84 [8]).

This implies psychosis is fun. But as one of my patients said, "Schizophrenia is the concentration camp of the mind." All my experience with patients tells me that she was correct in that appraisal. It is truly hell on earth (see book cover). Being in it is not motivated by a search for happiness, but an attempt to save one's life (6).

Third, Freud says that "Genetically, the superego is heir to the parental agency" (p. 164 [9]). After years of work, I found this statement to be misleading. It implies that the whole of the parental agency can be found in the superego. Actually, I believe that all that is in the superego are the hostile restrictions of the parent. Unlike my previous view, parts of both parents and an older sibling may also be in the superego. Although, one parent or sibling may have the majority of the restrictions, the pride, love, etc. that parent may feel for the child is left out of the superego.

This can be shown by the entirely different sound (literally) and material of the internal voices of the superego and the ego. Because Freud did not notice that distinction (I'll remind the reader that by his own declaration, he was not musical, which I think may be relevant), the relations between the superego and the ego are unnecessarily more complicated and I believe, inaccurate.

Granted, I had the advantage of having a clearer view than he did. The view he had was clouded by far more defenses (p. 100 [10]).

Freud's difficulty with understanding schizophrenics is illuminated by the following statement in a letter he wrote to Hollos, who apparently inquired why Freud had not interested himself in schizophrenia. Freud's response was,

> I admitted . . . that I do not like these patients, that I am annoyed with them, that I feel them to be so far distant from me and from everything human . . . (Is my behavior due to) an ever clearer partisanship toward the primacy of the intellect, an expression of hostility toward the id? A curious sort of intolerance which surely makes me unfit to be a psychiatrist.
>
> *(10, p. 319)*

I think that the judgment is an example of his overly harsh superego but does cripple to some extent his ability to recognize the nature of the unconscious of a schizophrenic.

One facet of his view on anality is his own analysis as described by a letter to Ferenczi: "My (heightened) productivity (during the early stages of World War I) probably has to do with the enormous improvement in the activity of my bowels" (Ibid., p. 240).

I cannot emphasize sufficiently how much more clear the ego-superego relations are, when one works with schizophrenics and especially schizophrenic children. The messiness of finger-painting is an excellent example. The unconscious is, so to speak, so much closer to the surface. Indeed, with children this is especially true by virtue of their age. Of course, my view would necessarily alter some of Freud's statements, but I have been of this opinion for so long that, when reading Freud, I automatically insert that caveat in my mind. In practice, it becomes much simpler to have a constructive dialogue with that idea in mind.

Anality and the Superego

Perhaps the most succinct statement that can be made of the connection between anality and the superego is "Cleanliness is next to Godliness." But for a full understanding of the implications, one must tease apart the full meaning of those words. "Cleanliness" denotes not only "without dirt." It means "order." It means some loss of freedom, loss of immediate instinctual expression. On a more conscious level, it means "no fun." It means restriction and an authority who controls, whether inner or outer.

"Godliness" also implies authority, and authority implies morality. It is God or his substitute who lays down the rules. He decides what is wrong or right. Again, a loss of freedom, No play. The characteristic of schizophrenic children that struck me most strongly is that schizophrenic children have no fantasy life in psychoanalytic terms. To such a child, everything is felt to be real. The refuge of fantasy is unavailable to him. The id (expresser of dirt, metaphorically) is completely controlled by the superego.

To truly understand the toddler's dilemma, I must remind the reader of something I discovered clinically and which Freud confirms. "in spite of all man's developmental advances, he scarcely finds the smell of his own excrement repulsive, but only that of other people's" (Ibid., p. 100). The baby cannot imagine that his mother's experience may be different than his own. I believe that the extent of that difference is a largely contributive factor to the damage of the child's mental health. Of course, the mother's different view of the child's excreta is only the literal view of their differences. There are also the symbolic differences that the child offers, like opinions, artistic expressions, etc.

The extent to which the mother feels and displays her disgust, horror, and repulsion is the extent to which the child will have to compare his own attitudes and subsequent loss of self-esteem.

Worse, the mother of the child who becomes schizophrenic, may add "No one will like you if you (fill in the blank)." Note how many contradictions of reality are in that statement, made by the one who is supposed to be an authority on reality. First, she is conveying to the child the idea that everyone feels like she does, when in fact, few people may feel that way. Secondly, she behaves as if she is acting in the child's best interests, when in fact the reverse may be true. Thirdly, she is implying that she is protecting the child, when in fact she may be being destructive. I fear that agreement by consensual validation removes any possibility of feeling certain, thus denying the patient any hope of removing anxiety. Since the "whole world" feels as she does, then if the baby continues to be fond of his feces and their odor, he must feel excluded. Worse yet, in order to avoid the fear of feeling excluded, he will exclude himself. He must give up his love (the equivalent of his dirt and identity). He must begin to feel about his feces as his mother does—repelled—or, pretend to feel that way.

Here we have the explanation of the bizarre list of characteristics that schizophrenics and, to some extent, neurotics feel are dirty. They are: love, truth, creativity, laughter, imagination, silliness (of an amusing kind), playing, and innumerable other idiosyncratic characteristics and behaviors which, in fact, according to most of society, are pleasant.

Obviously, the therapist's job is very difficult if the patient feels that truth is dirty. What an irony it is that the therapist's major tool is considered dirty, and therefore *unacceptable in polite society*. The result is that, often, a patient will not discuss what he feels is dirty for fear of alienating or offending the therapist. So, some of the most constructive and valuable parts of the patient's personality may not appear in our offices. I have never heard a patient say lying felt dirty.

Again, I must assert my great good fortune that when I began to work in a clinic, my boss felt I looked too young to work with adults, so I was restricted to working with children. I became known for my ability to slow hyperactive children down. Among my tools were finger paints. There, with my encouragement, repressions were lifted. It was quite remarkable how well children responded to an adult who could, with apparent delight, say "ooshy, gooshy" and swirl the paints around. (I was too inexperienced to make some relevant interpretations then, which I could make now.) But obviously mere encouragement to be dirty (with appropriate aprons and plastic tables) was remarkably and quickly therapeutic, to my surprise, for schizophrenic and obsessive-compulsive children. Squeals of delight in the playroom replaced running up and down the corridor. I think I didn't realize myself how quickly one child responded until one of the secretaries said to me "What did you do to that child?"

I often regretted that I couldn't do the same with adult patients but I do encourage adults to find sublimations and I did use verbal substitutes in collaborative fantasies. I might add that this solves the therapists' problem of boredom with having to painstakingly and slowly scrape away at obsessive-compulsive defenses. So, I am never bored.

The Pressure of Guilt

It is specifically the amount of guilt pressing down on the ungratified id that is the measure of how soon schizophrenia will appear and how severe it will be. Here, the saying "the straw that breaks the camel's back" is fitting.

If one can look at the matter as a physical metaphor, I think the issue becomes clarified. If someone is starving to death, it is the last crumb of food not taken in that kills. So, it is that one last blow of guilt from the superego, prohibiting the id and the ego one last bit of gratification, that I think is the precipitating cause of schizophrenia.

In the late 1950s or early 1960s, I saw a 16-year-old patient. I had seen Jason briefly when he was a child, just before I left the clinic and had little memory of his problem. When he came to me as an adolescent, he announced that he was going to save the world. The only obstacle to doing so, he told me, was that he needed a little bit of help from me to accomplish his objective. I was shocked and frightened to see the extent of his deterioration. He seemed to me to be on the verge of needing to be hospitalized. He confided to me his enormous guilt about his homosexuality (dirty love) about which no one knew.

At that time, homosexuality was considered an illness, a view that I accepted. However, I decided that Jason was better off being homosexual than psychotic. I think that more than a few of my colleagues would have been shocked at that decision.

I immediately began to encourage Jason to gratify his homosexual desires. Because he had positive memories of me when he was a child, he was less resistant to accepting encouragement than he might otherwise have been. It was amazing to me that very shortly after that, I heard nothing more of the task he had set himself, i.e., to save the world. That was a great relief to me, because I no longer felt pressure to have to save him from an imminent hospitalization. At the time, I didn't yet have enough confidence in myself to believe I would never have to hospitalize a patient. I was still quite inexperienced and so was surprised with what determination (and horror at what went on in mental hospitals) that problem no longer existed for me. We were able to comfortable discuss his homosexual relationships and other matters he brought up.

The Universal Fantasy of the Schizophrenic

The following is what appears to me to be the consistent fantasy of schizophrenics about feces. Any variation deviates very little from the following model:

The initial reality is that the child loves his feces and its symbols. The mother of the soon-to-be-schizophrenic child displays some variation of horror when it is presented to her as a gift. Enough of her emotion is expressed at the presentation that the child truly believes he has injured and/or is killing her.

The result is that which the child loves and presents as a gift transforms in his mind into a weapon, since the consequences appear to be so destructive. The result is a direct contradiction. The child is presenting the mother with what he sees as love, truth, creativity, and value; the mother sees only ugliness, destructiveness, and worthlessness.

The mother's contrary views of the child's expressions causes the following difficulties: The child has a natural desire to express himself, which is symbolized by the feces, but the flow of that expression is interfered with by the mother's view of feces as "bad" and "dangerous." This contradiction has very serious consequences because the child's expression is the essence of himself. It is his emotional DNA. Because of the "injurious capability" of those expressions, the guilt caused by the superego, "proves" to him that he is bad for having the wish to express himself, as shown by the way his mother reacts. The wish is symbolized by the earlier toilet training experience. It is the feces that the mother fears and which must be rejected by the child.

For example, "I want to go to the movies" must inherently make the child a "bad" person, since mother screams at him: "You are always trying to avoid your chores and leaving me to do them for you" in a tone of voice that implies it kills her to do the chores, or to live with the chores undone.

The result is that the child feels guilty for wishing to go to the movies. Additionally, he feels guilty for being angry at his mother's attitude toward his wish. The superego supports its position, by trying to convince him that he is superior to other children. This superiority promoted by the superego is all the more seductive, because his mother's rejection of his "bad feces" caused him to feel inferior. This grandiosity is experienced as "I am very virtuous because I don't even feel the desire to go to the movies, or if I do feel it, I don't give in to it like other children."

Therapy focuses primarily on the grandiosity, since that is the strongest resistance. Thus: "You think you are better than other children because you don't go to the movies. But aren't you really jealous of them because they do go and don't feel guilty? Further, what really happens to their mothers or yours for that matter, if their children go to the movies?" Then the therapist can suggest that the patient really loves his feces, and mother doesn't and what does that say about her? Further, do other people feel about his expressions the way she does?" This can show, that far from being like everyone else, as she pretended, she is the unusual, and irrational one. One 's child going to the movies has never been given as a cause of death on a death certificate.

However, the fantasy that the child's expressions are "bad" is not so easy to give up. One great advantage that this fantasy has is that it implies great power. That is, if he has so much guilt, he must be able to hurt others very badly. The guilt proves the damage he has supposedly caused. The advantage of that, is that he can revenge himself on his mother for all the pain she has caused him.

This is expressed as, "O.K. you think my feces are so terrible, I'll show you just how terrible I can be, or at least I can fantasize about how much I can hurt you." So he ends up wanting to believe that anything he does is truly destructive, ignoring reality. He unconsciously feels, "It's worth having such terrible feces, if only it would hurt or kill mother."

When I have made this interpretation, it is fascinating to watch and listen to the patient, when he has to express his disappointment, that his worst fear becomes an unfulfillable wish. I have to say, "The trouble is, if you really want to kill your mother you'll have to get a gun. Your wish isn't strong enough. Your mother was partially putting on an act, and you wanted to believe her."

When the patient can really hear you, it deflates the grandiosity. It releases the burden of the guilt, and causes the energy that the superego has controlled, to flow into the ego. The latter happens without further interpretation, and is, to me, an aesthetic experience. Thus, as the process goes on, the patient is relieved to discover that it is much harder to injure or kill someone than he had believed and wished it was. Further, there is no longer a compulsion to be superior to everyone else. He is at peace with the idea of going to the movies, his mother continuing to live, and the bubbles of guilt and grandiosity start bursting. It can result in "Oh, mother, do stop making a fuss about nothing," said in a tone implying that she is being silly. Of course, it is important that the therapist have a reasonably peaceful relationship with his own anality.

Clinical Material

Cassandra, a very seriously ill patient, has been speaking lovingly of her feces.

I: You really like your shit now.
C: I'm embarrassed to like it. (Embarrassment may follow the loss of guilt, similarly to the feeling of a recovered schizophrenic when he recalls his past.)
I: I'm so proud of you for admitting it.
C: If I really admit it, then I won't hold the world up anymore. (That burden accompanies the schizophrenic state.) I will stand up on the world. That is the big step. It's the first time I took that step. I'm better than that. That's why I couldn't take pleasure in my own shit. I was toilet trained and terrified of not getting to the potty on time. Once my father hit me and my mother called the police and my father blamed me and told the police that I was schizophrenic. He wanted me to go to the hospital and I wouldn't. I'm right to hate them.

Susan, another very seriously ill patient, expressed fear of being abandoned.

I: What happens if I don't abandon you?
S: You'll see I'm a slut. That I have bad bathroom habits.
I: So you're a dirty little girl (smiling).
S: (Laughs a great deal with obvious delight[1]) I like to be dirty, so others will bathe me. Counselors in camp bathed me. It was a sexual thrill. (Here we see the conflation of sex and anality and expressed in later life, of only relating physically, not emotionally, to men.)

184   "Out, Damned Spot! Out, I Say"

On another occasion:

I: Why do you never say how you feel about something? When you tell me about something, you never tell me how you feel about it. I always have to ask.
S: I say it in a detached way. When I did show feelings, I got punished and they gave me more medicine.

Kathleen, when she came to me, had one major fear, that I would send her to the hospital.

I: You haven't talked about your obsessions about dirt, which you complained about.
K: I don't feel clean. I am trying to get clean by obsessing. I try to rationalize the irrational. I'm such a wimp.
I: What is the real reason?
K: The real truth is not clean.
I: So you clean it by bullshitting and the truth is dirty. Why is that?
K: It really is so simple. Why can't I just tell the truth?
I: What does C. say about it?
K: It says "You try to make excuses."
I-C: Why do you call telling the truth, "making excuses?"
C: The truth is malleable.
I-C: I know the malleability of you. (referring to its lying)
I-K: I think it wants you to obsess to keep your mind off the truth.

Jane is a patient who closely identifies with her superego. Thus, though not so ill, she presents greater difficulties because of that identification. Her father is in an authoritative profession.

J: I have such disgust about dirt. It is unhealthy. Cleanliness is next to godliness. (She constantly complains about her roommates' messiness.) I did once have a stain on my culottes. My mother pointed it out. I was very scrupulous about that afterwards. After that no one knew I was menstruating.
I: You sound so superior.
J: You're probably right. I did have superior problems and perceptions to protect myself from being hated.

The patient who was in most constant conflict about anality was Carolyn. When she first came to me she had a paranoid delusion about other people's excrement. (She felt that someone had urinated in her shampoo bottle.) It was Carolyn who was most educative to me about the many symbolisms of anality.

The following are Carolyn's discussions of anality as her treatment (constantly resistant) progressed.

C: I had a dream of sex. I hug a penis. It felt great, but later I was sick with shame and they had to cut my toes off. I went to stay with L. My toes were dirty. They gave me a washcloth. It felt dirty and shameful.
I: What is your association to the idea that the punishment for dirty toes is to cut them off?
C: It's dirty. I had a dream of being in a garage face-down. I poured Tide in the crack of my friend's ass. I carried the memory of shit for a year. I tattled on a girl who smelled her finger from her ass. To gossip is to belong.
  (Later I learned that Carolyn frequently told negative stories about her peers to supervisors.)

Some weeks later:

C: Debting is throwing shit in a hole. (At the beginning of her treatment, Carolyn constantly fell into debt unnecessarily.)

Some months later:

C: I see myself at 2 or 3. I fill my pail with dirt. I am happy.
I: Why not come to me with your dirt?
C: You'll take it away or you'll change it. (This is a consistent fear that I find in schizophrenic patients.)
I: Why not keep it? (This was an error. I should have explored the transference here.)
C: Cause I always gave it to my father and I hate myself for giving it up. When I do it, I have the 'black hole.'[2] emptiness. That is the only way you will love me.
I: Will your father love you without it? (Here I am hoping she will see that changing herself, will not change her father's feeling about her).
C: No. *Dirt is myself, what I like.* (emphasis mine)
I: What dirt are you giving me?
N: That is the essence. When I did just that, I gave myself a black hole. I gave my soul.
  (My experience with patients is exactly that. Feces are equivalent to the soul, the identity, the emotional life. Giving it up causes unbearable terror.)

Some months later:

C: I thought my conscience really does want to kill me. I thought you were crazy, because you said it was destroying me. I thought a conscience is supposed to steer you right, and you said it wanted to destroy me.[3]
I: What happens if you take care of yourself?

C: That is scary. God will be angry. He needs his followers. Without them He wouldn't exist. (If one equates God with the superego, this is very insightful. In fact, I don't think I had ever quite realized it until she said it. But Carolyn doesn't realize the significance of what she has said. In fact, it is not infrequently the case that patients don't realize how significant their own discoveries are.) If this is true, then I'll be punished for not believing that God will protect me.

Some months later:

C: I do like shit. It is power.

A month later:

C: I have a fantasy of hugging you. I'm digging in the dirt, but I want you to clean it up. I like dirt. Ugh. I say "ugh" because I'm not supposed to like dirt. (When she can come to the point where the "not supposed to" of the conscience is dismissed, the ambivalence can be cleared up.)
C: My father called me shit. My conscience calls me a slob.

My most impressive lessons about the symbolic value of feces were taught me by Harry, a six-year-old brilliant schizophrenic boy, with whom I "babysat" before going into practice. It was summertime in the country. We would go into the woods where he occasionally had to defecate. But the next days were always a determined hunt for where the event had taken place, to make sure the defecation was still there. It was he who said to me, "My mother took my love away from me." In my naïveté, I denied that possibility, thinking "That's crazy even for a schizophrenic." Of course, I was wrong. It was from him I learned that all the gifts of a child are symbolic feces and I saw his adopted mother consistently reject them. Only if she accepts his gifts are they retained.

Indeed, I later learned that whether or not a child feared taking showers (because of identification with feces for fear of going down the drain with excrement) could be used as a method of a differential diagnostic tool for distinguishing between brain-damaged children from schizophrenic children. Brain-damaged children on a ward in psychiatric hospital had no such fears.

Conclusion

To return to Abraham, he says:

> The surrender of the excrement is the earliest form in which child "gives" or presents a thing: and the neurotic often shows . . . self-will in the matter of giving. Accordingly, in many cases he will refuse a demand or request made to him, but will of his own **free choice** (emphasis his) make a person

a handsome present. The important thing to him is to preserve his right of **decision** (emphasis mine).

(377 [11])

If anything, Abraham underestimated the importance of preserving the right of decision. That first decision is the precursor of whether or not the ego or the superego is in charge. If the child feels compelled and feels no right to decide, then the superego is the master. Depending on the quantity of affect attached, the severity of the caretaker's demand and the number of incidents involved, the initial evolution of the strength of the superego will be determined.

Conversely, if the child feels enough strength to decide, has little or no anxiety and gives (not surrenders), the strength of the ego will be increased. Of course, the stronger the superego, the greater the guilt since that is the coin of the superego. If the superego is too strong and the ego too weak, it will eventually collapse and the patient will succumb to schizophrenia.

Here I would like to give an example of how the superego prevaricates. I don't know how others would diagnose Diane, but she did have a great deal of anxiety when she came to me. She also felt dead, which to me is always an indicator of incipient schizophrenia. She was also a very easy patient to learn from since she appeared to be one of the least sick patients in my practice.

One day after she had been in treatment for several months, she told me that she had had a big blow-up with her father and was openly hostile to him for the first time in her life. Today, she told me that an idea occurred to her the previous night, that she wants to tell him that she hates him, though she had previously told her mother that she hated her father.

I asked how she would feel doing that. She said she would feel clean and was surprised to find she would not feel guilt. This kind of empty threat is generally the case. But it takes a lot of work to encourage the patient to try to expose it. This is a lesson to the patient that exposure of what is dreaded, very often brings a pleasant surprise. And the "dreaded dirt" looks quite different when it comes out in the open.

In terms of therapy, I must caution the therapist to be on guard against two seductive resistances. The first is pointed out by Freud, "'Natural ethics' as it is called has nothing to offer . . . except narcissistic satisfaction of thinking oneself better than others." It is that that the superego offers the patient in an attempt to ignore the reality of the pleasure and love of dirt.

The second is the threat of loneliness. The message is "I will never leave you." The implication is that it is the only one that will never leave the patient and others may. What the superego does not express unless very pressed is the reality: "I won't leave you. because without you, I am non-existent because I am only a fantasy." Of course, it doesn't point out to the patient how much more valuable, real and tangible and even possibly loving people are, than a destructive mendacious, hypocritical fantasy is, however, permanent.

As Shakespeare says "O coward conscience, how dost thou afflict me" (13, p. 136).

I close this chapter with a plea to the reader to read Abraham's chapter XXIII in his "Selected Papers on Psycho-Analysis," entitled "Contributions to the Theory of the Anal Character." The amount of seminal information that it contains cannot be exaggerated (20).

Notes

1 That kind of laughter that, when heard, is an obvious expression of relief at the exposure to someone in society of a never previously discussed subject with that affect.
2 See chapter 3.
3 Her view is the most common one but, in schizophrenics, we see how erroneous that view is.

References

1. Carey, Benedict. (2006). Lady Macbeth not alone in her quest for spotlessness. *New York Times*, September 12.
2. Abraham, Karl. (1921/1927). Contributions to the theory of the anal character. In *Selected Papers on Psychoanalysis*, Hogarth Press, Ltd., London, p. 377.
3. Ibid., p. 372.
4. Ibid., p. 373.
5. Ibid., p. 373.
6. Abraham, Karl. (1920/1927). The narcissistic evaluation of excretory processes in dreams and neuroses. In *Selected Papers on Psychoanalysis*, Hogarth Press, Ltd., London, pp. 320–321.
7. Abraham, Karl. (1921/1927). Contributions to the theory of the anal character. In *Selected Papers on Psychoanalysis*, Hogarth Press, Ltd., London, p. 391.
8. Freud, Sigmund. (1930). Civilization and its discontents. In *The Standard Edition of the Complete Psychological Works of Sigmund Freud*, Vol. XXI, Hogarth Press, Ltd., London, p. 84.
9. Ibid., p. 164.
10. Ibid., p. 100.
11. Abraham, Karl. (1921/1927). Contributions to the theory of the anal character. In *Selected Papers in Psychoanalysis*, Hogarth Press, Ltd., London, p. 377.
12. Freud, Sigmund. (1930) Civilization and its discontents. In *The Standard Edition of the Complete Psychological Works of Sigmund Freud*, Vol. XXI, Hogarth Press, London, p. 143.
13. Shakespeare, William. (1994). *Complete Works, Richard the Third*, Act Five, Scene Three, The Edition of the Shakespeare Head Press, Oxford, Barnes and Noble, p. 136.
14. Eissler, Kurt. (1971). Talent and Genius, 10a. *New York Times*, Quadrangle Press, p. 319.
15. Ibid., 11a, p. 240.
16. Freud, S. (1940). Outline of psychoanalysis. In *The Standard Edition of the Complete Psychological Works of Sigmund Freud*, Vol. 23, Hogarth Press, London, p. 185.
17. Ferenczi, S. (1925). Psychoanalysis of sexual habits. In *Further Contributions to the Theory and Technique of Psychoanalysis*, Hogarth Press, London, 1950, p. 267.
18. Shengold, Leonard. (1988). *A Hole in the Sky*, The Guildford Press, New York, p. 36.

14

OPPOSING OPINIONS AS TO TREATMENT OF WISHES AND HOPES PATHOLOGY

A Response to Salman Akhtar

I first became interested in this subject when my patient, Carolyn, told me that she hoped to get her mother to love her by going through various behaviors. In reality, her mother was already dead. I could not consider explaining this statement by saying she was simply misusing a word. In fact, I came to understand that the distinction between wishes and hopes is not at all a discussion of semantics, but one of profound psychological importance. Carolyn's statement was all the more interesting in that she worked in a very language-dependent job at which she excelled. An ordinary, psychologically healthy person who was reasonably intelligent could confuse hopes and wishes, but Carolyn was as likely to confuse those two words, or indeed, any two words, as an accountant would confuse addition and subtraction. It was for that reason that the error caught my interest.

I had the good fortune of beginning my career working with what were then called schizophrenic children. I say *good fortune* because in my view there is no greater opportunity to study the unconscious without obstruction than when one works with these children. They are so young, have such small egos and so few defenses, that they are the people who are closer to their unconscious than any other category of human being. No one expresses themselves more similarly to a waking dream than they do.

The most striking overt difference between them and normal children is that they do not play, so that no wishes are expressed symbolically and, indeed, rarely overtly. There are no cops and robbers, no lion taming, no fantasies of being the greatest baseball player in the world, taking care of babies, etc. Everything in their lives is literally true. Indeed, John Rosen believed that adult psychotics never dream at all, except about food. (1) My first little brilliant six-year old ran from the dinner table in terror when told that the mustard was strong.

The local International Symposium of the Psychotherapy of Schizophrenia group had a recent example of the lack of fantasy and play when the late Elaine Schwager presented a case of an autistic child. The presentation was called "The Relationship of Empathy to Symbolic Communication in Work with a Young Boy on the Autistic Spectrum." She was able to help this child get to the point of where he could fantasize, which I think is a very important accomplishment.

It doesn't take great psychological insight to recognize that the play of a child is inspired by his wishes. But if a child feels denied permission to wish, he is restricted to the "whips and scorns of time" (Hamlet, 688 [2]), against which he lacks the soothing ointment of wishes. The study of these children enables one to see how much of a prison that is.

If one can't wish, and on the day of a planned picnic it rains, one cannot play picnic to make up for the loss of the wished-for occasion. There is no fantasy of running after butterflies, swimming, or three-legged races. There is no fantasy of seeing other children or running for long stretches without boundaries. Or even a fantasy of seeing one's favorite Aunt Jane. Only undiluted pain. People who can't wish have no emotional concept of "possibilities." Life is dour, mechanical, hard and boring; as Hamlet says, the child will "grunt and sweat under a weary life" (Ibid. [3]).

Freud's view is by no means clear. On the one hand, he says, "The most frequent outcome of unconscious wishes that have been freed by psycho-analysis ... is that these wishes are **destroyed** (emphasis mine) by the rational mental activity of the better impulses that are opposed by them." But on the very same page, he says "the extirpation of the infantile wishful impulses is by no means the ideal aim of development" (XI [4]).

He shows he is clearly aware of how essential wishes are, when he points out that "Owing to their repressions, neurotics have sacrificed many sources of mental energy whose contributions would have been of great value in the formation of their character and in their activity in life" (Ibid. [4]). He solves the apparent contradiction by offering the idea of sublimation.

But the problem with severely ill patients is that even with repression, the wish can be so unacceptable to the superego that sublimation is not an option. Carolyn's hope that her dead mother love her can scarcely be called sublimation. A possible sublimation may be attempted by her trying to establish a positive relationship with another older woman, but Carolyn was not capable of that. She was too busy trying to punish me, the mother substitute, for her mother's unwillingness to care for her. It made her incapable of accepting more of what positive gain she could have gotten from a mother substitute. She wanted to force her mother to do what her mother clearly was unwilling to do, even after her death.

Here we must become clear as to the distinction between wishes and hopes in reality. In order to live reasonably comfortably in the world, we must be aware of and accept the existence of a wish within us that is impossible to attain. We must be free to know emotionally and intellectually that there is an emotional entity that is not subject to any restriction of reality. It is also important to be aware that one can even wish retroactively, i.e., "I wish that hadn't happened." Carolyn, if she hadn't been ill, could have wished, "I wish my mother had loved me." (Although Carolyn's mother had given in to all her temper tantrums, what Carolyn missed unconsciously was the mother's desire to give to make her child happy. Carolyn got her gifts by virtue of threats. I don't think Carolyn's mother was ever *willing* to freely give her anything.)

Indeed, a frequent example of that is the very common childhood fantasy of patients who feel they were born in the wrong family, that the babies had been mixed up in the hospital. This can easily be interpreted as "I wish I had been born in a different family." Indeed, it may be helpful to the patient if the therapist encourages her to play it out in session, so that she has a firm grasp of what it would have meant to her, and what she felt deprived of.

But only wishes that take place in the future have a possibility of being fulfilled. Even in that case, there has to be some realistic requirement present for the wish to be rationally defined as a "hope." The lottery will happen in the future, but one can realistically hope to win it only if one has bought a ticket. One can wish it were possible to win the lottery without buying a ticket, but one can certainly not hope for it.

The emotional difference between the two is, for one thing, a question of excitement. That kind of excitement is very possible at a horse race when one has put down a bet. One does not usually see such intensity when speaking of a wish. The wish is an expression of one's identity, but a hope requires some specific element of reality outside oneself to support it.

To put the matter in a different context: while participating in a wedding ceremony, one can realistically hope for a happy marriage. Certainly, it is possible. But what if one knows that one's spouse is already married to someone else, or has a previous history of spousal abuse, or is an inveterate gambler, alcoholic, or drug addicted? The reality is so grim that one can go into such a marriage only on a wish. Of course, if one is in denial, one can tell oneself that it is reasonable to hope, because one will work so hard at it that one's spouse will reform. But the fulfillment of that hope is far too dependent on someone else's wishes, motivation, and difficulty of execution. In this situation, previous behavior on the part of the other spouse makes what the one who hopes, to be, in fact, merely wishing.

In the political arena, the entry into the Iraq war seems, as more facts emerge, to have been more of a wish than a hope. That is hardly surprising, since the president had once been an alcoholic and was not treated for his alcoholism.

Discovering Salman Akhtar

The occurrence that inspired me to write about this subject was a personal meeting with Salman Akhtar and the reading of his paper "Someday" and "If Only"

Fantasies: Pathological Optimism and Inordinate Nostalgia, as Related Forms of Idealization" (1996 [6]). His abstract covers his thinking quite well:

> Fantasies whose core is constituted by the notions of "someday" and "if only" are ubiquitous in the human psyche. In severe character pathology, however, these fantasies have a particularly tenacious, defensive and ego-depleting quality. The "someday" fantasy idealizes the future and fosters optimism and the "if only" fantasy idealizes the past and lays groundwork for nostalgia. The two fantasies originate in the narcissistic disequilibrium consequent upon the early mother-child separation experiences, though the Oedipal conflict also contributes to them. Both can be employed as defenses against defective self-and object constancy as well as later narcissistic and Oedipal traumas. This paper attempts to highlight the metapsychology and behavioral consequences of these fantasies as well as their unfolding in the treatment situation.

For analytic treatment, Akhtar emphasizes

> six tasks ... (i) providing and sustaining a meaningful 'holding environment' (ii) affirmative interventions (iii) helping the patient unmask these fantasies and interpreting their defensive, narcissistic and sadomasochistic aspects (iv) rupturing the patient's **excessive** (emphasis mine) hope, analyzing the effects of such rupture, and facilitating the resultant mourning (v) reconstructing the early scenarios underlying the need for excessive hope and (vi) paying careful attention to countertransference feelings through such work.
> *(1996 [7])*

As I read the paper, and the prescribed treatment, I saw that the subject seemed to be in the general area of my thoughts about hopes and wishes. But the prescribed treatment made me feel that the patient would be going through something like an operation without an anesthetic. The word "rupturing" disturbed me greatly. But one must not imagine that Akhtar was oblivious to the pain. He says,

> They (such interventions) are neither conventional nor risk-free. They disrupt the transference dynamics and therefore are inevitably traumatic to the patient. Indeed, when their 'dosage' or timing is inappropriate—and this may not be entirely predictable—the resulting despair and psychic pain might lead the patient to become **seriously suicidal**.
> *(emphasis mine, Ibid. [8])*

In identifying with the patient, I felt as if I had been hit in the solar plexus. I thought to myself, "Isn't there a less painful way of handling this problem? Further, does it really solve the problem? What about finding the unconscious fantasy upon which these fantasies are built, so that the patient can have a chance to recognize them himself and sublimate them? Is not psychoanalysis built on the premise that such obsessive ideas are built on symbols?" Pointing out a reality that is in contradiction to the fantasy underlying "Someday" does not require training in psychoanalysis. Any reasonably intelligent layperson could do it.

Additionally, if (iii) has to be done, why is there a need for rupture? Further, I cannot understand how it would work. If the analyst "ruptures," does not the fantasy remain? Telling a patient, who believes he is Jesus Christ, that he is John Jones, will result in the patient perceiving the analyst as an enemy: one more person who doesn't understand him. The patient will become increasingly isolated.

Now I must interrupt myself by assuring the reader that I am not trying to disrespect Dr. Akhtar. Quite the contrary, I found him to be a very learned and compassionate person. But my life experience has been that I learn most from those with whom I disagree, because the experience forces me to discover the reasons for which I disagree, resulting in clarification of my own thinking.

As I continued to muse on the paper, I also wondered about Dr. Akhtar's use of the phrase "excessive hope." When one deals with such a severe problem, I cannot imagine that the difficulty is one of quantity. Rather, it seems to me to be one of quality. Something of substance must be amiss. For example, if one's sink has a leaky faucet and the drain is closed, one can be faced with the problem of a mess on the bathroom floor. But it is quite a different matter if the mess on the bathroom floor is due to frozen pipes. That is a qualitative, not a quantitative matter, and therefore must be approached differently.

Additionally, I wonder if the very patient and devoted Dr. Akhtar may not suffer from a problem that most of us who listen to bizarre ideas all day long sometimes have—something in us finally says, "Enough! I've got to bring some reality to this situation" because one starts to feel a bit mad oneself and a little frightened. I must plead guilty to have done this a few times myself, much to my later regret. Indeed, I have heard patients on a hospital ward say "I can't stand being with these crazy people anymore." I'm sure you have too.

Anna Potamianou, the author of *Hope: A Shield in the Economy of Borderline States* has a blurb that makes my point clear. "For most human beings hope is a positive benefit. Anna Potamianou shows how in the 'borderline' patient hope can become a perverted and omnipotent means of denying reality."[1] She gives both clinical and literary examples of how this happens and goes on to discuss the connections between hope and desire for these patients (1997 [9]).

Clinical Examples

Janice describes the following incident,

> If I came home from school, my mother would say "How was school?" and I would say "Fine" but there was nothing there.[2] I thought I didn't need her. I wanted to play with my friends.

My mother once said "I want to play." I was shocked because it was so unlike her. "Why?" I said. Once I came to the door and rang the bell. She asked me what I wanted. I said, "I want you to play with me." She was angry. I cried. I was scared. I feared I **wouldn't** have a mother."

The following is the dialogue between me and Janice.

I: You are using the future tense. That is much more tolerable than facing what is in the present. That is, that you feel you don't have a mother now.
J: Yes, **it gives me hope**. I keep hanging on. I can't accept it. If I concentrate on the present I will lose my bearing.
I: Let's see how that happens.
J: I was a lonely sad little girl. I wanted to be a tomboy and have no need of her and my dangerous father.
I: Instead of seeing your mother as she was, you tried to have no needs.[3]
J: I think of it as a tough exterior.
I: As long as you hold on to your fear, you hold on to your hope.[4]
J: If I allow the sad and lonely little girl to live, it gives me transparency and being present instead of veiled.
I: You felt that if you just live, you will be allowing your mother to kill you.
J: I hope I can keep this tender awareness of my self. It's also respectful of my self. There can be strength in tenderness and self-respect.

Janice's unconscious fantasy is that if she doesn't challenge her mother, the mother will become a real mother, i.e., maternal. To sustain the hope, she must remain passive. The price is loss of her identity, because this particular mother wanted Janice to be a replica of herself.

Kathleen is closer to insight than Janice. The following is a dialogue between her and me.

K: I have cut myself off from my mother (crying). I don't know if I can cross the gulf.
I: Is it possible?
K: I've been thinking of that. I don't think she is worth it. The last little bit of hope hangs on.
I: Maybe it is a wish. Have you thought of the fact that hope restricts your situation? But with a wish, the field is wide open. Do you see that?[5]
K: I really do (crying). I got cheated. I wish I was a different birth order.[6]

In the next session:

K: I can't accept what you said about my mother not loving me.[7]
I: Yes, you had problems in differentiating between hope and wish.

K: I think she brainwashed me into believing she loved me.[8] She always had explanations for what she did that hurt me.

This presents evidence of an important insight for us. It supports my theory that schizophrenia and other serious mental illnesses are caused by a mother (or other caregiver) who hates the child and lies about it. The mere presence of hostility is not enough. It is the lying that allows the child to go into such fantasies. However, we can see the usefulness of the work above in the following session, five months later:

K: I'm afraid you will make fun of me because I have a dream. I wish I could reconstruct the past. I have a lot of regrets where my mother is concerned. I wish we had connected. I wish we had been close. I wish I could accept the reality as much as the fantasy. Hope and dreams are now gone.
I: Just so you don't give up the wishes.
K: But so many wishes don't come true. I will be empty if I live that way.
I: You will be dead if you give them up.[9]
K: I did go all through my life saying, "I don't need it." when I couldn't get my wish. I thought if I do that I am fulfilled.
I: That is why you were so scared of being needy.
K: The relationship is over. No fixing anything. She couldn't change. I lost out on having a mother. When she was still alive, there was hope that things could get better. Wishes kept things going.
I: Did you think about the distinction between wishing and hoping?
K: Yes, as long as I understand that wishes may not come true, it's O.K. I have searched for a figure to admire like Dr. H (a professor she likes). But there are no women I really admire. Maybe someday I will. (Here she is looking for sublimation.) It's four months since my mother died. I was really saying good-bye.
I: Tell me what you wish she was like.

I think it is important to make sure that wishes are expressed aloud in order to support the patient's identity. Frequently patients will express wishes they were not aware of having had at all.

K: I would like her to have been less bitter, make a nice home, not put father down. She pretended not to have sex with him. She should have had more self-pity. Maybe it was at that point, when I saw that, is where I got disgusted at it, because she manipulated us.
I: So, you wished you had had a mother who felt sorry for herself. (Mother had had a very difficult husband from whom she was divorced.) You would liked to have been able to sit on her lap and if you were crying, she would say "There, there."
K: She was lazy. I was almost catatonic.[10]

Later in the session, I wondered why she had not used me for sublimation.

I: What about me?
K: You said I could call you anytime.[11] You gave me permission to be human, to feel.
I: But you don't seem to be treating me as if I have a maternal relationship to you.
K: I have. I will send you Christmas cards when treatment is over.

Unfortunately, the treatment ended abruptly for financial reasons, but she did send me some letters describing how much better she was (see Epilogue).

In terms of my differences with Dr. Akhtar, her unconscious fantasy was that her mother's expressed love for her was valid. I am not sure I did all that could have been done to raise all her wishes to consciousness, but I think I made a good start in helping her discriminate between hopes and wishes. Her other important accomplishments are not directly relevant to this paper.

Carolyn had a history of throwing her wishes out (see chapters on the black hole phenomenon), almost literally as if they were material objects. The purpose of discarding them was so that she would not have to face the fact that the unfulfilled wishes were not gratified. It was part of her grandiosity. The following are dialogues with her:

C: I am miserable. I got depressed thinking of 'no Mommy' (meaning an unloving mother). I feel everyone needs something from me.
I: But you complained that your mother didn't need you.
C: Maybe I misused the word 'need.' Maybe I meant 'want.'[12] She didn't want me. Now, I think of saying to you, "Can you help me?"

This startled me, coming from a patient who normally refuses help. It is subsequent to this that Carolyn began talking about her "black hole." She told me something that seemed incomprehensible. My attitude is that everything in psychosis makes sense, if only one knows how to figure it out. But that statement didn't make sense even in psychotic thinking. I couldn't understand how one lack could fill another lack.[13]

C: My hope is that mother loved me and you wanted me to get well. It didn't go.
I: They couldn't co-exist?
C: Because you represented the truth. The wish is O.K. now. Before it wasn't. Before, wishes didn't seem real.

A month later, she said she felt gruesomely (sic) unhappy when she couldn't get what she wanted. I volunteered, "When you can't get what you want, you give up the wish to the person who won't grant it. That way you think you won't have the pain of the ungranted wishes, but in reality, you lose yourself. Who you are, is what you want."

In the following session, she told me she woke up with the feeling of the "black hole." So taking a lesson from the last session, she said to herself, "I wish I could be with Boyd (current boyfriend) and the wish is staying with me. Then I realized I didn't have to be alone."

There is a very important lesson here. All of our patients complain of loneliness to some degree. But for those who complain about it bitterly, I recommend looking at the lesson to be learned from Carolyn here. I think this incident shows clearly that at least part of the patient's complaint is due to her having *missed parts of herself*. That is a loneliness that is truly more painful than the usual kind. It never ceases, and on that account alone, is more painful than the usual kind of loneliness. Further, it is certainly more present in psychotics than in other patients. So, I urge you to share this openly with your patient, and try to keep yourself and her, focused on what part of herself is lost, or more accurately what has not been available and experienced as lost. In reality, of course, it can be recovered.

To continue, in the next session, she reported a similar incident, though it left her puzzled. Referring to the "black hole" remedy, she said:

> I can't understand how it works. You said, 'What were you doing to yourself before you got your wish back?' The answer is, I was *splitting* myself.[14] The self I sent off is ghostlike. That is scary. Awful.

Some time later, we are still struggling with this problem, though to a much lesser extent. Responding to her idea that she feels I am God:

I: But you feel I am superior because you've made me into God, but having given me that much power is unbearable to you.
C: You are not God (angry). You make mistakes.
I: Yes. How do you make me into God?
C: I don't trust myself but I have God within me.
I: What do you lose if you give up being God?
C: Hope is the order of the world. For every effect, there is a cause. There would be chaos without it.[15] I lose hope in a good, caring, compassionate God. I lose hope that my parents will love me.[16]
I: How do you feel now?
C: Relief. I'm tired of having God and order in the universe and believe that my parents loved us children. If I acknowledge my hate, then I admit they didn't love me and there is no God. I can't believe they didn't love me. Maybe I'll just wish.

In case you are as confused as I was, trying to follow this back and forth, she says two months later, "I still want to hope, hope to get her to love me." Later, she says, "I kept deluding myself that I was my mother's favorite child. I didn't really believe it. I lived two lives, one wishing she loved me and the other knowing she didn't."

Carolyn had a fantasy, at least partly unconscious, that she had done something "bad," something never specified which caused her mother not to love her. That fantasy was invoked so that she could believe she could force her mother to love her. Carolyn believed that her threats by her temper tantrums were methods of forcing her mother to love her.

Much later, we see that the same kind of problem was going on in reference to her dead brother. In fact, her inability to recover from her brother's death 18 years prior, was her presenting problem.

She reads from her journal: "Val (therapist) is right. Pretending my brother is still alive is a lot of work. I never grieved over my brother's death. I denied it. I'm hoping he'll come back. If I give up hope, I fear he will never come back." Later I see I missed an important opening. She believed her hope would bring him back.

Carolyn puts in stark relief the role that hope can play, that is, that it can be used delusionally. We can see from this that we should be wary of the havoc it might wreak on other patients who are less ill. Additionally, we can see from Carolyn's history what dire consequences can come from not setting limits for a misbehaving child. She would have temper tantrums with her mother until she got her way. Carolyn's older sister warned their mother about her constant giving in, but to no avail. The result was that Carolyn could not tolerate the idea of an unfulfilled wish. From this came the "black hole," and the confusion about wish and hope.

However, the symptom of the "black hole" may not be confined to the overindulged child. I speculate that it may also occur with the child who was often denied the right to wish, as in "good boys don't wish for ice cream" or "good girls don't wish for their mothers to come back." I believe that I may have missed the fact that certain of my patients had this symptom because they had not verbalized it in precisely this way. With Carolyn, I had the advantage of an unusually verbal person.

Now what of the differences between myself and Dr. Akhtar? I can see why he got so impatient with patients who were constantly saying "if only" and "someday." They appear by that means to put the solution to their problems outside the analytic framework, and depend on external reality for a solution. It's as if they were coming to Dr. Akhtar saying "my life can only be fixed if the past can be changed, or when "someday" comes. I can't see how you can pull a rabbit out of a hat, but I'll be a good girl and play along." But Dr. Akhtar is not a magician. The analyst has no control over the occurrences of the patient's future life, much less her past.

Indeed, we have all heard patients complain: "You can't do anything to change my childhood, so what good are you?"

To which we can respond, "You are quite right. I can't change your childhood. but I can help you gain a feeling of greater control of the kind of situation you have endured, and thus find a way to respond in a way that is not so destructive to you."

For example, Janice needed to face the fact that her mother and her own fantasy were destroying her identity, and although she would never have the mother she wanted, she needed to learn to protect herself from her constant betrayal of her own wishes. If she could, she would undoubtedly be able to be angry when anyone tried to mold her, as her mother did, and she would not have to be devastated.

Kathleen had begun to solve her problems somewhat when she left me. She had begun to realize how phony her mother was and that a possibility existed of her meeting people whom she could respect. Indeed, I am remembering now that prior to Kathleen's coming to me, she had had a severe problem with alcohol, which she overcame by herself. As we know, alcohol abuse is known to be strongly associated with pathological lying and what laypeople call "wishful thinking."

Carolyn needed to further integrate the idea that throwing her wishes away, was destructive to her identity, in spite of her theory, that she had outsmarted everyone else in the world by avoiding all pain. *This is an example of the grandiosity with which the superego binds the patient to itself.*

In describing how these fantasies evolve, Akhtar again refers to "excessive optimism," which I previously described as viewing the error quantitatively, rather than qualitatively. I think that is the premise that leads Akhtar to make the technical error of "rupturing." Further, I think that error will confuse the patient. I can well imagine the patient asking, "How do you know how much is too much?" Putting myself in the place of the patient, I could not imagine an answer to that question.

I repeat, that the answer is to find the unconscious fantasy that lies behind the "someday" and "if only," I believe that those concepts are obstacles, not vehicles to freedom. The patient must be shown how binding they are, not fulfilling as they appear to him to be. Further, I believe they are teasers fed to the patient by a hostile superego that binds the patient to it, with "hopes" that are never fulfilled. It reminds me of the greyhound races, in which the dog is teased by a rabbit that he never captures.[17]

However, in "Constructions of Analysis," Freud gives us a skeletal idea on which we can base a treatment of schizophrenia. It is certainly not fleshed out, but gives us a hint of how one can proceed with treatment. Although Freud did not wish to treat schizophrenia himself, he gave us an idea of how those who are interested in doing it can proceed.[18]

Notes

1. I would have said "grandiose," not "omnipotent." See Chapter 2, "Infantile Omnipotence and Grandiosity."
2. Janice means that her mother was unresponsive.
3. Here we see that not only is she hoping for a mother who will really be maternal, but she is hoping to destroy her own needs. Indeed, the latter would seem to her to give credence to the former. This makes it appear to be not just a wish, but a hope.

4 I regret that interpretation which was given at a time when I was not as sensitive to this problem. I should have said the reverse: i.e., "as long as you hold onto the hope, you hold on to the fear."
5 I have written in my notes: Hope has to restrict itself to reality, but one can wish anything. I think this moment is the first time Kathleen got insight into the difference.
6 There were six children in her family. She was the fourth and felt she was neglected because she was not one of the older ones.
7 This is a condensation of what I actually said, which was, "You felt your mother didn't love you." But her condensation supports my difference of opinion with Akhtar on "rupture." Even inserting the word "felt" was not sufficient to keep Kathleen from rejecting the interpretation.
8 I think that insight can be explained both by the probability that it was already close to consciousness and that my intervention was useful.
9 Note I am speaking metaphorically here, which I prefer to do, when a patient is close enough to her unconscious to understand me. It has more impact than simply saying "feel dead."
10 Considering how she appeared when she first came to me, this is quite believable. At the first session as I said before, she told me that she had feared coming to therapy because she thought I would put her in a mental hospital and with great condescension assured me I could not help her. Her fears were realistic, because I think a psychiatrist certainly might have put her in the hospital.
11 I give that permission to all my patients to make sure that something unexpected doesn't happen which would cause them to be hospitalized. That permission is rarely taken advantage of.
12 How interesting. Another verbal error from the mistress of language.
13 See my paper on this subject, as well as Grotstein and Tustin (10, 11, 12).
14 I had never used that word with her and she is not a reader of Freud.
15 Carolyn cannot tolerate the idea of randomness.
16 Her father is dead.
17 See Levin, 1997, 2007. (13, 14)
18 Freud, 1937, XXIII, pp. 265–269.

References

1. Rosen, John. Personal Communication.
2. Shakespeare, William. Hamlet. (2015). In *The Complete Works*, Act III, Scene I, Barnes and Noble, Inc., China, p. 688.
3. Ibid.
4. Freud, Sigmund. (1910). Five lectures on psycho-analysis (Fifth Lecture). In *The Standard Edition of the Complete Psychological Works of Sigmund Freud*, Vol. XI, Hogarth Press, London, p. 53.
5. Ibid.
6. Akhtar, Salman. (1996). "'Someday' and 'If only. . . . Fantasies, pathological optimism and inordinate nostalgia as related forms of idealization.'" *JAPA*, 54.
7. Salman. "Abstract."
8. Ibid., p. 31.
9. Potamianou, Anna. (1997). *Hope: A Shield in the Economy of Borderline States*, Routledge, London and New York.
10. Levin, Revella. (1996). 'Black Hole' phenomena: Deficit or defense? A case report. *Journal of Clinical Psychoanalysis*, International Universities Press, Inc., Madison, CT.

11. Grotstein, James S. (1990). The 'black hole' as the basic psychotic experience: some newer psychoanalytic and neuroscience perspectives on psychosis. *Journal American Academy of Psychoanalysis*, 18: 29–46. See also chapter 8 and 9
12. Tustin, Frances. (1988). 'The black hole'—a significant element in autism. *Free Associations*, 11: 35–50.
13. Levin, Revella. (1997). Communicating with the schizophrenic superego. *Journal of the American Academy of Psychoanalysis*, 24: 709–736.
14. Levin, Revella. (2007). Communicating with the schizophrenic superego revisited: A new technique. *Journal of the American Academy of Psychoanalysis and Dynamic Psychiatry*, 35(3): 483–507.
15. Freud, Sigmund. (1937). *The Standard Edition of the Complete Psychological Works of Sigmund Freud*, Vol. XXIII, Hogarth Press, London, pp. 265–269.

15

THE EXCUSES FOR "SUPPORTIVE" RATHER THAN "ACTIVE" PSYCHOTHERAPY

In a future paper, "Toward a more Optimistic View of What Analysts Can Achieve," I will discuss the possibility that our aspirations for our patients are unnecessarily low. Now, it appears to me, more specifically, that we are not taking advantage of some vast discoveries that Freud offered us. In so doing, we have, so to speak, retreated from the battlefield. We have declared ourselves at least partially impotent.

The supposed basis for the prescription of psychotropic drugs for a psychotic, is a "chemical imbalance" of unknown or supposedly, as yet undiscovered composition. What is not asserted is that we (or I) don't know enough to resolve a psychosis psychoanalytically, at least in a particular patient. What is implied by such practitioners is, "*I don't know how to do it; Therefore, it can't be done.*" It is seldom described as, "*I don't know how to do it, so I will continue to try to explore new aspects of psychoanalytic theory to find it.*"

Indeed, in general medicine itself, the same kind of reasoning is often applied to physical illnesses, and ascribed to psychological problems. Examples are tuberculosis, cancer, ulcers, and no doubt many more. "*It can't be done. It must be in the patient's mind.*" Notably, such patients are rarely sent to some kind of therapist, counselor, or psychoanalyst. Rarely does the physician say, "*I am not smart enough to figure it out yet.*" When it can be blamed on a 'psychological problem,' as was so firmly believed when it came to ulcers, the physician's self-esteem is saved. Thus, the physician avoided the possible assault on his self-esteem, and/or guilt. (See *How Doctors Think*, Jerome Groopman, M.D., Chapter 6, 2007.)

In the past, we used to call neurotic patients 'too resistant.' I have not heard that excuse in years, apparently because enough people woke up to the fact that resolving resistances was the analyst's job. In recent times, the remedy has become the use of anti-psychotic drugs, or ECT, apparently when the patient became more rebellious than the analyst was willing to tolerate. Or, the patient required more work outside the analytic hour than the analyst was willing to offer. Indeed, I know of one analyst who had difficulty working with a patient who not only had psychological problems, but also had multiple sclerosis. The analyst decided to send her for ECT, adding to her already existing brain damage.

Failure to Attempt to Pull Out Roots

The interpersonal theory of psychoanalysis once used by the workers at Chestnut Lodge is, in my view, a kind of watered down psychoanalytic treatment. I use the term "watered down" because I got the impression from their workers that the professionals working there seemed to avoid the concrete language of schizophrenics. This led to a failure of emotionally contacting the unconscious of the patients. In turn, this led to basic problems remaining intact.

Many others worked in a variety of approaches (see following discussion). Hyman Spotnitz used a method he called "modern," in which he attacked the patient, making no distinction between the patient and his illness. Searles, of the interpersonal school, saw no harm in his hatred of the patient and makes the astounding statement that "we entered this profession in an unconscious effort to assuage our guilt" (Searles, 1979 [1]). In my view, such a person is unqualified to treat schizophrenics, because his guilt must necessitate hostility towards the patient. The therapist could not help blaming the patient for it, so the patient will suffer for his guilt.

Boyer and Giovachini use a more classical approach (Boyer and Giovachini [2]). Unlike Fromm-Reichmann (1950, 1952 [3]), who found interpretation of content to be of secondary importance, others including Bychowski and Rosen nearly approach classical analysis. There are innumerable others whom I believe it is valuable for a young therapist to explore. This would serve the purpose of discovering which approaches or bits of approaches best suit him or her. My own view is that the more closely the therapist can dig out the roots for each patient, the more likely the patient will advance even further and have results that last longer. This view is what is ignored by the behaviorist school, I believe. In my view, reliance on non-psychoanalytic techniques does not permit the patient to evolve to his or her maximum. To me, non-psychoanalytic techniques are supportive, not active, and leave the patient more vulnerable than is necessary. They declare the therapist, to some degree, helpless. The following, is to some degree, is an example of such treatment.

The Center Cannot Hold

This book was beautifully written by the brilliant Elyn R. Saks (Saks [4]). The following is a very condensed history. Her first intimation of mental illness came when she was eight. Later, she tried street drugs and was sent to a very rigid institution. Some years later, she attended Oxford and became overtly psychotic. She was referred to a Kleinian analyst—Mrs. Jones, but not medicated. Occasionally she was hospitalized, but no mechanical restraints were used because British hospitals rarely use them and have not done so for 200 years.

But when Ms. Saks wanted to go back to the U. S. to finish her education, Mrs. Jones handled the separation most unanalytically. There was no preparation for the separation. Mrs. Jones and her husband found it necessary to take a whole day to get Ms. Saks out of the office, Ms. Saks screaming and/or crying throughout much of that day. When she returned to the U.S., Ms. Saks spent the summer writing 10–15-page letters to Mrs. Jones.

The following is an example of her productions to her next analyst, Dr. Pritzer:

> People are controlling me, they're putting thoughts into my head. I can't resist them. They are doing it to me. I'll have to kill them. Are you controlling me? They're making me walk around your office. I give life and I take it away.
>
> *(Ibid, p. 132 [5])*

Ms. Saks does not receive any response from Dr. Pritzer. In fact, the only kind of response we see from Dr. Pritzer is when he set limits.

"I walked over to a big leafy plant in the corner and snapped off one of its leaves. 'See this is what I do to people!' Dr. Pritzer's stern response is, 'You should not have done that, Elyn, I like that plant. You are not to do that again . . .' He was setting limits" (Ibid., p. 134 [6]). I ask, is this analysis? Any interpretation would have been more helpful.

Of course, when she cracked in public, she was hospitalized. Ms. Saks says she later learned that 100 or so people die each year in the U.S. while being put in restraints (Ibid., p. 149). That certainly seems to me to be a good reason for psychoanalysts to keep their patients out of the hospital. Needless to say, she did not receive psychoanalytic treatment in the hospital, nor is there any mention of her analyst visiting her there.

Interestingly, her parents knew little of her condition. Through all her crises, "I had kept most of the details of my behavior, of the various diagnoses, away from my parents" (Ibid., p. 153). Her rationalizations are impressive—(1) She was ashamed. (2) She didn't want to worry them. They had other duties and children. (3) "I didn't want them interfering in my life." Incredibly, both physicians and her parents cooperated in the arrangement.

Ms. Saks says something that seems to me very appropriate, especially since I have said versions of "Why is any of them in this business?"

> Part of the problem was that I was behaving like a patient in psychoanalysis. When Mrs. Jones and I were working together, I was encouraged to say exactly what was on my mind, always, no matter how crazy it sounded—that

was how analysis worked. That was the **point** (emphasis hers).[1] Otherwise how would she [Mrs. Jones] know what was going on inside me? But the people at MU1O [the hospital] didn't want to know. If they couldn't tolerate what was in my head, **why were any of them in this business**? (emphasis mine) . . . Overall the sole message they seemed to want me to get was 'behave yourself' . . . say what's on your mind and there'll be consequences; struggle to keep the delusions to yourself, and it's likely you won't get the help you need.

(Ibid., p. 161)

On the other hand, Ms. Saks has had so little of customary psychoanalysis, that she rejects the schizophrenogenic mother theory with contempt. Those who read the book will discover that the schizophrenogenic mother turns out to be the father (Ibid., p. 169). I think proof of that is her father's statement:

'You have to stop thinking like this,' said my father firmly. I knew before he'd gotten to the next sentence that I was in for the familiar 'buck up-get tough' speech, variations of which I'd heard much of my life. 'This isn't terminal cancer, Elyn—and people have come back strong even from that diagnosis, you know. What you've got, that's a piece of cake by comparison. You can beat it with the right attitude. Stop feeling sorry for yourself.'

(Ibid., p. 183)

We never hear about an analyst saying to her, "You need a very good dose of feeling sorry for yourself." (I should insert regarding her 'weakness' that she managed to finish Yale law school and achieved a professorship.)

Though she did constantly argue with her ensuing psychoanalysts when her symptoms became severe and they wanted to medicate her. But she refused medication only because she thought they were a sign she was weak.

She continued her schooling and received treatment and medication with various analysts whose names she disguised. But still "I was having brief hallucinations, mostly at night—one of a large spider crawling up my wall, but mostly of people standing and staring at me." She said to herself, "They're not there. There are not really there. And even if they are, they're not really looking at you" (Ibid., p. 202). Thus, instead of getting treatment, she deals with her symptoms by denying them. When she complains of the side effects of medication, her analyst's response is "Should we up the Navane?" (Ibid., p. 203).

A few weeks later, she says to her analyst "The people in the sky poison me. I in turn will poison the world." I see her response to being poisoned as amazingly self-preservative. The analyst, however, says: "I think you are having thoughts that are scaring you because you need to be on more medication now" (Ibid., p. 204).

I will suggest just a few interpretations that might be made in response to these productions. I don't know the meaning of the spider but the analyst could have inquired. Denying people are staring at her, is certainly counterproductive. Her superego certainly is staring at her, without let-up, looking for something to criticize. When she has side effects from the medication, instead of lowering the medication, he wants to raise it. When she feels she is being poisoned, instead of asking about the nature of the poison, or declaring the poison to be lies she has been fed (which is what I have found consistently to be the accurate interpretation) he sweeps the scary thoughts under the rug with suggestions for more medication.

Quite consistently as she went from analyst to analyst, for various external reasons, whenever she produced seriously psychotic material, she was hospitalized or medicated. None of the analysts ever seemed to see the material as an opportunity. With the exception of the last analyst, who perhaps will interpret the material, nothing Ms. Saks writes about shows evidence that the analyst interpreted the material at all. Only Mrs. Jones responded analytically, but confined herself to pointing out only what she thought were projections. I experienced them as blaming the patient.

Another production was, "People are controlling me, they're putting thoughts in my head, I can't resist them. They're doing it to me. I have to kill them. Are you controlling me?" (Ibid., p. 132). This could have been interpreted as "Your father certainly did try to control you. You can kill him, by doing what you want to do. If you catch me controlling you, why would let me get away with it?" These interpretations weaken the superego, build the ego, and weaken the transference.

But should the patient be treated psychoanalytically? Leave it to the brilliant Ms. Saks to discover the 'professional' view of that at Yale. "Psychoanalysis, they explained, causes regression, and I was already too regressed; supportive psychotherapy, combined with medication was the way to go." Little did they know how unpsychoanalytic the treatment was. "I needed, in their view, to shore up my psychological defenses, not to delve behind or take them apart" (Ibid., p. 187).

If that is true, how was it that Freud found the interpretation of dreams so helpful? He brought the unconscious to consciousness. Why would not understanding 'poison' do the same for Ms. Saks?

At the end of the book, Ms. Saks finds a Dr. Freed.

> He comes right in on what I'm feeling, and helps me to understand how I sometimes use my psychotic thoughts to avoid the ordinary bad feelings that everyone experiences—sadness, rage, garden-variety disappointment. He also has more faith in the analytic process than I do. He thinks I might be able to get off meds entirely someday.

Through association with a psychopharmocologist she is on twice the recommended dose (Ibid., p. 325). I can't resist a caustic remark here: "Twice the drugs a day will keep the unconscious away, but the unconscious is exactly where the problem is, and how can you treat psychosis if you ignore it?

As to Ms. Saks' insight, when she gets breast cancer, "My father did not want to come and would not explain why . . . My parents not coming was a major blow. All my life, I'd idealized them . . . When I felt at death's door, and their first and last impulse was to stay where they were, I was crushed." She says, "I could no longer deny they're flawed (as are we all)," followed by three excuses (Ibid., p. 327).

Even her present insight is restricted to "whatever their faults (or ours), there was no shortage of 'I love you's' from my parents when I was a child, nor is there one now: To this day, they're openly affectionate with all of us," (9) continued with another page of excuses. She ends the book with another page of parental defense: "My parents and brothers gave me the love and support that allowed my life to proceed" (Ibid., p. 340). But her parents did not attend her wedding. Her friends did give her magnificent love and support. The deeper interpretations of pscychoanalysis would have uncovered this self-deception and cleared the way to better mental health.

Her way of handling her illness was to "keep reality on one side and delusions on the other" (Ibid., p. 183). No wonder she is exhausted. Is this what analysis taught her? But even Ms. Saks has a better solution, which unfortunately neither she nor her analysts, except perhaps Dr. Freed, took seriously enough. "Psychosis is a waking nightmare," she says (Ibid., p. 336). I can hear Tennessee Williams in the background saying "mendacity," and Freud saying "Amen."

Perhaps the final thing I can say about Ms. Saks that I think we should all pay very strict attention to is in regard to analysts' attitude towards patients. She says that in England doctors allowed her to make her own decisions. They only recommended. "Even at my craziest, I interpreted this as a demonstration of respect. When you're really crazy, respect is like a lifeline someone's throwing out. Catch this and maybe you won't drown" (80). I submit that supportive psychotherapy is not respectful. Her experience with Anthony Storr is a good example of this. (86–87).

Why Rush to Unnecessary Surrender?

It is hardly a secret that, for the past 35 or 40 years, certain writers have bashed psychoanalysis and pretty effectively undermined it in the public eye in the U.S. Oddly, some psychoanalysts themselves have helped to make it appear less potent and chip away at its reputation. The list of those people is too long to mention.

Repeatedly, I have asked myself, "Why?" The detractors have in effect said, "Let's not go too far. It's dangerous." They have disregarded Freud's dictum that psychoanalysis will make many more discoveries. Many insisted on the statement that Ms. Saks heard at Yale, "The patient is already too regressed."

Let me try to simplify the issue. It is a question of "Shall we pull out the roots of the pathology or push them down?" Freud's answer consistently was "Pull it out so we can examine it, understand it and have an opportunity to resolve it."

Nowhere in the 24 books of the Standard Edition did I find a statement that recommends repression.

The "push down" school says, "Oh, no, we dare not pull it out. It might explode. It's better to push it down, and let the patient resign herself to never having an opportunity to truly understand herself. Some pathological material will have to remain undisturbed. We have to repress some of it."

Obviously, I belong to the "pull out" school, which I believe was a given in Freud's mind. In 1991, the New York Psychoanalytic Society presented a panel entitled the "Use of Medication with Patient in Analysis." I regret to say that of the six members, five were in favor of using medication. After the presentation, I said,

> I recall the experience I had at the International Congress in Montreal four years ago. At the time, Herman Beland, then President of the West German Psychoanalytic Association, presented a case of a psychotic, suicidal woman. In the treatment of that case, which turned out very successfully, he used only a very small amount of medication and even that was used only for a few days. The case, presented at a plenary session, was greeted with great enthusiasm . . . certainly the analysts in other countries cannot be that much brighter than we are.

The international situation is not that much different now than it was then, so I have no reason to alter my statement. I must confess that there have a been a few times where I set limits like one of Ms. Saks' analysts did. I lived to regret that I did not interpret instead of doing what is essentially a repressive measure. An example of how one doesn't have to set limits was when one of my patients kept shouting endlessly. I feared for my ears and my neighbors. I was tempted to set limits, but pulled myself together and said "What are you trying to hide?" The shouting stopped and I got a very direct answer in much lower decibels.

If we resign ourselves to the "push down" school, aren't we saying that Freud's work was of little value? His understanding of the unconscious was for the purpose of decreasing the suffering of his patients. Shall we inch closer to the cognitive and behaviorist schools, whose positive results are so temporary? Shall we join the schools of treatment who behave as if there were no such thing as an unconscious? Isn't such massive denial a sign of pathology?

Why are we, Freud's descendants, so eager to join his opponents? I take this question seriously and I have no firm answer. I can only say "it is fear," but I am not at all sure of what. Since I have never felt fear of a patient's unconscious myself, I can claim no great insight. But I do believe that those who have it, can make an effort to understand whether it is a rational of irrational fear.

I see no reason to see it as other than irrational. From my position, I feel we should, in order to maintain our integrity, try to understand it and therefore resolve it. Let us not condemn Freud's great essential contribution, the unconscious, to the dust bin.

At the Salzburg conference, Freud commented, "Psychoanalysis was not possible with dementia praecox patients: all that could be done was to use what had been learned from neurotic patients as a guideline to the symptoms and then confront the psychotic patient directly."

Clearly the idea that psychoanalysis was not possible with dementia praecox patients, was meant in the sense that they could not be asked to lie down and free associate, but they could be confronted directly, which is exactly what John Rosen described in his book *Direct Analysis*.

Note

1 Unfortunately, she leaves out the value of interpretations, if she knows it.

References

1. Searles, Harold. (1979). *Countertransference and Related Subjects*, International Universities Press, New York, p. 28.
2. Fromm-Reichman, Frieda. (1950). *Principles of Intensive Psychotherapy*, University of Chicago Press, Chicago, p. 131.
3. Boyer, L. Bryce, and Giovachini, Peter L. (1967). *Psychoanalytic Treatment of Characterological and Schizophrenice Disorders*, Science House, New York, pp. 136–138.
4. Saks, Elyn. (2007). *The Center Cannot Hold*, Hyperion, New York.
5. Ibid., p. 132.
6. Ibid., p. 114.
7. Ibid., p. 153.
8. Ibid., p. 161.
9. Ibid., p. 183.
10. Ibid., p. 202.
11. Ibid., p. 203.
12. Ibid., p. 132.
13. Ibid., p. 120.
14. Ibid., p. 325.
15. Ibid., p. 327.
16. Ibid., p. 9.
17. Ibid., p. 340.
18. Ibid., p. 325.
19. Ibid., p. 336.
20. Ibid., p. 80.
21. Ibid., pp. 86–87.
22. New York Psychoanalytic Society. (1992). The use of medication with patients in analysis. (Published in the *Journal of Clinical Psychoanalysis*, 1[1])

16

TOWARD A MORE OPTIMISTIC VIEW OF WHAT ANALYSTS CAN ACHIEVE

The question I am raising in this paper is inspired by work with borderline and schizophrenic patients, and concerns an aspect of our counter transference of which we are usually unaware, namely our construction of-and therefore acceptance of reality. The question can be put simply enough: are we settling for a lower level of achievement for our patients than is obtainable? Certainly, there appears to be good reasons for being pessimistic about what is obtainable. When our patients come to us, they are suffering from apparently important deficiencies. They suffer from anxiety, are either emotionally flat or labile, and prone to overexcitement.

If they can work at all, they are not working optimally at their jobs, object constancy is probably minimal, shaky, and what constancy has been achieved is undermined by their own pessimism and resignation. Further, inevitably they are, in varying degrees, skeptical of what we can do for them. Let me begin by raising the possibility that by making assessments like the foregoing, we are unconsciously influenced by what they assume is their prognosis. Especially true, in this era of psychiatric drugs, where the height of psychiatric aspiration often seems to be to "cover the symptoms." I have a suspicion that privately, analysts say to their intimate colleagues, or else, even more privately to themselves, "He (or she) can only achieve a limited amount of health. He has been too damaged."

But exactly here, when we are assimilating whatever tale of impossibility comes from the patient, we should think to ourselves that, though this indeed sounds like "misery," our field began by not accepting "misery" as an end-state. I am referring specifically to hysterical misery, and to Freud's famous dictum that his goal was to transform "hysterical misery into common unhappiness" (Breuer and Freud, 305).

Some readers will object that the hysterical misery Freud refers to is somehow different, that it was pretend play, an affair of the imagination, a false illness. But let us recall that at the time it was not so clear that hysterical misery was not fate; at the time, it seemed just the opposite. For who could take up battle against a disease of the nervous system and expect to win? Similarly, with our patients nowadays, even though their traits realistically seem to be the product of their deficits interacting with an often harsh social world, we do them no service to accept a lowered horizon, before we have exhausted the investigation into what it was all about. Freud proceeded to make a psychological investigation regardless. So should we.

Other readers will challenge me on a different basis: they will say not all patients achieve happiness. Resignation can be part of maturity and in any event, is better than the endless dashed hopes, bitter recriminations, and other storms that must accompany a life of false hopes. To this, I reply simply, that not all my patients achieve happiness. And the ones who don't, must indeed learn to live with it. Nonetheless, I advocate taking a second look, and a third, and a fourth, etc., at the patient's glum appraisal, and being as wary as possible about its contagion into our own reservoir of hope. This line of thinking derives from my early work with severely ill patients which I was able to witness, and some of which I was able to do myself, who achieved really profound changes and proceeded to live worthwhile and fulfilling lives.

I was young at the time and this experience had a profound effect on me. I learned something invaluable about what was possible. But most analysts are not fortunate enough to have had this experience played out before their very eyes. And it is that much more understandable if they have fallen victim to what I am suggesting is a counter-transference problem. Indeed, their own analysts may have fallen victim to that problem, so that their own analyses proceeded under a false assessment of what constitutes optimal results, or at least, this has been reported to me by many analysts. The result, at any rate, is that as a field we have settled for goals that I believe are set too low. Every one of my patients has insisted near the beginning of their treatment, that he (or she) must surely be the sickest patient I have ever tried to treat. They seem quite deflated when I must inform them that they do not win the prize. Surely, this is a most interesting form of grandiosity.

The Reality Principle and Its Discontents

A different way of putting the question I am raising in this paper is "What is the greatest amount of pleasure and the least amount of pain that is consistent with good mental health and how can we help a patient attain it?" I doubt that few would argue that everyone would wish for the maximum attainable degree of happiness in their lives. But how much and what kind of happiness is attainable, consistent with the least amount of pain? As a sub-question, I am also asking: "How much of unpleasant reality must be accepted in order to achieve this goal?"

In raising this latter question, I am implicitly not restricting myself to the assumption that accepting unpleasant reality is always a requirement. In doing the latter, I give myself a kind of freedom which analysts do not usually permit themselves, i.e., to delve into areas which have been 'forbidden' to us by basic theory, and basic assumptions.

Freud has often been viewed as pessimistic regarding how much happiness humans can achieve. He writes, "Generally speaking, our civilization is built up on the suppression of instincts. Each individual has surrendered some part of his possessions—some part of the sense of omnipotence or of the aggressive or vindictive inclinations in his personality" (Freud, 1908). Clearly, he is saying that important painful loss is necessary for civilization to maintain itself, and the individual to adjust himself or herself to it. Of course, the idea of the death instinct is another obvious example of his pessimism (Freud, 1920).

Implicit in this view is the assumption that civilization has the last word on reality, and thus, on the modicum of misery all must endure. Freud's opinion is severe but clear: civilization is what is necessary for man's survival and the restrictions that civilization puts on society are the least amount of restriction necessary for man's happiness. Strachey's introduction to Freud's "Civilization and Its Discontents" states that Freud's theme is the "irremediable antagonism between the demands of instinct and the restrictions of civilization" (Freud, 1930).

Personally, I question the irremediableness and perhaps even the antagonism. Elizabeth Young-Bruehl and Faith Bethelard also question it. They say, "Which demand of what instinct? Which demands of what civilization?" (Young-Bruehl, 1997).

My first argument with Freud's assumption is to point out that not only every nation, but even every city in that nation makes subtle or even not so subtle distinctions as to what is acceptable. These standards, however, can differ markedly from other nations and cities. For example, in Italy, one person shouting at another is quite frequent, is not looked at askance and subsides fairly quickly without ending a relationship. In upperclass England, such behavior would be shocking. Germany differs from the United States in that, in the former, asking favors of a stranger if one does not have a dire emergency is frowned upon. But, in the latter, it is quite acceptable for instance to ask directions if one is traveling. Much of what is acceptable in New York City would doubtless be unacceptable in Salt Lake City. What is accepted in Salt Lake City might be laughed at in New York City.

Beyond variations in custom, there are individual differences in conformity and non-conformity, as well as in the degree of conscientiousness. Beyond that, and of special relevance to our work, is the variations of the kind of condemnations found in each individual superego. Is there an analyst who has not heard a patient say "But society does not accept X," to which the analyst's silent response is "Where does that irrational idea come from?" But each patient, at least at the beginning of treatment, believes that their own superego is an accurate reflection of what 'society' demands, not seeing that that representation is only indicative of their own parents' idiosyncrasies.

As our work with a particular patient progresses, we find more and more that the 'society' which that particular superego 'represents' is inconsistent with the patient's happiness to an unnecessary degree. It not only unrealistically denies the patient pleasure, but following its dictates frequently evokes hostility from most of the people in his or her environment. One of my patients recently expressed great surprise to discover that most people enjoyed her positive responses to them. Her father had responded to her positive responses with "That's phony," in a voice that made it clear that he believed that such behavior was not acceptable in 'society.' In general, he seemed to be a person who was contemptuous of anything that made anyone else happy. And then there are those patients whose perfectionism endures despite the clearest sort of feedback. In the workplace, compulsivity, when expressed as perfectionism, may cause an employer to complain about how long the employee takes to complete his tasks. But, in the patient's mind, 'society' would be outraged at possible mistakes.

I find that, in general, as patients used the word 'society,' and in the terms of what it 'forbids,' they are clearly using it as a part of what we call the superego, but externalizing it so that they themselves don't recognize it. As such, I think we need to be on our guard when patients use that word, and be skeptical as to whether or not it has value for humanity or will be more likely to deprive humanity unnecessarily of freedom that will enrich our lives.

I received support of the following practitioners by lesser known of their statements. Freud speaks about bringing "about the slow demolition of the super-ego" (Freud 1940). Alexander says,

> We now see that our therapeutic endeavors must be directed against a two-faced over lordship on the part of the superego . . . an anachronism in the mind. It has lagged behind the rapid development of civilized conditions, in the sense that its automatic, inflexible mode of function causes the mental system to continually to come into conflict with the outer world . . . This task is carried out by limiting the sphere of activity of the automatically functioning superego, and transferring its role to the conscious ego.
> *(Alexander, 1925)*

Ferenczi contemporaneously agrees: "the business of a real character analysis is to do away . . . with any kind of superego, including that of the analyst" (Ferenczi, 1928). My own contribution to this concept has been to invent a technique to weaken the superego of schizophrenics in order to accomplish the above discussed goals and permit the ego to reign over the personality (Levin, 1997). But further discussion is not germane here; what we are interested in is less the aspect of internalization, and more the sense of reality that accrues to the dictates of the internalized authority.

I should explain again to the reader that my questioning of the value of the acceptance of reality was inspired by my work with borderline and schizophrenic patients—patients who, in a manner of speaking, had trouble with reality testing. It is these patients, who more than others who are ill, gave me an opportunity not afforded to their analysts of those less ill, to see how unrealistic superegos can be. Yet, despite obvious failures to accept many realities, I found my patients in some ways, were so accepting of reality that they were emotionally paralyzed. This manifested itself in their anxiety. Examples of this are embedded everywhere in the commonplace anxieties of everyday life: "If I wear this outfit, someone might not like it." Or "If I invite Mary to my party, she might refuse." Such anticipated rejections are, of course, within the realm of the possible, but reasonably healthy people do not find themselves immobilized by them. My patients often do. And their immobilization was not experienced as a conflict—whether to do this or that—but rather as though they were bumped against a wall, or a ceiling, and needed to pull back within themselves lest they hurt their head or arm or whatever. In other words, they had bumped against a reality and what I was hearing, if I was lucky enough to hear anything, was part of the process of recoil. And yet, one could not really argue with the patient's rendition of reality. Joan might really not like the outfit. Mary might well not come to the party. And so on.

So, I came to the strange conclusion that, in some ways, if one takes being realistic literally, psychotics can be more realistic than non-psychotics. Realistically many obstacles can lie in the way of our patients' goals. But it appears to me, that very often the greater the psychopathology of the patient, the more he or she may be aware of those obstacles. While conversely, the healthier person may be blind to much of the realistic hindrance. This view led me to the importance of infantile omnipotence.

Omnipotence and Grandiosity

I think Joan Riviere puts it well when she says, "Omnipotence has been a vague concept, loosely and confusedly bandied about, hazily interchanged with narcissism or with phantasy-life, its meaning and especially its functions not clearly established and placed" (Riviere, 1936).

I have written elsewhere on this subject (Levin, 1986) (chapter 5), so here I will merely briefly recapitulate. In essence, I have found myself forced to assume that infantile omnipotence is necessary for healthy development. Ornstein has described omnipotence exactly as I have, an "unrealistic feeling of confidence" (Ornstein, 122). If omnipotence is sufficiently interfered with because of inadequate sensitivity by the mother to the infant's wishes, and an incapacity to help the infant gain gratification, he will in defense, develop grandiosity. Perhaps the most important distinction between the two, as the child grows, is the following: the child who successfully goes through his period of infantile omnipotence becomes a confident child, and as his confidence leads to both the development of skills and trust in relationships, it increasingly becomes anchored on a realistic basis, with the result that infantile omnipotence recedes into the unconscious. But the child whose feeling of omnipotence is interfered with too much, because the parent is intimidated by it, becomes grandiose, which is expressed as being compulsively competitive, hostile, anxious and contemptuous of others.

Kathleen, a patient on the verge of a schizophrenic break when she came to me (and aware of it) had the following insight: "When I've been insisting I can't be cured, I've really been saying my sickness is so brilliant that you can't cure it." I later discovered that as a child and teenager, Kathleen constantly viewed herself as stupid. Her mother had been so jealous of Kathleen's intelligence that the child repressed her realistic appraisal of her abilities. Gradually, as I interpreted both her grandiosity as her 'incurability,' and how she had denied her intelligence, she realized she could not possibly fail at college, began to be confident of her intelligence, and graduated with honors.

The important point about this distinction is that infantile omnipotence is clearly not reality. The child's wish or cry certainly does not in itself produce the bottle. But *feeling* that it does brings about an unrealistic lack of anxiety, which I believe is necessary to good mental health. If, on the other hand, the normal infantile omnipotence is rejected and subsequently repressed because of parental hostility or jealousy, apparently realistic anxiety results in grandiosity in other parts of the personality.

It is my thesis that we, as a profession, are too prone to distrust the unconscious' strength of drive for health—and we insufficiently trust the instinct for self-preservation. We are too likely to say, "This trauma or these circumstances are so damaging that our patient cannot find his potential for self-fulfillment. His confidence, his trust, his whatever is crushed beyond redemption." We treat such 'hopeless' patients as if a limb were amputated, instead of merely buried. I have had patients who say just that when they have improved. One example is Carolyn's "black hole" symptom, which I have argued should be understood in terms of a defense rather than a deficit.[1]

I submit that, as long as one is alive, the instinct of self-preservation cannot be crushed, if only because it is instinctual and in that sense, biological. Mental health researchers are now more and more assuming a predominantly biological etiology for psychological illness (a view of which I am quite skeptical) but surprisingly ignore the biological origin of the instinct for self-preservation. Certainly, Freud seemed most impressed by the self-preservation instinct, since it is noted 56 times in the Index of the Standard Edition (Freud, 1974).

Reality or Defense?

Thus, the patient may experience the feeling of having his instinct of self-preservation crushed, as expressed in such statements as "I will never be able to have a good relationship because my father died when I was so young," or "because my mother hated me." An example of someone who one would have thought would—at best—lead an average life is Bill Clinton. He never met his father and had a far-from-desirable step-father, yet he accomplished and is still accomplishing a great deal.

However, I submit that it is the defense against the emotional trauma that causes the arrested development and not the trauma itself. For example, one patient's "emptiness" may have prevented adequate mourning for a lost father. Another patient may wish to believe that her mother's hatred of her is "proof" that she was "bad," in the hope that if only she became "better," her mother would love her. Of course, the patient can never find a way of being "good enough."

The work of the analyst is to look with sufficient persistence for the defensive fantasy and expose it to the ego. I am very ready to accept the idea that this can appear impossible, and frequently is, most difficult. The patient may sound very realistic. One wonderful rationalization is age. "I am too old" says one 43-year-old patient, who is also emotionally very ill. But when I hear the same complaint, bemoaned in the same plaintive voice from my 30-year-old and 23-year-old patients, I come to the conclusion that there is no such thing as "too old." If I had any doubts before, they were erased this past year by a successful treatment of an 87-year-old woman's paranoid delusion.

We need to be very careful not to be seduced by a patient's *depressive certainty*. I have yet to see a severely ill patient who did not advise me, very soon after entering treatment, that I cannot help him or her. Looking back on the tone with which this advice is usually given, I realize how sympathetic to *me* that tone is. It is always said, as if I were a poor, well-meaning, but clearly naive person. The implication being that it is the patient who has accepted this tragic "reality."

Speaking of my supposed naïveté, I see how seductive that attitude can be when I listen to 77-year-old Hannah, a new patient who is a refugee from Nazi Germany. She tells me how reluctant she is to share her pain with me, since I am obviously so innocent. How realistic her statement sounds! After all, I was not chased from my native country in fear for my life. I soon discover that her mother, who fled with her, also had to be protected from unpleasant realities.

Bathsheba was another patient who was also very concerned for me, and had good reason to fear I could not help her (see chapter 6). She was extremely suicidal and had seen 11 therapists before me. But she is now no longer suicidal and has made a very good marriage. Neither Bathsheba, Hannah, nor the previously mentioned Kathleen, who boasted of her incurability, are any longer resigned to their illness; they are determined to fight for their health. I, of course, grant the exception of their unconscious resistance. But in their eyes, I am no longer that fool who mistakenly thought they could get better.

Projective Disidentification

Relevant to this issue of reality acceptance is the question of *who owns what* in the patient's assessment. That is, we also have to consider what is owned by the other, having been put there by the patient through projective identification.

The role of projective identification in foreclosing reality is touched on in a recent essay by John Steiner, "The Aim of Psychoanalysis in Theory and Practice." The burden of Steiner's argument is to draw our attention to how the patient cannot fully accept the split-off fragments of self that have been expelled onto the object via projective identification, *unless and until* the patient also accepts separation from the object. The patient and the analyst are thus inevitably in a tricky situation as they try to undo projective identification. It would seem a simple business for the patient simply to reclaim those parts of the self that have been put into the object. But projective identification serves not only to rid the self of aspect of self that are intolerable to the other, in one way or another. It is also a means of controlling the object. That, in turn, involves a denial of the object's rejection of those aspects. So, in giving up the defense, the patient must also accept rejection of the object. And this entails mourning.

> It is clear that projective identification itself obscures the reality of the separateness between self and object, and it is this reality that is re-established if the projections can be returned. The patient often find this situation puzzling and unfair. He cannot take back the projection unless he can mourn and he cannot let the object go and mourn it unless he can take back the projections.
>
> *(Steiner, 1077)*

What is there to argue with here? Steiner's is a most courageous attempt to tackle a difficult task and has much to commend it. Yet, he falls into what I believe is the trap of the depressive position's "reality." He says, "The motive for projective identification can be varied—but the result is always a denial of separation." I submit that if the problem were only managing separation of subject and object, it would not be nearly so difficult. One could mourn and be finished with it. The problem is just what Steiner called "projection of split-off fragments" (Ibid.). It is painful to lose an object. But it is impossible to resign oneself to loss of emotional pieces of the self. The problem, in other words, is that the object will leave and take parts of the self with it.

What I have not seen in the literature nor discussed in Klein, as far as I know, is that the motive for giving up pieces of the self, is the fact that originally the object has rejected those pieces. If the patient then gives them up, whether out of fear of separation or for other motives, then he is leaving them in control of the object. This in turn obliges him to maintain a permanent tie to the object. Whatever it is the object rejects, be it intelligence, love, creativity (or whatever it is that the patient experiences the object is rejecting)—it is no longer his. He no longer has control over it. But the instinct for self-preservation will fight that.

This degree of relinquishment rarely happens. Few patients will accept it. Those who do will be truly in the depressive position, in the literal sense. That is, they will leave their treatment unnecessarily depressed. Steiner puts the matter quite succinctly when he says "the reality of dependence on the object has to be acknowledged and the reality of the loss of the object has to be faced in order for mourning to be worked through, and both are often vehemently resisted" (Ibid.).

However, if the patient accepts the fact that at the center of the relinquishment is a piece of himself, it will ameliorate the pain of the parent's rejection of him, and he will not find the loss of the object so unbearable. The loss of the object, if that is all it is, can be accepted with a reasonable degree of mourning. Indeed, one can infer that if the patient is mourning seemingly without end, or resists mourning at all, it is because he cannot to leave an emotional part of *himself* behind, not because he cannot accept separation from the object. What is called for in these situations is projective disidentification, if I may use that term.

Omnipotence, again, is part and parcel of healthy adaptation; it is an expression of the instinctual life and is well described by Ornstein as "unrealistic confidence." It is, in another way of speaking, the healthy inner buffer, hardwired into our make-up, that we have in encountering "reality." Omnipotence is not an obstacle to dealing with reality. Indeed, if one consults Freud's original formulation of the principles of mental functioning, one will see that he speaks of the "reality principle" as "safeguarding" the pleasure principle. In my terms, negotiations with reality serve to modify one's omnipotence, but also to confirm it.

Grandiosity is another matter altogether. As I have argued in Chapter 2, grandiosity arises when omnipotence has failed and defensive efforts are needed. It is a secondary formation that hardens around the original breech in omnipotence; its characteristics are not only hostility to the other, but also unwarranted superiority. Grandiosity cuts one off. Interestingly, grandiosity need not be grand. It can also be poor, or downtrodden, or long-suffering, as with a patient of mine whose secret consolation was that she could tolerate more pain than anyone else in the world. It can be a mixture of suffering, renunciation, and fantasy vindication, as it was with the patient who had "God in her pocket." She could "prove" this was so, provided she could continue to deny having the wishes that were never fulfilled. Another patient had "total" control over her mother by virtue of never admitting to herself that she had a brain, a very good one in fact, of her own.

Grandiosity does indeed interfere with the assessment of reality. But, if looked at closely, the interference is of a negative sort. This is obvious enough if the grandiosity takes a negative form, such as the patient whose secret consolation and superiority lay in her ability to tolerate more misery than anyone else on earth. For such a patient, a negative assessment of reality, and pity for the poor therapist, is a matter of course. The most common form, in my experience, hides in patients with the strongest superegos. Although filled with guilt, they also believe they are morally superior to everyone else and that grandiosity informs the resistance to reducing the strength of their superego.

The interconnections between grandiosity and projective identification are usually there to be discovered, provided one can get an initial foothold. That is, a patient will readily explain how having an indissoluble connection with a parent made him feel on top of the world, equipped him to endure no matter what. That lack of separation and the grandiosity go hand in hand. But you cannot readily get to either side of it meaningfully until you have established that there is something else about the patient that has been rejected—first by the parent, and now by the patient himself. I maintain that you cannot reach this dimension without confidence (indeed to have the derivative of one's omnipotence) that theoretically, at least, the patient is wrong in his conviction that he can never really succeed or have a life of his own. The patient will present as though infantile omnipotence has been lost, but in fact it can be rediscovered. The therapist's job is to find the structures, part grandiosity, part projection, part fusion with the object that show where it has been hidden from sight.

Steiner's view of the therapeutic centrality of relinquishing wishes is not novel. Freud also speaks of the desirability of "renunciation of wishes" when he speaks of a woman's desire for a penis. He points out how resistant a woman can be to giving up her wish for a penis; even when she intellectually accepts the reality, the wish "persists in the unconscious." I often consider the possibility that Freud mistook a woman's desire to have penis *in* her for a desire to have one on her. That is a wish that *can* be fulfilled. The only solution that Freud offers is through the sublimation of an intellectual profession. Again, as I said in relationship to Steiner's relinquishment of objects, I believe that this cannot be done, or if it is, the result is a pathological depression.

For purposes of clarification, let me hasten to state that I have never believed Freud was correct in his views regarding penis envy. I think, rather, that what appeared to be penis envy was in part due to the restrictions of the culture of the time, and in part a male's difficulty in believing that what was so precious to him would not be desired by the gender that did not have one. By the same token, one could make a case for the unconscious desire of men for female breasts, which are so much more evident even when a woman is clothed, which men find so attractive, and which have such an important function.

Rather, I brought up the question of penis envy because it is in that area that Freud most clearly states the concept of relinquishment of wishes. I think that no matter which wish one discusses, whether the patient wishes to give up a wish, or the analyst encourages him to do so, it is a recipe for frustration and/or self-deception. I think the most honest and least harmful statement one can make about any unwelcome wish is "*I wish I didn't wish for that.*" In so stating, one must recognize that that statement will bring only clarification. As I said in relationship to Steiner's "relinquishment," I believe this cannot be done, or if the attempt is made, the result is a pathological depression. One's wishes are part and parcel of one's identity. As such, for the analyst to ask the patient to renounce his instinct for self-preservation, one might as well ask him, to symbolically stop breathing!

Rather, the analyst must help the patient. remove the obstacles to that wish fulfillment. One example is the Oedipus complex, which Steiner also discusses. In general, he supports Money-Kyrle's belief in the persistence of Oedipal pathology, that the patients "adhere to the unconscious belief that, instead of giving up his Oedipus complex, he can realize it with the analyst's help and so be master of the world" (Ibid.). I think, in this case, that it is the patient who is right and the analyst who is wrong.

Before I explain what I mean, I should quickly make clear the extent to which Steiner and I do agree. Steiner maintains that "the classic description of the dissolution of the Oedipus complex as a result of castration threats from the father"—here, appropriately, Steiner cites Freud (1924)—"leads not to a true resolution but to a psychic retreat based on grievance." (Steiner, 1079). I couldn't agree more. Likewise, I agree that much of what passes for analysis of the Oedipus complex proceeds on a version of the same dynamic. I cannot believe that the Oedipus complex can dissolve because of "the absence of the satisfaction hoped for, (and) must in the end, lead the small lover to turn away from his hopeless longing" (Freud, 173). If such a thing could happen, there would be no such thing as psychopathology, since most of the pain rests on the conflict between what the patient thinks and what he feels.

I believe that psychoanalysis has, perhaps, not really recognized why the Oedipus complex is not ordinarily a problem in everyday living. How is it, for example, that so many people are not neurotically fixated on the Oedipus complex? I would submit that it is because their Oedipal wishes *have* been fulfilled. Certainly, they have not been fulfilled because the parent of the opposite gender has had sexual intercourse with them. Rather, it is because the child has felt generally loved and emotionally possessed without the expression of his personality controlled by the parent of the opposite gender. He has felt that love to be unconditional. He has felt that parent to be receptive to his wishes. He has felt free to hug that parent physically. Further, he has not felt that the parent of the *same* gender resents that relationship, nor fears that the child might surpass him or her. In short, he has felt from an unconscious point of view, that the parent of the opposite gender was *his* or *hers* without objection from either parent.

When we speak of a physical object as "mine," we are implying that we have control over that object in the sense of being able to use it as we wish (respecting, of course, its own inherent qualities). In an abstract sense, the same is true of people. I do not mean that we can literally command one's parent to fulfill a wish, though it is interesting to see some two- and three-year-olds do exactly that quite successfully. Rather, we hope that the child feels that the parent supports him in his strivings and desires for self-fulfillment.

If a child does not have such a parent, he will feel later in life to some extent that *no one* is his. He feels inhibitions in touching other people, either emotionally or physically. A successful analysis will enable the patient to be free to make attempts to establish relationships that can lead the patient to acquire a spouse that he feels will be his or hers. Or, it will permit the patient to feel that the spouse to whom he is already married can become his. Certainly, one of the neurotic symptoms we frequently see is competition between husband and wife instead of pride, leading, of course, to hostility. This is the result of the fact that one or both of the couple do not feel that the spouse is truly his or hers.

I may be accused of being old fashioned, or sexist, or both, but I would submit that the Oedipus complex became seen as literally sexual because it was a male who perceived it. Do I need to point out what writers of fiction and screenwriters already know? Namely, that when women are attracted to men, they usually don't initially imagine themselves having intercourse with them. Rather, they imagine affectionate speech or hugging. So, I will propose the idea that the sexual intercourse that is implicit in how we speak about the Oedipus is *symbolic of closeness*. What this means in practice is that the little girl who is able to climb on to her Daddy's lap most of the time when she wants to does not feel frustrated in her Oedipal desires.

As with the Oedipal situation, so with reality. I maintain that it is the analyst's function to find a way to help the patient remove the obstacles that lie in the way of wish fulfillment, and to resume development in a way that allows omnipotence to flourish. I would also accept Ticho's idea that "Psychoanalysis is a treatment method that aims at the removal of the causes of such an interruption so that development can be resumed" (16). Whether or not one accepts the proposition that sexual intercourse is an Oedipal symbol, it is still incumbent on the analyst to try to remove the obstacles in the way of finding a partner with whom the patient can build a lasting romantic relationship.

This is done by exposing the defenses. For example, for the patient previously mentioned whose father died when she was very young, the analyst must focus on the emptiness that prevented mourning, i.e., helping the patient regain aspects of herself that were hers. Rather than 'build' a fantasy father out of projected pieces of herself. This will enable the patient to then find 'fathers' in other men in the world. This does not mean that she will find a father who will literally hold her on his lap or carry her. But it will enable her to go to men for advice, for sympathy, for protection and for love.

I find it difficult to believe that a child of four or five years old has a such a specific sexual desire, or such an enduring sexual desire, that cuddling would be insufficient. Does she really feel that she needs to have a penis in her vagina (which she may very well not even know exists), in order to feel satisfied? The Oedipus complex is an example of a supposedly unsatisfiable wish that can be satisfied in a healthy child. Further, she can fulfill her dreams of marrying her father and giving him a baby by finding someone that is very similar to him. We are all familiar with how often that happens.

There is an old song that has the lyrics, "I want a girl just like the girl who married dear old Dad." This is a healthy expression of an ability to use another woman as a symbol for his mother and find it completely satisfactory. In a healthy person, a reasonable clone of the parents of the opposite sex will do very well. As we know, the ability to transfer is not limited to transferring on to the analyst.

The pain of Oedipal jealousy is caused by parents who did not symbolically have sex with their children. Or to put it another way, what Young-Bruehl and Bethelard call the "cherishment" was lacking (23). We need to help a patient overcome the psychological obstacles in the way of cherishment, which arise as a result of his not being cherished as a child. That achievement, which may seem impossible to him, can be a dream come true.

I have a patient who had been hospitalized for her schizophrenia. She had neuroleptic malignant syndrome, so her psychiatrist could not treat her with drugs. He told her that his work with her would be an attempt to "seal over" her illness. I submit that we can do much better than that. This brilliant woman has the right to have her illness as well as her dreams interpreted. As she told me: her identity lies in that material. Can I do less than help her unearth it, so that it is available to her in her future life?

Summary

In summary, I am saying that accepting all that is unpleasant is not total reality, nor is it an acceptance of all unpleasant reality necessary to good mental health. Rather, good mental health is achieved by removing the neurotic obstacles to wish fulfillment. But this necessitates that the analyst not be wedded to literal reality and that he or she have a healthy respect for the symbolic abilities of the unconscious.

I am suggesting that we set our sights higher. More can be done in terms of helping our patients achieve happiness than we have assumed. I am not suggesting that more can be done with every patient in every area. No analyst can do a perfect job with any patient, let alone with all patients. However, I do believe that, theoretically and perhaps practically, more can be done than has been done heretofore. We must be careful to recognize that our patients' cynical view is part of their illness and not permit ourselves to be seduced by it.

I am very grateful to the late Joseph Sandler for his and Anna Ursula Dreher's book: *What Do Psychoanalysts Want?* It was a great inspiration to me in the course of working on this paper. Fortunately, I was able to inform Dr. Sandler of my delight in his work before his passing.

Note

1 See chapters on "black hole."

References

1. Ferenczi. (1928). The elasticity of psychoanalytic Technique. In *Final Contributions to the Problems and Methods of Psychoanalysis*, Hogarth Press, London, 1955, pp. 87–101.
2. Alexander, Franz. (1925). A metapsychological description of the process of cure. *International Journal Psycho-Analysis*, 6: 13–34.

3. Freud, Sigmund. (1895). The psychotherapy of hysteria. J. Breuer and S. Freud, *Studies in Hysteria, The Standard Edition of the Complete Psychological Works of Sigmund Freud*, Vol. II, Hogarth Press, London, p. 305.
4. Freud, Sigmund. (1908). Civilized sexual morality nervous illness. In *The Standard Edition of the Complete Psychological Works of Sigmund Freud*, Vol. IX, Hogarth Press, London, p. 186.
5. Freud, Sigmund. (1920). Beyond the pleasure principle. In *The Standard Edition of the Complete Psychological Works of Sigmund Freud*, Vol. XXIII, Hogarth Press, London.
6. Freud, Sigmund. (1924). "The Dissolution of the Oedipus Complex." Vol. XIX, S. E., p. 173.
7. Freud, Sigmund. (1930). Civilization and its discontents. In *The Standard Edition of the Complete Psychological Works of Sigmund Freud*, Vol. XXI, p. 60.
8. Freud, Sigmund. (1933). New introductory lectures. In *The Standard Edition of the Complete Psychological Works of Sigmund Freud*, Vol. XXII, Hogarth Press, London, p. 125.
9. Freud, Sigmund. (1940). An outline of psychoanalysis. In *The Standard Edition of the Complete Psychological Works of Sigmund Freud*, Vol. XXIII, Hogarth Press, London.
10. Ibid., p. 180.
11. Freud, Sigmund. (1974). General subject index. In *The Standard Edition of the Complete Psychological Works of Sigmund Freud*, Vol. XXIV, Hogarth Press, London, pp. 225–405.
12. Levin, Revella. (1986). Infantile omnipotence and grandiosity. *Psychoanalytic Review*, 73(1), Spring Bibliography (2).
13. Levin, Revella. (1996). Black hole phenomena: Deficit or defense? *Journal of Clinical Psychoanalysis*, 5(1).
14. Levin, Revella. (1997). Communicating with the schizophrenic superego. *Journal of the American Academy of Psychoanalysis*, 24.
15. Money-Kyrle, R. (1968). Cognitive development. *Int. Jour. Psychoanalysis*, 49: 691.
16. Ticho, E.A. (1972). Termination of psychoanalytic treatment goals, life goals. *Psychoanalytic Quarterly*, 41: 315.
17. Ornstein, Paul. (1997). Omnipotence in health and illness. In Carolyn Ellman and Joseph Reppen (Eds.), *Omnipotent Fantasies and the Vulnerable Self*, Jason Aronson, Inc., Northvale, NJ and London, p. 122.
18. Ibid., p. 129.
19. Sterner, John. (1996). The aim of psychoanalysis in theory and practice. *International Journal of Psychoanalysis*, 77(Part 6).
20. Ibid., p. 1075.
21. Ibid.
22. Ibid., p. 1077.
23. Young-Bruehl, Elizabeth, and Bethelard, Faith. (1997). *Cherishment culture*. Lecture to the New York Psychoanalytic Association, Symposium on "Psychoanalysis and culture," March 15.

17

THE BURNED-OUT THERAPIST

This paper is an elaborated version of a talk I gave in Chicago for the ISPS in 2004. Paradoxically, I chose this topic because I realized I knew nothing about it when a few people in our local chapter complained of feeling "burned out." I had never experienced even a whiff of a such a feeling, but it aroused my curiosity.

I had been treating seriously disturbed people for many years. I had never in all those years experienced burnout. My feeling was, "How can that happen? It's like a contradiction in terms. How can something so exciting make a therapist feel burned out? It's as if one said "Beautiful spring days depress me." To me it was a foreign concept. The apparent contradiction intrigued me. For months and months, the thought of it nagged me. But I was stuck with "How can this be?" and made no insightful progress.

One handicap I had was that a wonderful article on the subject was not published until December 4, 2006, in *New York Magazine*, entitled "Can't Get no Satisfaction" by Jennifer Senior. She did a wonderful job of researching this subject. She quotes the work of Barry Farber, a psychotherapist and professor at Columbia University who did his dissertation on the subject. Prior to that, Herbert Freudenberger researched it. The result was his 1974 book *Burnout: The High Cost of High Achievement*. Others soon followed. A sub-specialty of psychology was born. Senior says,

> Almost all the research that had been done on the subject, and there's been quite a lot, was on the people in the 'caring professions'—nurses, public-school teachers, legal-aid workers, social workers, clergy. Because many of these people were idealists and because they worked with the hardest-luck cases, they were highly susceptible to disillusionment.

Those who burned out were not only physically and mentally exhausted, they were cynical, detached, convinced their efforts were worthless. They held themselves in contempt. Worse, they held their clients in contempt. They began to loathe the same people they originally sought to help.

Christina Maslach, in her book *Burnout: The Cost of Caring*, quotes a Florida social worker: "I recently received a call at night, and while I was getting dressed, I was screaming and cursing those motherfuckers for calling me with their goddamned problems" (2).

Senior quotes Alden Cass who provides what I think is the best insight into the problem. "Their expectations of success are through the roof and when their reality doesn't match up with their expectations, it leads to burnout—they leave no room for error or failure at all in their formula." This reminded me of what one young therapist reported to me. She said she was disappointed with her work, because she was sure that I could have cured her schizophrenic patient, and she couldn't. She had previously discussed this patient with me, so I was quite surprised that she said that. I was quite sure it would be practically impossible since he lived far out of town and could only occasionally come into New York. I had given her some ideas about his problems, but was extremely dubious of an eventual success unless he moved to New York. That is an example of unrealistic expectations. One does have to recognize practical limitations.

Another view of burnout is noted by Aylia Pines, a researcher in Israel who sums up the problem as "'the failure of existential quest'—that moment when we wake up one morning and realize that what we're doing has appallingly little value." Farmer calls burnout "the gap between expectations and reward." If that is the problem, then surely one reason I never felt burnout was because I was certain any gain I could make in a schizophrenic's life was more than the other therapies I saw them receive. When I began, there was only institutionalization, shock therapy, lobotomies, and the beginnings of Sullivan's work, which did not seem singularly impressive to me. Later I will discuss how and why my expectations rose. But today's situation, as far as psychiatrists go, seems little different. Psychiatry in the United States says schizophrenia is incurable and patients will have to be on drugs for as long as they live. If I believed that, not only would I have burnout, I wouldn't even begin to treat such patients any more than I would work with retarded patients. One simply can't get enough satisfaction. There is too little improvement possible. Supportive therapy bores me. Thus, by accident, I avoided the possibility of burnout.

But now I will return to my ignorance of 2004. To try to solve my problem, I thought I would begin by speaking about how a therapist would like to feel about her work. She would like to awake in the morning and think to herself, "Oh, today I'm going to see Jane, who had that exciting insight last session. I wonder if it will cause her to feel less anxious or lead to some other improvement that I can't even imagine now. Or will that insight expose a problem that neither of us were aware of?" All of these have happened to me.

Another possibility: "I am so curious to find out more about my new patient Gregory. He doesn't appear to be as sick as the referring therapist told me he was. Was she wrong, or does Gregory just have an interesting way of hiding his problem?" Once that happened to me in a way I will never forget. A very bright patient came to me, telling me that he believed in "gods," with a small "g," he hastened to add. Nine months after he began treatment, he called me one midnight to tell me that he had received a possible threat to his health and was about to kill his fiancée and himself. I discovered that he was so knowledgeable and clever that he knew that if he told me he had a conventional Godly hallucination, I would realize how sick he was. I always find it amazing that some patients don't want you to know how serious their problems are, for fear you will not treat them. Would they go to an oncologist and be afraid to tell the physician they found a lump?

One may awake one morning and think of the patient who is doing so much better and would now be so much easier to work with than she had been in the past, but you have to let her go. What a pleasure she would have been to work with now! But she is now so healthy it would have really been socializing. And you ask the age-old question, "Why don't healthy people ever consult me?" That is the little joke I offer when patients tell me that I would throw them out, if I knew how sick they were. I find consistently that patients all want the prize for being the sickest I have ever seen—I am so cruel that I consistently deny them that honor. First of all, it's the truth. Secondly, it deflates their grandiosity a little. I think it also makes them less certain that I won't be able to help them.

I was still stuck in 2004 until I saw a video of Harold Searles's work. Listening to what Searles had to say broadened my picture of the happy therapist. When Searles spoke, I couldn't help noticing how many complaints he had. I got the impression that he was not so much interested in helping the patient as focusing on how he could endure the session. My picture of the happy therapist is that, on the contrary, he is stimulated. A happy therapist can be frustrated that the hour is over too soon, just when things were getting 'hot.' Unlike Searles, who is rigid about his schedule, the happy therapist is angry at the clock, not at the patient.

The happy therapist is stimulated by the questions that come to mind. For example, "What a surprising thing my patient has just said. Is that truly a pathological idea or is it a stunted striving for health? What parent does that idea come from? Is that why my patient is so hesitant to speak? Why does she persistently tell me it is easier for her to talk to her friend, than to talk to me? I really learn once again how important it is for all of us to be able to express hostility and how damaging it is for anyone not to be able to. She is so much happier, since she stuck in her face in mine and screamed at me and I only flinched slightly."

A happy therapist doesn't worry about her adequacy, except perhaps momentarily, because she doesn't set herself up as a model. If you let your patient put you on a pedestal, you will come down with a crash, and your patient will be even more pessimistic. The happy therapist is committed to the idea that the patient has to find her own self, unburdened by this grandiosity, and resists cooperating with the patient's pathological urges to copy her, instead of discovering her own self.

It was after watching the whole Searles video that the light in my mind went on. I felt I understood why therapists burn out. I saw that Searles was trying to thread his way in what he felt was a jungle for which he had no map. That leads to constant anxiety on the part of the therapists, not to speak of bewilderment on the part of the patient.

The happy therapist knows she can get lost, but only in a very circumscribed area. She doesn't worry about the patient having a psychotic episode that she can't handle, or committing suicide. This is because the happy therapist has confidence in her basic framework and her ability to know where to look for answers if she doesn't immediately know how to solve a problem. She is quite sure that the patient won't commit suicide, because she knows that the patient knows she is quite available.

Of course, sometimes one learns the hard way. A patient of mine crashed when I left on vacation once. Thereafter, when I went on vacation, I called two patients twice a week in order to reassure them of my availability. And they knew when I would call them. That knowledge acted as a kind of life preserver. Separations are always the most dangerous times for the mentally ill. But in these days of sophisticated technology, it is an avoidable risk. Sometimes all that is required is the patient's knowledge of one's phone number.

The light that went on after I saw the Searles video was that in order for a therapist to have that kind of confidence, she has to have a theory in which she believes and that protects her from the feelings of helplessness that Searles complains of. How often we speak of the patient's anxiety! But how can the therapist work well and comfortably if she is constantly afraid she is "screwing up"? And how long can she go on feeling she is screwing up without feeling burned out?

The question then becomes, how can a therapist find a framework that will sustain her? My answer is: each therapist must find her own way. She must familiarize herself with all the theories and find out which one makes the most sense to her, which one fits her own personality and seems to make sense to her patients.

I can only relate my own experience to you, for whatever that is worth. Conditions for learning were much better when I began to find my way than they are for you, at least in the United States.

I started in 1954, just before Thorazine came on to the scene. We had a chance to study patients "naked," so to speak. Drugs do what they are supposed to do: cover up problems. The result is that one can't see what one is doing, so to speak. I always picture myself at my sewing machine and I think, "How could I possibly sew in a straight line if I can't see the needle?" If the patient is drugged, the dynamics look muddy.

If the patient is on drugs, neither you nor the patient are clear as to what is going on. I had an opportunity to see non-medicated patients 24/7. I saw the immediate results (or non-results) of my interpretations. It was a perfect laboratory.

I had just gotten my master's degree and been trained in what was then called the "neo-Freudian" approach, what is now called "object relations." It made a great deal of sense to me. I recall that, as students, we used to make jokes about Freud. But when I went to work in this lab that I referred to, the patients responded with a "so what" attitude to Sullivan's work. However, Freud got a very definitive response, much to my surprise. Of course, nothing gives one greater conviction than seeing changes happening in front of one's own eyes.

I learned to speak and think in the concrete terms in which the patients spoke. They responded. That was how I learned. Truly, in this situation, the customer is almost always right. Indeed, I would advise you to assume that that the patient is always right until proven otherwise. It's far safer. For example, the patient feels she is being poisoned, if that is what she complains of. It is up to you to figure out how.

Of course, Freud may not work for you. You may not find it works for your patients. But you will not work happily or effectively until you find a theory that suits you. You may even find a theory that is entirely yours. But it needs to be something you can count on, in order to prevent burnout. Of course, you may get a sudden inspiration whose origin you don't know. Well, it probably came from your unconscious, a very reliable source, so be grateful for it. Creativity is not only not a bad word. On the contrary, it can be a blessing.

So, my words of wisdom are these: unlike Searles, you don't have to be miserable. You can enjoy your work. Get yourself in a position physically, intellectually, and emotionally of not being afraid. Hopefully you will rarely have cause to be angry with your patients. If it happens too often, find out what you are doing wrong. Searles was angry at his patients, not their sickness.

You can enjoy your work. I envy you. I wish I were young again and could work for 50 years more!

References

1. Senior, Jennifer. (2006). Can't get no satisfaction. *New York Magazine*, New York, December 4.
2. Maslach, Christina. (2003). "The Cost of Caring." Malor Books, Cambridge, MA, p. 121.

18

HOW TO DECREASE YOUR CHANCES OF GETTING HURT OR KILLED WHEN WORKING WITH A SCHIZOPHRENIC PATIENT

I have deliberately not entitled this paper "How Not to Get Killed, etc." because I could hardly guarantee the reader that he or she would not get killed. I can only provide experiences and a theoretical approach to the problem that have served me well. Also, I believe that I can claim some authority on this subject, in that I have worked with schizophrenics for 50 years and have occasionally been in some danger. Further, I was initially handicapped when beginning my career by the fact that, I believe, I was more generally fearful of being physically harmed than most people. Since I avoided having to hospitalize a patient, or call the police, I believe I can offer some useful suggestions.

Interestingly, to my knowledge, nothing has been written on this subject, at least in terms of how to handle the problem psychologically. This, in spite of the fact that the public cases I am mentioning are only the most recent ones that I am aware of. A few years ago, one psychiatrist, Dr. Wayne Fenton, and one psychologist, Dr. Kathryn Faughey, have been killed in the northeast of the United States (*New York Times*, October 8, 2008). Further, Dr. Bruce Ivins, the suspect in the well-known anthrax cases, told his therapist of his wish to kill her and others (*New York Times*, August 2, 2008).

Let me begin with the Fenton case. I hesitate to critique Dr. Fenton's approach to the matter, because it is not considered *comme il faut* to malign the dead. On the other hand, given the kind of man Dr. Fenton is described as being, conscientious, devoted to his patients, and a man who, as one colleague described him, "was willing to go to the place where a person needed help" (*Washington Post*, written by Cameron W. Barr, September 8, 2006), I think he would have appreciated our learning how to protect ourselves, better than he did.

I have read several reports of the incident and although they seemed to conflict, I will do my best to relate to you what happened. For unclear reasons, another therapist asked Dr. Fenton to see the patient, Vitali Davydov, concerning his resistance to taking his medication. The patient was a 19-year-old boy with a twin brother. According to Derek Valcourt of Baltimore (WJZAP),

> Fenton met with Davydov Saturday, and had set up an appointment for later that week. But after Davydov became angry while discussing his medication for schizophrenia and bipolar disorder, another session was hastily arranged for Sunday. When Davydov and his father arrived for the Sunday afternoon appointment, Fenton told the father he would tell Davydov that it was important to take medication. Fenton also said he would try to encourage the teen to take the medication with an injection, not orally.

I think Fenton made three errors there which may have led to his death. First, one must always assume that any schizophrenic is paranoid. Fenton fed into that paranoia by seeing and talking to the father alone. Talking behind someone's back is the most fertile field for paranoia to grow. If a parent is involved, I never see or talk to the parent alone. I see both together, telling the patient that I will not discuss him unless the patient is present. If I see them both later in the treatment, I make sure that any subject I discuss with both is with the patient's permission. Schizophrenics, not just neurotics, have a right to have the first rule of psychotherapy observed: confidentiality.

The second error, as I see it, was to speak of injections at all. An injection of anti-psychotics has no antidote. Whatever destructive effects that medication may have must be borne for 30 days. I consider that torture. My view is that if one must stop a patient from becoming violent and can't handle it any other way, one can use a straitjacket or restraining sheet. At least one is only immobilizing the patient's body. He is still free to think and feel whatever occurs to him. As prisoners often say, "You can imprison my body, but my mind is still free." Injections imprison the mind and subjectively threaten identity. Nelson Mandela is a case in point.

Fenton's third possible error was to offer the patient medication when he was already refusing it. I understand that Fenton was trying to keep the patient from harming himself or others. But the patient had already declared his discomfort with medication. What the patient, who is already suffering, heard when Fenton offers him medication is "Shut up. Don't bother me with your pain." Is that a totally unrealistic view?

Benedict Carey, in an article in the *New York Times* (September 19, 2006), quotes Mrs. Fenton as saying that Dr. Fenton was the "most non-threatening person you ever met." That may well be true, but to Davydov, he was a killer. Carey says, "So-called anti-psychotic drugs effectively blunt symptoms of psychosis and tend to reduce the risk of violent outbursts, psychiatrists say. But the medications are mentally dulling . . . and many patients either stop taking them or refuse them altogether." Carey quotes Dr. William Carpenter, who makes a very good point, "As doctors, we think patients ought to do what we think they should do." This is where I think Fenton's grandiosity interfered with his judgment.

The patient probably felt not only that he ought not do what Dr. Fenton suggested. He probably felt he dared not do it. He felt that Fenton did not know what was best for him.

But Carey also quotes Dr. Thomas H. McGlashan, a close friend of Dr. Fenton's, making a statement with which I thoroughly disagree. He says,

> When a patient is revving up and paranoid, instead of becoming imperious or dogmatic or rigid, I might admit that I'm kind of nervous too. If you're scared, you let the patient know that. Because a lot of their behaviour is coming from their perception of being threatened. If you let them know that you are feeling threatened, vulnerable and not interested in controlling them, that can help defuse the situation.

I am certainly not in favor of "imperious, dogmatic or rigid." The problem with that is, as I have discussed before, the patient will not see you as being on his side since you will be too busy defending yourself from him. There are other alternatives.

Another bit of advice with which I disagree is Dr. Fuller Torrey's statement: "Most say that the best way is to use common sense," quoted by Lyndsey Layton of the *Washington Post* (September 5, 2006). I assume his definition of "common sense" is trying to talk logically to the patient. I fear that is exactly what Dr. Fenton may have done, as in "Look here, young man, you really need these drugs to keep you out of trouble. And they will make you feel better soon," despite the patient's denials of that view, in effect treating the patient as if he were stupid.

Next, I will discuss what little I know about Dr. Kathryn Faughey. I should not neglect to mention that Dr. Kent D. Shinbach, a psychiatrist, was badly injured when he tried to rescue her. Following Dr. Faughey's wake, one patient described her as "more of a life coach. We didn't do analysis. She was comfortable giving advice." Other patients described her therapeutic behavior as clearly not preservative of the transference.

The irony of Dr. Faughey's killing was that her murderer was not even her patient. Rather, the patient was in search of his own therapist whom he could not find and, for reasons we don't know, killed Dr. Faughey instead. I have no problem with Dr. Faughey's being a "life coach," but it does concern me that people who are treating mental patients don't know how to handle such emergencies. This case touches me further to some extent, more than simply the death of a colleague, because one of Dr. Faughey's patients is a friend of a friend of mine. I have twice previously heard from patients how much they suffered, seemingly unable to recover, when their therapists died—even when the death wasn't violent.

Next, we have the case of Bruce Ivins, the suspect in the well-known anthrax case. Here, we have a good example of how not to handle this problem, although the therapist was fortunately not killed. The *Times* article does not state whether Jean Duley (the therapist) consulted colleagues or a supervisor, though, apparently,

Ivins' threats were ongoing. The patient attended group counseling and had apparently been seeing a psychiatrist. An article in the *Times* by Sarah Abruzzese and Eric Lipton (August 2, 2008) says, "In court records, filed after Ivins discussed his plans to kill his co-workers, a social worker who led the session, Jean Duley, said that Ivin's psychiatrist had called him 'homicidal, sociopathic with clear intentions.'" She went on to say that the Federal Bureau of Investigation was looking at Ivins and that he would soon be charged with five murders—the same number of fatalities in the anthrax attacks. "He is a revenge killer," Ms. Duley told a Maryland District Court judge in Frederick as she sought a restraining order against Ivins. "When he feels he has been slighted, and especially towards women, he plots and actually tries to carry out revenge killings. If that isn't a rejection and a useless one at that, I would like to know what is. He had been treated with antidepressants, anti-anxiety and anti-psychotic medication."

Ivins said of his psychiatrist: "He's not that easy to talk to and doesn't really pick up on my problems." The case ended in the patient's suicide, as the government closed in on him.

Theory

When Ms. Duley speaks of her patient as a "revenge killer," she, at last, demonstrates some insight, but apparently has no idea of how to use that information on behalf of her patient. Through the years, I have gradually come to realize that all intentions to kill or actual killings are partially revenge killings. The question is: revenge for what? The general answer is: for feeling killed, or experienced threats thereof. Obviously, since the patient is still physically alive from an objective point of view, he must feel a threat to his emotional life, his identity—that which distinguishes him from others. To a schizophrenic—that is, in his concretistic thinking—psychic death, the fear of being confused with someone else, or experienced loss of pieces of his self are equivalent. The patient feels that something has been taken from him, which he feels is essential to his identity.

I believe that it is incumbent on the therapist to ascertain which quality he feels has been taken from him, and how it was that he came to be deprived of it, why he allowed it to be taken from him and how he can regain it. That is the simple recipe of how I believe this problem can be resolved.

I can hear the reader say, "That is all very well as a theory, but how do I go about it?" I shall answer that question to the best of my ability, but first, having so strenuously objected to Ms. Duley's handling of the problem, let me point out a necessary precondition.

As in all of my discussion of the problems of schizophrenics, I believe that it is necessary for the therapist to demonstrate that she is on the patient's side. Dr. Schwaber, in a letter to me dated January 4, 2009, says,

> What you said in your paper is very much in keeping with my own position of which I've written, about locating the patient's perspective and finding

its inherent legitimacy. I think that is what you mean by being 'on the patient's side'. But it has to be felt by both therapist and patient as real, not pro forma, to truly be on her or his side, the therapist must struggle to locate it, so that the patient feels it is deeply understood (6).

Indeed, I believe one must do one's best to convince the patient by deed, not mere protestations. My view is that the patient has come to consult me in the hope that I can relieve him of his pain; implicit in that view is the assumption that his interests are paramount. Putting a restraining order on the patient, as Ms. Duley did, not only "proves" to the patient that the therapist is not at all on his side, and is only there to protect society and herself. Going to the police obviously falls into the same category. The patient experiences the therapist as being against him. The therapist can rationalize that she is saving the patient from doing something that will ultimately have negative consequences to himself, but, as they say in the vernacular, the patient feels that is "b.s."

This is an example of how invoking "reality" in (such a case) is pointless—a tactic I imagine both Dr. Fenton and Dr. Faughey did when they were attacked. "I don't hate you. I don't want to harm you. I'm only trying to help you by calling the police." Such statements only infuriate the patient, who feels that the therapist is insulting him by lying to him. Being "on his side" means looking at the world he as sees it, as I believe the following advice shows.

It is my belief that it is better to simply state to the patient: "If you want to kill me, you must feel like you are being killed, or already dead yourself. Let us explore how you are being killed and why you are letting it happen." This statement accomplishes several goals. It shows the patient that you are on his side, you are trying to "save his life," and that you have tools with which to approach this problem. Further, it assumes that, since he allowed it, he has the power to disallow it. The therapist must understand that that patient only wants to kill because he is desperate, hopeless, and knows no other way to save his own life. His desire to kill is emotionally no different from the reader's desire to kill a criminal who points a gun at his heart.

I did come across two opinions that differ from mine, and which I feel it is incumbent upon me to address. Arthur Hyatt Williams has an article in *Psychosis, Understanding and Treatment* entitled "Murderousness in Relationship to Psychotic Breakdown." Williams is to be commended for having done very thorough research on the subject. He points out what I think is a very important issue: he differentiates between those people whom a murderer merely wishes to murder from those he actually murders.

> It was clear that the victim, in a panic, increased the anxieties of his assailant in one way or another, so that the interaction escalated into the murderous deed itself. In other cases, the victim-designate was able to contain, to tolerate and to communicate with the would-be assailant without hatred or panic.

(Hyatt, 9)

Williams and Bion (8,9) explain the problem in terms of projective identification. Bion says, "the patient's fear of committing murder owes much of its intensity to his belief that he has already been guilty of it" (Bion, 8). I must interject here, that although in general I am a great admirer of Klein, I have always had problems with the concept of projective identification, because I could never perceive where the motivation came from. I am willing to concede that may be my own intellectual failure, but the result is that I have never found the concept particularly useful. I feel obligated to inform the reader that a theoretical difference exists. But since this is primarily a practical chapter, and neither Bion nor Williams offers suggestions as to how to protect oneself, I will continue to present my own point of view.

One Crisis

In the introduction, I spoke of the following patient. It was an experience I had when I was a naïve 27-year-old. I was working in a rural area, in a rented house, for John Rosen. My patient was a postpartum psychotic whose precipitating behavior was that she tried to kill her husband with an axe. Our work had been going on for four months. I was fortunate, for purposes of learning, in that she was my only patient, and an English major—she used her words carefully and accurately, thus giving me an optimal opportunity to learn the language of schizophrenia.

It was summertime when the following incident took place. Her back was to the kitchen, where the knives were. She and I were the only people in the house and the phone was out of order. We were standing near the back screen door opposite each other. She was holding my hands in a tight vise with my body tightly up against her body.

She was much improved from the time I had begun working with her, although I was making many novice mistakes. I had a great investment in her health, having worked so hard and well with her; I'd become quite fond of her. But, as I said previously, I was unusually afraid of being hurt physically. I most strongly did not want all my work to be for naught. I had apparently hit one of her emotional nerves. She was 5'8" and weighed about 185 pounds. I was 5'4" and weighed about 120. Further, she had the advantage of psychotic strength.

The one advantage I had was that, due to her obesity, I felt I was the more fleet. I believed I could pull my hands down hard, gain release, and run to the nearest village about a half a mile away. But that would have surely ruined the therapy at the very least. At worst, she might have put herself in physical danger. Both of these alternatives were unacceptable to me. I was so naïve and stupid (to this day I cannot understand how I could have made such a judgment) that, without thinking of another alternative, I rejected that option. I had been taught that if I was in physical danger, I was to get one knee up and punch it into her belly. But she held me so close to her, I couldn't get my knee up. All I could think of at the moment was to call her name, as if trying to bring her to her senses—of course, this was utterly useless. Then, I remembered that I had also been taught to make a transference interpretation. So I said, in a loud, firm voice, "I am **not** your mother."[1]

She dropped her hands. We sat and waited for the men to come home. Hindsight tells me that my later discovery that she felt she had had to sell her soul to her mother for food ("being forced into prostitution") was on point. That was why she wanted to kill me and that was why the transference interpretation worked. I was not demanding that she give up her "soul." I was trying to restore it to her.

All good and fine, but what do we do to avoid crises, and find a substitute for the patient's wanting to kill someone who is "killing" him?

Killing as a Failure in Communication

My first insight into this problem came when I was relatively young, seeing a patient named Lindsey. She was a young lesbian who described her adoptive mother as having breasts of stone. Lindsey told me she wanted to drop a bookcase on her mother but was horrified at the idea of telling her she hated her. If I recall correctly, the threat to drop the bookcase seemed rather imminent. I guess that is why it is so vivid to me, because I can still recall the picture in my mind of the bookcase falling on Lindsey's mother and the disaster that would have ensued. What was striking to me was the question of why she believed that telling her mother she hated her would be more destructive than dropping the bookcase on her. When I suggested that she express her feelings to her mother, Lindsey responded, "I could never tell my mother I hated her—" shocked that I would consider that possibility. The implication was that if she said that, she would be terribly uncouth. That's why the bookcase option seemed more acceptable. Apparently being "uncouth" was considered abhorrent in Lindsey's home. Since dropping bookcases had not been discussed, one could consider it less destructive than telling her mother she hated her. I met Lindsey's mother once. I do remember feeling that with her, all proprieties must be strictly observed.

Before you laugh at considering these options, think of a two-year-old being told firmly, "You should never tell anyone you hate them. That is very rude." Children that age take instructions very concretely. Note that an alternative is not given. Other behavior, like "Don't throw bookcases at people'" is not mentioned. Of course, you can say, the option would not come up because a two-year-old isn't strong enough to do it. An adult knows that, but a small child in the omnipotent stage doesn't know it and might consider it an option.

You could say, "You don't have to tell people not to throw bookcases. It's too obvious." But at the age of two, a child is not capable of reasoning out many consequences, or even having a clear idea of what death is, much less knowing that the victim might suffer a fatal subdural hematoma as a result. At two, the consequence of telling someone you hate them is that mother will be very angry and may throw you out with the garbage. So, if throwing a bookcase at someone can get rid of someone's painful hostility, directed at you, why isn't that a reasonable solution?

Why I am using such a young age as an example? Lindsey knew she was a lesbian no later than the age of four, and very probably earlier, so my example seems appropriate.

The case of Lindsey is an example of the destructiveness of repression or suppression. I am indebted to Dr. Evelyne Albrecht Schwabel for reminding me that in her discussion of another analyst's work with a suicidal patient, she cites Freud's admonition; he warns us about the danger of suppression of material:

> To urge the patient to suppress, renounce or sublimate her instincts the moment she admitted her erotic transference would be, not an analytic way of dealing with them, but a senseless one. It would be as though, after summoning up a spirit from the underworld by cunning spells, one were to send him down again without having asked him a single question. One would have brought the repressed into consciousness, only to repress it once more in a fright. Nor should we deceive ourselves about the success of any such proceeding. As we know, the passions are little affected by sublime speeches. The patient will feel only the humiliation and she will not fail to take her revenge for it.
>
> (Schwabel, 7)

I would quibble with Freud only to the extent that his admonition might well be extended beyond the transference. Unfortunately, I have no notes on that discussion with Lindsey. Since she expressed her alternatives so distinctly, I'm quite sure I would have encouraged her to express her hatred in some fashion to her mother, for the purpose of defusing the situation. Lindsey was being "killed" by her mother's edict not to express her feelings.

The Reality Behind the Fantasy

I recall one more case, which came as close to disaster as the case with the first patient I spoke of, but in a different way. Edward was a brilliant young man, referred by another patient, named Keith. Edward was so clever that he never admitted he had conversations with God for fear that I would think he was crazy. Denial of psychotic symptoms is a frequent occurrence with schizophrenic patients, for the very reason Edward gave. Edward did admit, however, to having relations with "gods" (he majored in medieval history). He was well defended, so I was unprepared when he called me up at midnight one night to tell me he was going to kill himself and his fiancée. The precipitating factor was that he received news that was a possible, though not an imminent, threat to his life and/or health.

My emotional response to myself was: "No, I cannot call 911 and have him taken to the hospital. At the very least, it would ruin his life to have that on his record." This time I knew what I would need to do. Fortunately, Keith (the patient who referred him) lived nearby and was sufficiently larger than Edward. I knew that if things got physical, Keith would be able to control Edward. I called Keith and told him to put his pants on, go to Edward's apartment, get the fiancée out of there and hold Edward down until I could get there. I called Edward immediately to tell him of my plan and arrived as soon as I could in my housecoat.

I worked with Edward until about 3 a.m. when I felt it was safe to send Keith home. Keith was wonderfully cooperative through this whole incident. I stayed until 5 a.m. Edward and I planned to have him see me every day that week, taking Valium and having a friend come with him to my office every day. When he came, he said to his friend, in my presence, "If I jump her, you jump me." Within a week, we had the situation fairly under control. Neither he nor I felt he (or I) were in danger any longer. Unfortunately, I have only one note about the material under discussion. He says, fantasizing that he is talking to his mother, "You're a bad mommy." I wrote "That is the first time hostility is consciously turned outward." My note is entitled "The Final Session in Psychosis."

He wrote me several letters. The letters are rather long, so I will report only those factors that are relevant to the subject of fear of being killed. He wrote,

> In the first stage, I was nuts. By nuts I mean I was doing things that I didn't want to do, and not knowing why I did them . . . all I know is that what I was doing was making me unhappy, very unhappy. It was also practically impossible to do what I really wanted—damned frustrating. At the same time, what I was doing was making me happy. That is the wacky part. Because I truly believed that what I was doing was good and right for me. Even more than that, I believed that it was vital to my physical survival to believe in exactly this way.

A month later, he writes:

> I finally gained conscious knowledge of how I kill my emotions . . . A device my parents used to control me was that they would raise all possible logical objections to what could happen and prod me (I feel like they somehow forced me) to consider them. After concentrating on all these things that could go wrong, I would begin to feel afraid of my desire, and often would drop it as harmful or illogical.[2] I would begin to actually feel all the bad feelings that might ensue. The funny thing is that in my mind, it was a defense mechanism. I am going to protect myself against bad feelings when something goes wrong by feeling the feelings in advance.

In another letter, dated a year later, where he is more used to introspection, he describes his attitude toward teasing and being teased.

> I realize that I view teasing as exposing someone's weakness. If I am teased, it is because I am weak. I am tremendously frightened by this, since I consider

that my weakness will lead to my being killed by my mother, who wants me dead. This need to defend myself in a life and death struggle which was very real in my childhood, gave me no sense of security and led to my constantly being alert to attacks. I see quite clearly that this is the central reason for much of my defensive behavior and it is quite important to explore further.

I should point out that his emphasis on defensive behavior is entirely his, since I don't talk that way. But I do remember there was much discussion in sessions about his constant fear of being killed by his mother. I am sure that only by various maneuvers did he manage to prevent that actual occurrence.

Other Examples

Awareness of wishes is essential to a feeling of identity. Additionally, the ability to have knowledge is also vital. The following are a few examples:

One patient says, "If I throw my mother out of me, what will replace it, is my wish to live." My response to that is that her continuous questions about where she belongs, are now answered by saying she belongs in her own body.

Another patient says, "I let my mother take away my self-respect, my identity (her words, not mine) from me." The patient would not interfere with her mother's fantasy that she is doing the best for her. Interestingly this patient had an autistic child. She resented whenever he showed a will of his own. This child was incapable of using the concept "I." She felt he was hers, because he was "dead," like the car with which she had an accident.

A six-year-old schizophrenic told me his mother took his love away from him. I took care of him, at the very beginning of my career, so I thought that was crazy even for a schizophrenic. I found, of course, that I was wrong. His mother rejected his "offerings"—opinions, pictures, physical accomplishments—anything with which a child might come running to his mother to say "look at me!" When he moved his bowels in the woods, where we took walks, he would go looking for them the next day.[3]

Practical Suggestions

If you are unsure of your safety with your patient, make sure you are the one closest to the door. I have always arranged for a "babysitter" with patients I don't know—someone who arrives before the patient and sits in the waiting room, staying until after the patient leaves.

I make a point of never *taking a history* at the beginning. Rather, I ask the patient about what pains him. I avoid taking histories because I want the patient to feel free to express his emotions, without being forced to answer factual questions. This enables me to establish a connection with the patient in the first session. The history will come out later, as necessary. Not taking a history establishes a relationship, instead of keeping the patient at arm's length. This technique enabled me to treat an imminently suicidal patient (Bathsheba) very successfully.

I believe, as in any psychotherapeutic intervention, the therapist must use his or her own best judgment. I would strongly advise against using any technique just because some authority suggested it. I think it is most important that the therapist evaluate the situation as only he or she knows it, with their own rationale. The fact that I never called 911 doesn't mean that you shouldn't do so if you find yourself in a situation that frightens you. However, I think it costs you nothing emotionally to have an unobtrusive, relatively large man in the waiting room for the first session, just so the patient knows you are not alone. I say this regardless of the gender of the therapist. I also believe that when a patient comes in complaining of being poisoned, the first two things out of your mouth should not be (1) "Here is a prescription" (which he will experience as "shut up") or (2) "You are not being poisoned" (which denies his experience and may make him more anxious). I think those two statements are quite risky.

Certainly, other people may have other suggestions as to how to handle potentially alarming situations. I urge you to listen to all of them and evaluate them. This problem is not going away. And "Kendra's Law" punishes the victim.[4] So I feel this paper is important from a sociological point of view. If society begins to think that killing is a necessary and insoluble part of schizophrenic behavior, these patients will be totally relegated to pharmacopeia and be considered hopeless. And all the knowledge we have gained in understanding schizophrenia will be lost. I find the thought of that heartbreaking.

I would like to thank Daniel Mackler for piquing my interest in writing about this subject and for Googling the newspaper articles for me. I would also like to thank Mrs. Lee Miller for encouraging me to expand the paper so that I was reminded of patients to whom this subject applied. I would also like to have thanked the late Dr. Murray Jackson for advising me that Europe also suffers from this problem, but far less so from patients who are psychodynamically treated.

Notes

1 Later experience taught me that "loud" is necessary in order to overcome the noise of the voices inside the patient's head. "Firm" is necessary in order to avoid sounding hostile.
2 Suppression of wishes leads to loss of identity.
3 See chapter 13.
4 Kendra's Law is forced injection of psychotropic drugs for people who refuse to take drugs, in New York State.

References

1. Barr, Cameron, W. (2006). "Psychiatrist is slain, as caring fixer of others." *The Washington Post*, September 8.
2. Carey, Benedict. (2006). "Mourners recall slain doctor, as caring fixer of others." *The New York Times*, September 19.

3. Freud, Sigmund. (1914). Observations on transference love. In *The Standard Edition of the Complete Psychological Works of Sigmund Freud*, Vol. XII, Hogarth Press, London, p. 164.
4. Layton, Lindsey. (2006). "Devoted to most severe cases, raise risk of personal danger." *The Washington Post*, September 5.
5. *New York Times*. (2008). News clippings, August 2 and October 2.
6. Schwaber, Evelyne Albrecht. (2004). On: Miscarriages of psychoanalytic treatment with suicidal patients. *IJPA*, 85(Part 1): 198.
7. Schwaber, Evelyne Albrecht. (2008). Personal Communication, January 4.
8. Bion, W.R. (1993). *Second Thoughts*, Jason Aronson, Northvale, NJ, p. 82.
9. Williams, Arthur Hyatt. (1995). Murderousness in relationship to psychotic breakdown. In Jane Elwood (Ed.), *Psychosis: Understanding and Treatment*, Jessica Kinglsey, London and Bristol, PA, p. 91.

19

TECHNIQUE

Dos and Don'ts

This book is devoted only to the treatment of schizophrenics, and, theoretically, it is also applicable to depressives. I am defining a schizophrenic as one who feels dead or feels he is in danger of dying. He may be actively suicidal. The therapist will have to use her judgment as to whether such a patient is suitable for the recommendations in this book. By this I mean that, if the therapist is too frightened to work with such a patient, she should not do so. If the therapist fears the patient will commit suicide before the next scheduled session, and she has no confidence that she will be able to prevent it, the therapist should not work with such a patient.

The rest of this chapter will not be in any particular order. Rather, it will be composed of suggestions that I have learned through a very long career.

I consider a patient no longer schizophrenic when his existence is no longer an issue with him.

I have never had a patient commit suicide, nor have I ever had to hospitalize a patient. I do my best to keep patients out of hospitals because I have heard too many stories about the damage done to patients in those institutions—forcing patients to take anti-psychotic drugs or submit to ECT—without informed consent.

1. I have never sent patients to a psychiatrist for a prescription for drugs, except Edward, for his emergency and then it was only Valium. The following are the two important reasons:
    a. The drugs will cause the patients to be out of touch with his unconscious, which is exactly their purpose. But it is their unconscious that I wish to reach. While some patients may be more comfortable when taking anti-psychotics, the patients will not receive the full impact of my interpretations.

b. Secondly, he will not be able to communicate to me the full strength of his response, so that I am handicapped in the sense of not knowing how effective I am when I make an interpretation, and he cannot receive the full benefit of what I am offering.

One patient once told me the most important reason she had confidence in me was that she could see I was not afraid. She apparently had sensed in her previous therapists that they were afraid of either her material or her wish to commit suicide. Of course, there is no button to push in order to make oneself confident. But it may be helpful if the therapist understands that schizophrenia is not a trap for the non-schizophrenic person. That is, if one voluntarily allows oneself to descend into material that is ordinarily unconscious, one can get out whenever one wishes. Obviously the same is not true of the patient. It is really quite similar, psychologically, to going up and down in an elevator.

2. I think it is also helpful if one truly orients oneself as to whether the material one is offered, belongs to the id, the ego, or the superego. The superego is the domain of the "should," the "have to" and the "must"—the anti-identity, the rules, the restrictions, the deceptions, and the enemy. The id is the domain of the wishes, the lack of necessity for the rational, the total freedom, and of course, creativity; the world of the baby. The ego is the domain of the rational, the identity, and the decision making.

Working with schizophrenics means one allows oneself to think concretely, not figuratively. That is why one hears puns. For example, I heard one patient say "to take care of" not only in the normal sense, but also in the sense meant by a mafioso. This patient keeps saying she wants to kill herself. I say to her, "You are already dead because you won't pay attention to your feelings. You ignore them, so you feel dead." In that statement, I connect the concrete and figurative when she says she is dead. She is condensing, because she is not saying she feels dead, which is what a non-schizophrenic would say about her energy level (Freud, XXIII, 1).

I grant her feelings of death and I point out that she can become "alive" by allowing her feelings to come to consciousness. Note here that I never say to her, "You are not dead." If I were to say that, I would show her I don't understand her and cause her to feel more isolated. Isolation is one of the most important, painful and persistent feelings a schizophrenic has to contend with. With schizophrenia, one can do what is not possible in a non-schizophrenic state, i.e., go from dead to alive. The therapist has to be able to think in this apparently irrational way. This kind of thinking is shorthand for what I call "schizophrenese" to professionals. I will respond to the patient in his own language: "Yes, your conscience wants you to be dead. Are you going to let it boss you around?" When I've uncovered the repressed feeling resulting in the patient's "death," I might say "Your mother wants you to be dead. Are you going to let her have her way?"

3. Whose side the therapist is on is very important. The whole therapy is a battle to weaken the superego, and allow the ego to get stronger. So, the therapist must consistently behave and feel that she is on the patient's side. It is definitely not the Freudian suggestion of neutrality, which is applicable to neurotics. The patient is very frightened and needs to know that he has absolutely dependable support. That is the reason for the patient to have the therapist's phone number and to be able to reach her within a reasonable time. It is amazing how infrequently the permission is taken advantage of. The mere knowledge that it is available appears to be sufficiently fear-reducing.

4. One characteristic that is absolutely necessary for a therapist to possess is an ability to tolerate non-responsiveness. Very often, one will be met by silence. One may also be met by patient's refusal to tell the therapist where she is wrong in one detail. Often, patients are unwilling to divulge some pathological material. They have already had the experience of being met with the contempt of many people to the expression of pathological material. This difficulty is at least partially solved by telling them I have never had to hospitalize a patient. That is translated in their minds as "No matter how crazy I am, she won't put me away." The result is they can tell me things that they might otherwise not disclose, thus making my job easier.

Speaking of problems in disclosure, I was once referred a patient named Donna by another patient, Jane. In making the referral, Jane told me how resistant to therapy Donna was. When Donna came, she would tell me little else but her name and address, and then wanted to leave the therapy after ten minutes. I decided *I* would have to do the talking. So, I gave her a layman's description of the ego, the id, and the superego in some detail. Her response amazed me. She asked me if she could come four times a week.

Of course, my approach was risky because I knew so little about her. But by sticking to theory that I knew, I made her feel that I understood her at least to some extent. This incident points out the necessity for the therapist to be creative. I have tried during the whole of my career to try to understand courage: its presence or lack thereof. Certainly, courage on the part of both therapist and patient makes the work much easier. The therapist needs it to some degree, when she is faced with material unfamiliar to her. And the patient needs it to face his fears, rational or irrational. I must confess that, as much as I have tried, I have never been able to understand why some people have it and some people don't.[1]

But, of course, the patient must eventually face his fear of the superego threats. The only thing that makes that at it at all possible is the presence of the therapist, and her confidence that nothing terrible will happen to the patient if he faces his fears. Of course, he will have to face the reality that the figure whom the superego represents, has been hostile to him since childhood and has done a great deal of damage to him. Certainly, that will be painful, but of course that reality has to be faced emotionally, so that he can get well.

Presumably, by the time he is in a position to face that fear, which is done gradually, the therapist will be pretty knowledgeable about what the patient has to face, and can gently help him face it. Of course, that doesn't make it easy, but it does make it possible. If there is a way of making it easy, I haven't found it. If my reader knows a way, I would welcome any suggestions.

The result is very gratifying for both therapist and the patient, as mentioned previously. It will be verbalized as some variation of "I feel like Rip Van Winkle." The patient will feel much less helpless and no longer a slave to his guilt. "The nightmare is over" is how the patient will experience it.

5. The general attitude of the therapist toward the patient is extremely important, of course. There are, or were, two very prominent authorities who had negative attitudes toward patients. One complained that, inevitably, the therapist would feel responsible for the patient's pathology—I never felt that way and always wondered why he did. Of course, when a patient is hostile, unless one has done something deliberately to provoke him, one must maintain a firm conviction that the hostility is due to the transference and treat it as a defense. That is, ask how the patient would feel if the therapist did not feel hostile toward the patient. One will get some surprising answers. One therapist expected to feel hostile and forgave himself for feeling hostile toward the patient.

The other prominent therapist deliberately provoked the patient in an attempt to elicit hostility from him and then called it transference. Transference, however, is by definition misplaced hostility originating from objects of childhood. I see no point in such provocation.

Freud was well aware of his own attitude. In a revealing letter, he wrote to the mother of a schizophrenic son, who asked why he did not treat schizophrenics. "I do not like these patients . . . I feel them to be so far distant from me and from everything *human*. A curious sort of intolerance" (Eissler, 3; italics mine). I can personally forgive him for that, given that he lived in Vienna, which was renowned for its high level of culture and civilized attitudes, despite its undercurrents of anti-Semitism. Additionally, he suffered from the problems that I discussed in the chapter called "Five Errors."

I am stubborn in my position that successful treatment of schizophrenics must have as a requirement the therapist's affection for the patient and an ability to be on his side against those who have harmed him. As one patient told me, "Schizophrenia is a concentration camp of the mind." That's a position that requires empathy and sympathy.

My advice to would-be psychotherapists of schizophrenic patients who don't like schizophrenics is to walk away. This road will lead you nowhere but to unhappiness for both you and the patient.

6. When you are talking to the superego, be sure to always look *away* from the patient. Otherwise, he may think the hostility and ridicule with which you address it is directed at him, instead of his superego.
7. Try very hard not to burden your patient with your own problems. He has a right to feel you are totally devoted to him during his sessions. I'm sure you wouldn't burden your baby or toddler with the problems you are having with your landlord. Be sure to leave your phone number with your patient when you go on vacation. When I went to Europe, I told my patients the day and time when I would call them.
8. With patients who have separation anxiety, which is most patients at the beginning of treatment, I have used the technique of buying a "Val Doll" (Val is my nickname) and giving it to the patient. This reduces the pain of having to wait for the next session. The patient can talk to the doll at any time, day or night. The therapist must remember that the patient has a great deal of anxiety. The doll is a tangible comfort that gives the patient enough peace to address basic problems. I don't think one can successfully treat schizophrenia without at least two sessions a week.
9. Do not lie to your patient. They have good antennae for untruths. You must remember: they were raised on lies. The method you are using to treat them is telling the truth. The truth may cause pain, but it reduces anxiety and permits one to be more rational.
10. People often ask me what I think is the cause of schizophrenia. I always reply that it is a combination of hate and lies. Both elements are required. Hate alone causes only an unhappy neurotic but lying about it is what confuses the patient. I do not think it is caused by a chemical imbalance. The improvement of my patients without the use of drugs supports that view.
11. As mentioned in the previous chapter, the following elaboration on history-taking may be helpful. Your patient has a great deal of anxiety when he first comes to you. He is worried about what you will think of him and if he can explain himself. He will most probably want to hide the worst of his problems from you. It is surprising how many patients don't want you to think they are "crazy," even though that is what they have come to you for. This can be true even well into the treatment.

You must learn to tolerate a large block of your ignorance about facts and even feelings when you first see a patient, because he wants to talk about what is most disturbing to him, not to satisfy your curiosity. You will have to contain yourself until it becomes appropriate to ask a question, which may well come many sessions later.

This approach is contrary to his going to a physician for a physical problem. But if you start asking questions, your patient will soon become angry with you and leave you. He does not have the patience to satisfy you, because he is having such a hard time telling you what he wants to tell you. Therapy begins in the first session. It is therapeutic for him just to be able to talk to someone whom he hopes will understand something about what he feels. You can say something to the effect of, "you must have felt hurt (angry, frightened, etc.) when that happened to you."

At the end of the first session, do offer something to the effect of, "I think I can help you with X problem. Do you want to come back?" Never presume that he does want to come back. Let him know that he is free to make his own decisions.

I hope that you feel as much excitement and gratification in your career as I have in mine— and may you suffer from the same problem I have often had: how to keep yourself from jumping up and down in your seat when your patient makes a major discovery before you expected it. You want to yell "wow!" but fear that will interfere with the transference, and you have difficulty controlling yourself.

12. A family member of one prospective patient insisted that the patient could not come to me, because the patient trusted no one. All my arguments to the effect that schizophrenics never trust anyone were of no avail. But, of course, schizophrenics never trust a therapist. Some of the distrust is quite rational. They have seen therapists who try to argue with their delusions by being rational. That makes the patient feel misunderstood. All the delusions are valid, but not in the sense that the average person can understand them. They are only rational to the unconscious and it is up to the therapist to figure it out.

Another rational reason not to trust the therapist is that the patient has never seen the therapist before, so he or she has no evidence for trusting that the therapist can help him. But probably irrationally, he has already transferred the hostile superego on to him. The therapist must be prepared to work with a patient who may not trust her for a very long time and not let her feelings be hurt. The suspicions and hostility have nothing to do with her. It is silly to expect a patient to really trust the therapist until he has arrived at the "the nightmare is over" stage. People who say that the therapy can be successful only if the patient trusts the therapist are asking for the impossible if they are working with schizophrenics. Once I did some really inspired work with one patient. But she insisted that I was not the reason she felt better. She said it was a fortune teller who helped her. Sometimes the resistance is very strong. Sometimes I wish I had the emotional equivalent of a pneumatic drill. By the same token, I never had a patient who did not initially assure me that I would not be able to cure him and I will end up putting him in the hospital. Additionally, few patients demonstrate gratitude.

I suggest that the therapist put herself in the place of a mother who sees her child being misled and tortured. She then reacts as most mothers would. She attacks the attacker. But in this case, she makes sure that she is not defensive.

The problem with a defensive reaction, such as "That is not true" or "Shut up," is that it only permits the superego to attack again and does nothing to weaken it. One must make sure that one goes on the offensive. "Shut up" is especially destructive in that it permits the superego to go into hiding, which gives it time to strengthen its weapons.

I do not try to be polite or civilized. I can use any kind of vulgarity. Patients enjoy that demonstration especially because they never had the courage to attack the seemingly "sacred" object. Patients are shocked when I speak disrespectfully to their superegos. But then they laugh and are relieved. I compare it to spitting on a religious object and it certainly surprised the superego. One incident I remember is when I scolded my patient's superego for its objections to the patient's sexual interest. I said to it, "Oh, you're just jealous. For heaven's sake, you (superego) don't even have a body." That really intimidated the superego and silenced it.

The therapist must be prepared to work very hard in most cases. In short, her motivation must be greater than if she works with neurotics. My motivation was a strong sense of curiosity. I'm sure other therapists' motivation would vary. If the therapist has a need for appreciation, I would discourage her from trying to work with these patients. But to the extent I am successful, I do feel gratification in my having relieved great suffering. It is that, that is my goal. The therapist must have sympathy for the patient's suffering, and must understand that, frequently, there is more torture than is evident on the surface.

Grunberger said,

> Even if we admit that mastery of the unconscious borders on the illusion of the narcissistic omnipotence, and if we grant that the readiness to regress to that stage and find oneself in familiar surroundings is often referable to a structure that is more or less susceptible to regression, one that is fragile in the face of certain practical tasks as well as sensitive to the messages coming from the unconscious, the fact nevertheless remains that persons belonging to this category often make excellent analysts. They are also strangely related, in terms of their structure, to poets, artists, and creative scholars, whose intuitive understanding of the unconscious was appreciated by Freud—he said that he learned more about the unconscious from them than from anyone else.
>
> *(4)*

This matches my idea of a good therapist for schizophrenia.

Note

1 Leo Rangell suggests browsing through his two-volume book on the "Human core," *The Intrapsychic Base of Behavior*. International University Press, 1980.

References

1. Freud, Sigmund. Conditions in analysis. In *The Standard Edition of the Complete Psychological Works of Sigmund Freud*, Vol. XXIII, Hogarth Press, London, p. 267.
2. Rangell, Leo. (1980). *Human Core: Intrapsychic Base of Behavior*, Vol. 2, International Universities Press, Madison, CT.
3. Eissler, Kurt. (1971). *Talent and Genius*, Quadrangle Books, New York, p. 319.
4. Grunberger, Bele. (1971). *Narcissism*, International Universities Press, New York, p. 197.

20

SIDE EFFECTS OF ANTI-PSYCHOTIC DRUGS

I have known for years that neuroleptics taken over a period of years will cause neurologic damage resulting in "tardive dyskinesia (up to 40%), tardive dystonia, anticholinergic poisoning, restless agitation, confusion, disorientation, tachycardia, and grogginess (known by patients as appearing like a zombie)" (1). But what I didn't know, until recently, is that psychiatric drugs can also produce an *increase* in psychosis as a result of the neurological damage caused by anti-pyschotic drugs (Whitaker, 2). That is, a patient may start out with a relatively mild degree of psychosis, but the drugs, because of their increasing damage on the brain, will cause greater degree of psychosis.

There is a law that states that a patient must be informed of the side effects of medication. But, it is a custom of psychiatrists *not* to inform the patients of these side effects, in spite of the fact that the patients have frequently sued psychiatrists and drug companies for this failure to inform (3).

Worse yet, if the patient has been on anti-psychotic drugs for a long enough period, and then they try to stop, they may get an *increase* in involuntary movements. If this happens, the only way to overcome this problem, is to resume taking the drugs.

I thought I knew so much about how schizophrenia was being treated in this country until Robert Whitaker opened my eyes to a whole new phenomenon. As an example, Zyprexa causes very serious weight gain (Whitaker, 4) "Although several studies funded by NIMH and the British Government have found that patients on the whole, don't do any better on Risperdal (one of the newer anti-psychotics) and the older atypicals (Ibid., 5)." A patient complains that she always has trouble getting along with people.

> Risperdal exacerbates that problem. She says, 'The meds isolated you. They interfere with your empathy. There is flatness to you, and so you're uncomfortable with people all the time. They make it hard for you to get along.' ...

In addition, this patient is developing tardive dyskinesia, i.e. her tongue is rolling over in her mouth.

The same patient commented, 'I would have been more productive without meds.' Another time, she lamented 'that with a life on anti-psychotics, you lose your soul and you never get it back.' 'The things I remember looking back, is that I was not really that sick early on. I was really just confused. I had all these issues, but nobody talked to me about that. I wish I could go off meds even now, but there is no help how to do it. I can't even start a dialogue.'

(Ibid., 6)

Another patient who managed to get off drugs says, "It was fabulous I was surprised to find out who I was after all these years" (Ibid., 7). I find that is a persistent complaint of patients on drugs, i.e., the loss of *identity*.

A further side effect very rarely mentioned is Neuroleptic Malignant Syndrome, which results in death. It is caused by the administration of overdose of anti-psychotic drugs. (8)

One condition remains clear in Whitaker's book. All the physical treatments of schizophrenia depend for their tests of efficacy on the *psychiatrists*' opinion of the patients' state of being. These evaluations are generally evaluations of how aggressive and hostile, or overexcited the patient is. They do not depend on the *patient's* subjective experience. This leaves the patient viewed as a thing, not a person. Such evaluations seem irrational to me, since schizophrenia is an emotional disease that is most accurately described by the person experiencing it, namely the patient. They appear to be evaluated by the degree of the disturbance they cause the *psychiatrists*, not the patient. That will not solve the problem. They forget that the patient is the authority on what he feels.

I urge you to get Whitaker's book *The Anatomy of an Epidemic*, which is a brilliant and precise exposé of the situation. What I was not aware of is that years of imbibing anti-psychotic drugs cause so much neurological damage that the patients become *more* psychotic. Whitaker makes a painstaking and very convincing case for that argument (see also Whitaker, *Mad in America*).

References

1. *Tardive Dyskinesia, Task Force #18*. American Psychiatric Association, Washington, DC, p. 15.
2. Whitaker, Robert. (2010). *Anatomy of an Epidemic*, Crown Publishers, New York, pp. 64, 82, 99–102.
3. *Dan Rather T.V. Show*. (1983). CBS, November 28.
4. Whitaker, Robert. (2010). *Anatomy of an Epidemic*, Crown Publishers, Washington, DC, p. 13.
5. Ibid., p. 18.
6. Ibid., p. 20.
7. Ibid., p. 30.
8. Henderson, Victor W., M.D., and Wooten, G. Frederick, M.D. (1981). Neuroleptic malignant syndrome: A pathogenic role for dopamine reception blockade? *Neurology*, 31, February: 132–137.

21
EPILOGUE

Four years after Kathleen left me, she wrote me the following letter:

> I think that I will always have just a tiny bit of the obsessive/compulsive perfectionist in me—that's just me. . . . In my case, I'll never be 'normal.' Whatever the hell that's supposed to mean! I've experienced the horror of mental illness, and a near breakdown. I came much too close to the abyss to ever fit the mold of the completely well-adjusted person—if such person exists. I know something of the terrifying chaotic horror that Conrad mentions in *The Heart of Darkness*. I know too much of pain and fear. I am very fortunate to be as healthy as I am. Funny how resilient some of us are.
>
> Don't get me wrong Val (my nickname). I'm a happy contributing member of society with a healthy marriage, and a small, but tight circle of friends. I have the respect of my supervisors and colleagues . . . my ability to confront my mother's failure and point the accusatory finger of shame at *her* took the load of guilt and grief from my shoulders. What a relief this has been.
>
> This epiphany paved the way for future progress. I no longer allow people to take advantage of me or other people. . . . I tell it like it is. As you might guess, some people don't like such outspoken ways, but I'm not out to become Ms. Popularity. Too often, the price is too high.
>
> This way of life took years, Val, but you helped plant the seeds. Whenever I demurred at blaming my mother, or didn't question my bullying conscience, you dug and picked and nagged, forcing me to face my cowardice. No matter how dense or stubborn I was in therapy, you never let me off the hook. You demanded that I question all of my beliefs (all mothers love their children) and mindless assumptions about the world in general (everyone thinks that crazy people are evil or bad). . . . I suffered from loneliness, but never regret. In the process, I beat down my conscience.

> What strikes me most about my therapy is how easily you accepted me. I was an absolute mess when I came to you. Crazy. Scared to death. (In the first session, she was frightened to come to me because she feared I would hospitalize her.) Despairing. Isolated in my illness. Nothing I said shocked you. You respected me and let me talk things through without the usual saccharine that therapists give. . . . You allowed me to be as ugly and mean as I wanted. Yet you were ruthless when I tried to hide something. . . . When I see mentally ill people, I feel nothing but empathy and mercy for them, and hope they will heal without drugs or shock therapy. I pray that a miracle will happen and that they will be lucky like me. . . . I 'forgive' myself from being human and becoming sick.

I can't agree that Kathleen needs to be obsessive-compulsive. But external factors interfered. On the other hand, what therapist does not have the cockles of her heart warmed by such a letter!

INDEX

Abraham, Karl 37, 101, 174, 176; children, demands adaptation 176
Abruzzese, Sarah 232
Absetzung 28
active psychotherapy, excuses 202
affirmative interventions 192
"Against Therapy" (Masson) 104–105
aggression, release 104
agranulocytosis 11
Akhtar, Salman 68, 189, 191–193; analytic treatment 192; perspective 192
aloneness, feeling (prevention) 32–33
anal cruelty, interpretations 93
anality 52; clinical material 183–188; input (Freud) 175; schizophrenia, relationship 176–180; superego, impact 179–180; symbol 177–178
Analysis of the Self, The (Kohut) 29
analysts, achievement (optimistic view) 210
analytic process, faith 206
"Anatomy of an Epidemic" (Whitaker) 7
Anatomy of an Epidemic, The (Whitaker) 250
antagonism, impact 212
anti-identity 242–243
anti-psychotic drugs: impact 230–231; side effects 249; usage 202, 241
anti-Semitism, undercurrents 244
anxiety: cause 155; removal 180
Aspects of Internalization (Schafer) 124
atypicals 7

bad feelings: avoidance 206; protection 237
Barr, Cameron W. 229

being good, achievement 176
Beland, Herman 208
Bender, Daniel 104–105
Bergler, Edmund 146–148
Berkowitz. D. 40
Bethelard, Faith 212
Black Force, experience 161–162
black hole 172; creation 66–67; feeling 197; symptom 198, 215
black hole phenomenon 56, 135; addendum 68; case report 57, 58–65; discussion 65–67
blaspheming, enjoyment 141
Bonapart, Marie 114
boredom, therapist problem 180
brain, voice 155
brain-conscious dialogue 48
Brenner, Charles 141
buck up-get tough speech 205
Burnout: The Cost of Caring (Maslach) 225
Burnout: The High Cost of High Achievement (Freudenberger) 224
Bychowski, G. 10, 101, 203

"Can't Get No Satisfaction" (Senior) 224
Carey, Benedict 174, 230–231
caring profession 224
Carpenter, William 230–231
Cass, Alden 225
character pathology, severity 192
Chassequet-Smirgel, Janine 116
chemical imbalance: concept 7; postulation 146

Chestnut Lodge 6, 91
childhood: change, impossibility 198–199; fantasies 191
children, demands adaptation 176
classical analysis, immunity 100
cleanliness, denotation 179
Clinton, Bill 215–216
communication: failure, killing (impact) 235–236; inability 242
community, patient return 104
compassion, feeling 70
Compassion and Self-Hate (Rubin) 147
competence, growth 32
compromise formation 141
concretization, language 101
confidence: feeling, realism (absence) 214–215; loss 37
confusion, creation 95
conscience 124; identification 21; term, usage 145; verbalization 127
conscience, statement (I-C) 49–50; black hole phenomenon, examples 61, 62
conscience, statement reversal (C-I) 48, 49–50; black hole phenomenon, examples 60–65, 68–69
conscious knowledge, gaining 237
consciousness 172; omnipotence, feeling 34; rage 146; repression 236
"Construction in Analysis" (Freud) 12, 95
conviction, maintenance 244
conviction (support), undisprovability (impact) 78
countertransference 136–137
courage, understanding 243
creation, impact 78
Creation, myths 177
criticism, restraint (purpose) 37
Curtis, H. 86

death instinct 113–115; doubts, maintenance (Freud) 114; misperception 152; pure culture 14–15
death struggle 238
defeat, resignation 110
defecation, omnipotence 177
defense 56; case report 56, 68; exposure 221; mechanism 237; process 20; reality, contrast 215–216
defensive behavior 238
deficits 56; case report 56, 68; maternal bonding/attachment, deficits 66
delusion 50; patient error, convincing 12–13; reality, separation 207; transference, equivalence 86–87

demons, introduction 124
depression: impact 53–54; pathological depression 219; suffering 54–55
despair, paranoia (word substitution) 79–80
deterioration 181
Deutsch, Helene 29
Devereux, George 104
Devil, terror 13–14
differentiations 73; statement, importance 133
direct analysis 94
Direct Analysis (Rosen) 86, 101
Direct Psychoanalysis 95
Direct Psychoanalysis II (Rosen) 99
disillusionment, susceptibility 224
dreams: example 99; interpretation 143; mechanism 12; psychoses, equivalence 10, 119
drugged state 169
Duley, Jean 231–232

education, description 28
ego: death, schizophrenic superego attack 152; development 73; disease 95; distrust 122–123; domain 242–243; growth 157; material 130; self-criticism 120–121; superego 48–50; superego, attack 96
Ego and the Id, The (Freud) 45, 145
"Ego and the Superego" (Freud) 115
Ego-Ideal, The (Chassequet-Smirgel) 116
ego-syntonic results 45
Eisenbud, Jules 103
Eissler, K. 44–46, 144, 163, 244
Elavil, side effects 11
electroconvulsive therapy (ECT) 5, 91, 202; application 100; submission 241; treatment 5–6; usage, avoidance 7
emotion, expression 181
emotion, quality 136–137
emotional conditions, impact 77
emotional courage 171
emotional differences 191
emotional DNA, essence 182
emotional involvement, focus 19
emotional material, sharing 31
emotional pressure 63
emotional problems, handling 85
emotional response 236–237
emotions (death), conscious knowledge (gaining) 237
emptiness 58
English, O. Spurgeon 102, 104
Eros, rest 114

erotic transference, admission 236
exception, psychology 57
excessive hope 192, 193
excitatory processes, expiration 115
existential quest, failure 225

Fairbairn, W.R.D. 124
faith 73–79; defining 79; destructive consequences 77–79; encouragement, emotional conditions 77; impact 72; irrationality, exposure 140; maintenance 80; problems 74–75; trust, distinction 73
faith-motivated people, reasoning 87
fantasy (fantasies): core 192; dumb fantasy 40; homosexual fantasies 62; murder, relationship 33–34; reality 236–238
Farber, Barry 224
Faughey, Kathryn 229, 231, 233
Federn, Paul 7, 10, 44, 92, 95
feedback 213
Fenichel, O. 37
Fenton, Wayne 229–230, 233
Ferenczi, S. 144, 175, 177, 179
finger-painting, messiness 179
foolishness, feeling 29
foreign body 148
foreignness, threat 148
"Formulation Regarding the Two Principles in Mental Functioning" (Freud) 28
free association, psychosis 98
Freudenberger, Herbert 224
Freud, Sigmund 10–13, 210; death instinct, doubts 114–115; definitions 177–179; errors 110, 177–179; mental structures, understanding 28–29; neutrality suggestion 243; psychology, application 91–92; schizophrenic understanding, difficulty 178; structural theory/consequences, errors 108; suicidal patient, discussion 236; victim 112; wishes, relinquishing 27–28
friend/foe, recognition 48
Fromm-Richmann, Frieda 7, 10, 44, 92, 151, 203; loneliness, expectation 152
frustration: constancy 122–123; suffering 95–96
functioning superego activity, sphere (limitation) 213
"Future of an Illusion, The" (Freud) 77

gambling 82
Gediman, Helen 119
genetic explanations, skepticism 173

ghost, becoming 65
Glassman, David 22
God: anger 59; belief 59–60; conversations 236; feeling 197; hallucination 226; pocket, location 57, 61, 66, 70, 126, 135, 172, 218; protection 170; requirement, absence 64; superego dialogue, example 49–50
grandiosity: defense 35–36; hostile quality 36; identity, relationship 148–149; impact 218; infantile omnipotence, difference 27; irrationality 39; omnipotence, distinction/relationship 36–38, 214–215; projective identification, interconn3ection 218–219; reduction 135–136; self-discovery, example 149
gratification 31
gray voice 111, 150
greatness, delusion 37
Greenacre, Phyllis 100
Groopman, Jerome 202
"Group Psychology and the Analysis of the Ego" (Freud) 115
Grunberger, Bela 16, 247
Grunebaum, J./H. 73, 74
guilt: assuaging 203; conscience, impact 174; dissolution 37; feeling 157; handling 138–139; imputation, patient rebellion 145; pressure 181–183; threat 155
guilt, sense 110; noise 145

happiness, attainment 211–212
Harris, I. 38
Havens, Leston 150, 153
Heart of Darkness, The (Conrad) 251
Hegeman, E. 151
historical truth, fragment 12, 95, 126
Hoch, Paul 5
homosexual desires, gratification 181
homosexual fantasies 62
Hope: A Shield in the Economy of Borderline States (Potamianou) 193
hope: excessive hope 192, 193; wishes and hopes pathology, treatment 189
hostile introject, domination 161
hostility: encouragement 172; usage 156
How Doctors Think (Groopman) 202
human being, production 177
humiliation, feeling 236
Hurvich, Marvin 161

id, wishes identification 21
id-ego alliance 48–49

identity: change, possibility 78; feeling, awareness (importance) 238; grandiosity, relationship 148–149; loss 250; primitive beginning 175; threat 148–149
identity, loss 250; fear 150–151
"If Only Fantasies" (Akhtar) 191–192
illness, handling 207
immortality, measure (guarantee) 78
immunotherapy 120
incurability 215
Index of the Standard Edition 215
indifference, change 23–24
infancy, megalomania 27
infant, social achievement 82
infantile omnipotence: betrayal 21; clinical examples 30–31; grandiosity, difference 27; loss 219; reality, contrast 215; repression, relationship 31–35; requirement 214–215; substitution 33
infantile reaction 175
"Infantile Sexuality" (Freud) 45
information, gathering 72
insane (treatment), Freudian psychology (usage) 91–92
insanity, laughter 98
instinctual satisfaction, temptations 122–123
insulin, application 100
internalized authority, dictates 213
International Symposium for the Psychotherapy of Schizophrenia 105, 190
interpretation, problem 21–22
intolerance 178
introject 124; death threats 161; domination 161
introspection, habituation 237–238
irrational anxiety, cause 155
irrational belief 79
irrational idea, origin 212–213
isolation, breakup 49
Ivins, Bruce 229, 231

Jackson, Murray 7, 239
jealousy 40
Judaism, usage 48
Jung, Carl 7

Kanzer, M. 87
Karon, Bertram 6, 7, 44, 105
Keller, Helen 60
Kernberg, O. 29
Kerr, John 7, 119

kinetic power 36–37
King George III (porphyria) 5–6
Klein, M. 29, 32
Knight, Robert 13
Kohut, H. 29, 40

Layton, Lyndsey 231
Levin, Revella 161; responses 161–162
Lewin, Bertram 100
Lidz, T.R. 13, 83
life and death struggle 238
life coach, role 231
Lipton, Eric 232
Lithium: side effects 11; usage 47
logic, absence 136–137
loneliness 58
"Loving and Beloved Superego in Freud's Structural Theory" (Schafer) 14, 123
Luster, Martin 5

Macbeth (Shakespeare) 153
Mackler, Daniel 239
madness, history 5–7
Malcolm, Janet 24
man: higher nature, complaints 112; virtuosity 122–123
Maslach, Christina 225
Masson, Jeffrey 104
material, suppression (danger) 236
maternal bonding/attachment, deficits 66
McGlashan, Thomas H. 231
McKinnon, Catherine M. 86, 104
McLean Hospital, establishment 5
medication (usage), patient anger (reaction) 230
Meissner, W.W. 78, 79, 83
Menaker, Esther 78
Mendelson, M.D. 151
Mendel, Werner 13
mental illness 195; treatment, sociology 7–9
mental life: repression 112; spontaneous illnesses 119
mental life, spontaneous illnesses 10
mental structures, understanding 28–29
mentor, ego distrust 122–123
method 12, 95
Michelangelo, fantasies 38
Miller, C. 74, 79
Miller, Lee 239
mind, concentration mind 178
Miracle Worker, The (Sullivan) 60
misery, acceptance 210

mission 53
Mohacsy, I. 151
Money-Kyrle, R.E. 37, 219
Monroe, Ruth 1
moral factor 110
moral sense, shock 112
moral treatment 6
"Moses and Monotheism" (Freud) 77
Most Dangerous Method, A (Kerr) 207
"Most Dangerous Profession, A" (Kerr) 7
mother-child relationship 66
mother-child separation experiences 192
mother, helplessness 177
mother/superego, self-identification 171
murder: fantasy, relationship 33–34; fear 237
murderers: differentiation 233; inquiries 176
"Murderousness in Relationship to Psychotic Breakdown" (Williams) 233
murderous rage, direction 95–96

naïvete 216
narcissism: injury 176; interchange 214; transformation 175
narcissistic disequilibrium, fantasy origination 192
narcissistic neuroses, resistance 143
narcissistic omnipotence, illusion 247
narcissistic traumas 192
negative change 157
negative therapeutic reaction 110–111, 145
negative transference: problem 24; reactions 101
neglected patients, presentation 57
neo-Freudian approach 228
neurosis, examination 53–55
neurotic, psychotic (difference) 90–91
neutrality, Freudian suggestion 243
New Introductory Lectures of Psychoanalysis (Freud) 121
new job, acquisition 171–172
non-pleasure, value 176
non-psychoanalytic techniques 203
non-psychotic, realism 214
non-responsiveness, toleration (ability) 243
non-schizophrenic state 242
Nunberg, Herman 92, 93, 95, 97, 103

object, rejection 217
objectivity, affirmation 103
Observations of Direct Analysis (Rosen) 102

obsessional neurosis 123, 145
obsessive-compulsive defenses, erosion 180
Oedipal conflict/traumas, impact 192
Oedipus Complex (Oedipus complex) 15–16, 144, 219–221
offerings, rejection 238
omnipotence: derivatives 36; failure 31; grandiosity, distinction/relationship 36–38, 214–215; narcissistic omnipotence, illusion 247; realism, absence 35; repression, cause 38–42; sense 29, 212
omnipotentiality 34
oneness, impact 78
opinions, opposition 189
"Optimum Conditions for Treatment of Psychosis Unrelated to Diagnosis" (Rosen) 99–100
oral interpretations 97; usage 92–93
oral problem 41
Ornstein, Paul 218
Ostman, Per 105
Outline of Psychoanalysis, An (Freud) 119
owner (case), schizophrenic superego (promise) 153

pain/death chances, decrease (crisis) 234–235
paranoia 79–82; case illustrations 80–82; impact 72, 85; observation 153; psychoses, treatment 150; reduction 135–136
paranoid person, description 79
parents, anal/urethral identification 175
pathological depression 219
pathological material, expression 243
patients: anger 230; colleague, dialogue 161–163; connection, establishment 238–239; DNA personality, mismatch 147; emotional appreciation, fear (interference) 137; excessive hope, rupture 192; hostility, absence (Rosen) 103–104; interaction, pain/death chances (decrease) 229; lying, avoidance 245; pathology, responsibility 244; poisoning complaints 23; state of being, psychiatrist opinion 250; support, therapist discovery 232–233; torture 152; trauma 192; trust 86–88
penis: envy 219
penis: loss 75–76
Perls, Fritz 150
per-Oedipal material, symbol 97

person, container (concept) 140
phantasy-life, interchange 214
physical danger 234–235
physical survival 237
Piers, G. 120
pleasure principle: dethronement 28; dethronement, absence 33; immutability, conviction (Freud) 28
pleasure, value 175–176
porphyria 6
positive transference 60–61
possession, feeling 17
postpartum psychotic 234
Potamianou, Anna 193
potential threat 36–37
primary narcissism, deficits 56
projective disidentification 216–222
projective identification, grandiosity (interconnection) 218–219
psychiatric drugs, skepticism 105
psychic death 232
psychic growth 161
psychoanalysis, patient behavior 204–205
psychoanalyst, therapeutic action 146
psychoanalytic moral 67
Psychoanalytic Psychotherapy Study Center (paper) 22
psychoanalytic relationship: case illustration 75–77; faith/paranoia/trust,: impact 72
psychopath, becoming 122
psychopharmacological drugs, side effects 11
psychosis: dream, equivalence 10, 119; mysteries 90–91; nightmare 207; resistance 143; resolution 100; understanding 90
psychosynthesis, achievement 16
psychotherapeutic interventions 239
psychotherapeutic manpower, usage (increase) 93
psychotherapy: efficacy, underestimation 75; supportive/active psychotherapy, excuses 202; trust, usage 82–83
"Psychotherapy of Hysteria, The" (Breuer/Freud) 210
Psychotherapy of Schizophrenia (Scheflen) 103
psychotic: neurotic, difference 90–91; realism 214; treatment, oral interpretations (usage) 92–93
psychotic fears 62
psychotic material, production 206
psychotic patient, identification 57

psychotic thoughts, usage 206
psychotropic drugs, prescription 202
pull out theory 8
Pumpian-Mindlin, Eugene 34–35, 38–39
push down school 208; therapy 13

Quakers, moral treatment 6

rational, ego domain 242
rationality, usage 125
Rat Man, grandiose fantasies 39
real, characterization 69
reality: attack 82; contradiction 12–13; defense, contrast 215–216; delusions, separation 207; depressive position 217; infantile omnipotence, contrast 215; principle/discontents 211–214
reality-principle, introduction 33–34
reality testing 86, 115–116, 144; reliance, absence 147–148
reasons 113
recovery, resistance 110
recriminations, impact 211
regression 100
relative morality, Christian Right abhorrence 155
relinquishment 219
repressed impulses, discovery 145
repression 112; cause 38–42; cause, creation (impact) 78; destructiveness 236; impact 175; infantile omnipotence, relationship 31–35; perception (Freud) 41; setup 175
revenge killer, theory 232–234
Riggs, Austin 6
Risperdal, side effects 249–250
Riviere, Joan 214
roles, reversal 51
root, extraction attempt (failure) 203
Rosen, John 10, 86, 189; attitude, change 92; community, patient return 104; concerns 3; delusion, understanding 93; genius 22; historical reflections 90; intentional assumptions 101; patient hostility, absence 103–104; psychosis, resolution 100; psychotherapeutic manpower, usage (increase) 93; theoretical formulations, reactions 103; theoretical talent, absence (example) 95–96; theoretical underpinnings, weaknesses 102; therapeutic success 101
Rosenfeld, Herbert 44
Rubin, Theodore 147

Index **259**

rules: impact 64; infraction 141
rupturing, technical error 199

sacred object, attack 247
Saks, Elyn R.: Freed perspective 206; history, condensation 203–207; production, example 204; schizophrenogenic mother theory, rejection 205
Satran, G. 151
Savage Sleep (Rosen) 100
Schafer, Roy 14–15, 123
Scheflen, Albert 103, 104
schizophrenese 25
schizophrenia: anality, relationship 176–180; cause, opinion 245; cessation 51–53; comprehension/amelioration 119; psychotherapy, possibility (Freud perception) 11; therapist description 24
schizophrenic: clinical experience, absence 178; dreamer, awakening 10; mistrust 246; paranoia 230; problems 232–233; superego 213; treatment 241; treatment, rationality (usage) 125; tuning out 54; understanding, difficulty (Freud) 178; universal fantasy 181–183
schizophrenic, neurotic level: case study 44; marathon 46–49; neurosis, examination 53; referral 46; schizophrenia, cessation 51–53; treatment 49–51
schizophrenic behavior, importance 13
schizophrenic break 215
schizophrenic children, interaction 189
schizophrenic patient, interaction: pain/death, chances (decrease) 229; theory 232–234
schizophrenic patient, opportunity 84
schizophrenic superego: ego death 152; identification 167; interchange, example 167–169; lies 152; owner care 153; truth, admission 153
schizophrenic superego, communication 119, 143; case examples 122–137
schizophrenogenic mother: father personage 205; theory, rejection (Saks) 205
Schwaber, Evelyne Albrecht 232, 236
Schwager, Elaine 190
Schwing, Gertrude 101
screaming, provocation 51
Searles, Harold 29, 40, 101–103, 203, 226–227
self: delineation, oneness (impact) 78; fragments, splitting 217; sense 78

self-awareness, suspension 125
self-control: difficulty 246; pathological characteristic 37
self-criticism 29, 120–121
self-defense, fear 81
self-destructiveness 46
self-determination, primitive right 176
self-esteem 39
self/object constancy, defect 192
self/object separateness (reality), projective identification (impact) 217
self-perceptions, opposition 121
self-preservation, instinct 215
self-reliance 60
self-satisfaction, feeling 176
Senior, Jennifer 224
sensitivity, inadequacy 214
separation, denial 217
separation-individuation phase 139
sexual material, oral/anal interpretation 103
Shinbach, Kent D. 231
shock treatments, usage 100
Silver, Ann-Louise 152
Singer, M. 120
Skolnick, Marvin 150–151
"Someday" (Akhtar) 191
"Sophocles and Oedipus" (Vallacott) 77
speech, hammering style 59
sphincter morality 120, 175
Spotnitz, Hyman 4, 20, 203
Steiner, John 77, 217, 219–220
Stone, Leo 101
Strachey, J. 146
strangers, relationships (formation) 81
structural theory 113; discarding 141
structural theory/consequences, errors 108
structure, relevance (examples) 16–19
stupidity, feeling 29
sturm und drang (feeling) 136
subdural hematoma, occurrence 235
subjective chaos, reduction 48
sublimation, option (absence) 190
submission 176
suicide: committing 160, 241; predisposition 216; seriousness 192
Sullivan, Annie 60
Sullivan, Charles 96
Sullivan, Harry Stack 1, 10, 22, 44
superego: accusation, failure 155; anality, relationship 179–180; anger 151; assumptions (Freud) 144–146; attack 96; clinical material/presentation 157–160;

colleague/patient dialogue 161–163; conversations 112–113, 138, 171–172; death, warning 156–157; demotion 123, 213; derivation 109–110; destructive criticism 156; destructiveness 155; dialogue, example 49–50; domain 242; duplicity 113; extinguishing 123; faith, irrationality (exposure) 140; flow 52; friendship, pretending 155; frightened 111; function, severity 15; hatred, reaction 156; higher nature 112–113; id-ego alliance 48–49; identification, absence 171; identification, switching 169; insights, importance (absence) 170; lies/tricks/manipulation 156; loving side 14; modification, reassurance 44–45; murder, ego (impact) 95–96; muteness, discussion 110; nature 151–154; negative connotations, irreversibility 155; obedience 149; parental agency 178; patient dependence/isolation 156; perspective (Bergler) 146–148; rationale, vagueness 138; reality testing 144; sadistic nucleus 121; schizophrenic superego, communication 119; self-manifestation process 146; strength 176; stupidity 110–112; superiority 182; term, usage 145; threat 156; understanding 48–49; weakening 51–52, 135

superego, communication 125, 245; analyst guide 154–155; indirect eye contact 156; rules 156–157; usefulness 149–151

superego voice: loudness 139–140; recognition process 155–156

supermorality 115

supportive psychotherapy, excuses 202

surrender, rush (reasons) 207–209

suspicion, implication 79

tardive dyskinesia 249; patient development 250

tardive dystonia 249

Task Force Report #18 (APA) 11

temper tantrums 198

therapeutic alliance/stereotype, establishment 83

therapeutic relationship, maintenance 86

therapist: acceptance 252; burnout 224; cooperation 161; superego dislike 155; trust, absence 246

therapy: dislike 169; faith, problems 74–75; patient trust 86–88; push-down school 13

Thorazine, usage 227

threat, perception 231

Ticho, E.A. 221

Torrey, Fuller 231

transference 136–137; analysis 109; change 23–24; delusion, equivalence 86–87; dynamics, disruption 192; impact 244; interference 246

trust 82–88; case illustrations 85–86; faith, distinction 73; impact 72; necessity 86; patient trust 86–88; possibility, patient discovery 83–84; usage 82–83

"Trust Based Therapy" (Boszornenyi) 82

truth: presence 95; recommendation 153

truth-telling 109

Tustin, Frances 56, 200

"Two Classes of Instincts, The" (Freud) 45

tyrannical superego 144

unconscious: control 90–91; education 102; mastery, admission 247

undisprovability, impact 78

unhappiness 210

universal meanings, interpretation 102

unrealistic confidence 218

untruths, antennae 245

"Use of Medication with Patient in Analysis" (New York Psychoanalytic Society) 208

Valcourt, Derek 230

Valium, usage 237

victim-designate, impact 233

virtue, reward (forfeit) 122–123

Viscott, David 10

watered down, term (usage) 203

weakness, exposure 237–238

Whitaker, Robert 7, 249–250

wild analysis 84

Williams, Arthur Hyatt 233

Williams, Paul 148

Williams, Tennessee 207

wishes 169; destruction 190; renunciation 219; throwing, history 196

wishes, relinquishing 27–28

wishes and hopes pathology: clinical examples 193–199; treatment 189

wishful thinking 199

words, importance/idiosyncratic meaning 23

Young-Bruehl, Elizabeth 212

Zyprexa, side effects 249